Dear James

SECRETS OF SUCCESS FROM
A MANAGEMENT MAVERICK

D1332177

Caspian

Caspian Publishing
London

First published in 2000 by Caspian Publishing Ltd.

Millbank Tower
21-24 Millbank
London SW1P 4QP

Tel: 020-7828 0706
Fax: 020-7592 8923
www.realbusiness.co.uk

A catalogue record for this book is available from the British Library.

ISBN 1 901844 20 X

Designed by Jenny Eade
Cover photograph by Will Webster
Illustrations by Cheshire Publicity
Printed by St Edmundsbury Press

CONTENTS

Very few people know more about the arts of managing a family business than John Timpson. He started as a shop assistant in the shoe company founded by his great-grandfather; ten years later, after a boardroom battle between his father and his uncle, he saw the company pass into the hands of the UDS conglomerate.

After successfully running a chain of fashion shops under the UDS umbrella, Timpson found himself promoted to be managing director of the old family firm. Then, when UDS was itself swallowed up by the Hanson Trust empire, John Timpson bought back his company in what, at the time, was one of Britain's largest-ever management buy-outs.

For all his respect for heritage and family (business) values, Timpson does not suffer from nostalgia. Seeing no future in the shoe shops that were the company's foundation, he sold them off. Timpson became a shoe repair chain and, on that new cornerstone, its chairman built a raft of related services – notably key cutting – delivered in a customer-friendly culture by a highly motivated and well-incentivised workforce which has, to date, multiplied profits six-fold and made the business a market leader.

The experience Timpson gained and deployed in the course of his remarkable corporate odyssey is set down in this book. Its context – the bequest of a working lifetime's accumulated wisdom to his son and heir – could not be more personal. But the themes and the lessons that it imparts with such lucidity are universal. To those who run Britain's businesses, large and small, I have a simple message: read this book and take its many insights to heart. You and your companies can only benefit.

Andrew Lorenz
Business Editor
The Sunday Times

Acknowledgements

I am grateful to Michael McAvoy who first suggested that I should write this book. To Barbara Mason and Christine Hickman who turned my dictated and scribbled notes into a typed manuscript. To John Turner for most of the illustrations and to Caspian, particularly Stuart Rock and Jenny Eade, who turned it into the published product. I am grateful for the encouragement that I have received from the team on *Real Business* in my role as a monthly columnist on that magazine.

I thank Kit Green who gave some encouraging and constructive criticim when I showed him the first chapter I had written, and Mike Williams and Martin Tragen who checked the technical accuracy, particularly in matters of property and finance.

I owe a fundamental debt of thanks to all the people who work at Timpson who run the business for me and have provided me with something to write about – with special mention to James for having the courage to work for his father and provide the basis of this book.

Finally, a word of apology to all my family and friends who have endured my book writing during weekends and holidays – as Alex said, "Thank Goodness it's finished!"

Although this book is written to James I have written it for all my family, especially Alex

The Timpson story

CHAPTER 1

Losing control

Dear James

Don't ignore
the experience
of history !

Everything went so smoothly for the first 29 years of my life. At the age of 17 I followed in the footsteps of my father and grandfather. I started as a sales assistant in the business my great-grandfather founded when he had opened a shop in Manchester in 1865.

During a year between school and university, I was taught how to sell shoes and look after customers, I tried to repair shoes and at our shoe factory in Kettering I learned how shoes were made. University holidays were spent as a shop assistant. Having graduated, I discovered my degree meant little to colleagues in the family firm. Members of the family always started at the bottom and I was no exception but promotion was almost certain to be rapid. At 26 I arrived in the boardroom as the director responsible for buying ladies' footwear. The business had 250 shoe shops, 150 shoe repair workshops and a shoe factory making 22,000 pairs of shoes a week.

In September 1972, everything suddenly changed.

Change of chairman

William Timpson had become a public company in 1929. By 1960, when I joined the firm, the family holding had been reduced to 55 per cent. My great-grandfather who founded the business had 12 children. My grandfather had four. Many of the shareholders were distant relatives who could pass in the street without recognising each other.

From the time of its flotation, the company had enjoyed an unbroken run of success, under the guidance of my grandfather, Will Timpson, the chairman, supported by his half-brother Noel as managing director. Will supplied the flair and was good with people, visiting shops on a regular basis. Noel was the tough businessman, a strict disciplinarian desperately keen to become chairman.

Noel got his wish in 1960. But his term of office was tragically short-lived. Within months of taking the chair he died while gardening at his home in Cheshire. Although Noel was over 60 and Will was nearly 80 no succession plan was clear. Two family directors remained, my father Anthony, whose main responsibility was shoe buying, and his cousin, Geoffrey Noakes, who controlled the shoe repair business.

As a stop-gap solution the company secretary, Gordon Akester, became chairman. My father was deputy chairman as well as being the joint managing director with Geoffrey Noakes. When Gordon Akester retired, three years later, my father became chairman with Geoffrey Noakes as deputy chairman. They continued to be joint managing directors.

People close to the business thought the new management structure was an unfortunate compromise. My father and his cousin Geoffrey were complete opposites, neither totally appreciating the other's strengths and never truly working as a team.

My father inherited Will Timpson's rapport with the staff, visiting shops on a regular basis. He was a successful shoe buyer and thoroughly understood the footwear market. He did not, however, match his father's flair. He was comfortable as the caretaker of our family business but had no passion for ideas. The business was unlikely to create major changes under his leadership.

Geoffrey, on the other hand, did want change. He wanted to be the top dog. His ambition was to succeed my father as chairman. My father had been warned by a previous director: "Look out for Noakes; he is out for all he can get and does not care who he tramples on."

Difficult trading

The scene was set for disharmony at a time when the company needed strong leadership. The sixties became progressively more hostile to Timpson. The shoe shops had a strong customer appeal in the north of

11

England but little presence in the south. The closure of shipyards and coalmines and the decline of the textile trade took business away from the Timpson heartland. New competitors appeared on the scene, particularly Marks & Spencer, Littlewoods and British Home Stores, together with increased competition from mail order companies. The biggest threat came from Charles Clore's rapidly expanding British Shoe Corporation.

Timpson experienced a significant drop in shoe sales. Its traditional suburban shopping areas were being redeveloped and replaced by the new pedestrian precincts. The business did not do enough to update its property portfolio. It became progressively more difficult to find enough orders to fill the factory at Kettering. Built in 1923, it had become a burden to the business. Buyers had to distort the range of stock to keep the factory on full production. The shoe repair shops were also in difficulty. After an uninterrupted run of success since the business started shoe repairing in 1903, demand suddenly disappeared. Cheap imports, synthetic soles and the demise of the stiletto heel fashion all brought bad news. The total demand for shoe repairing fell by 15 per cent for three years running.

Company reports issued throughout the sixties described a business in stagnation. My father recognised that Timpson was now following, not leading the industry. He saw himself in a static market with increasing competition.

In 1963, father came to my University at Nottingham to talk about our business to a group of students. Afterwards he was cross-questioned by my senior tutor and professor. They wanted to know why he didn't diversify. "Why don't you go into cameras?" they asked. (Dixons, who were then just retailers of cameras, was a stock market favourite). Father didn't want to change the business he had inherited from his father and grandfather. Our expertise was in shoes and we should stick to shoes.

During the sixties Timpson profits hovered around £1m. The British Shoe Corporation increased its share of the shoe retail market and the Timpson stronghold in the north became a weakness.

Up to 1963 the success of the shoe repairs had strengthened Geoffrey Noakes' power base but when that business ran into trouble, he sought wider responsibility. In 1968, he took charge of marketing. This was a strange appointment. Geoffrey (who liked to be called Colonel Noakes) had no experience of the retail business and absolutely no marketing flair. He had a military management style with standing orders and set procedures. He found an ally in 1969 when he met Professor Roland Smith from the Manchester Business School.

Geoffrey asked Roland Smith to run a senior management course at the Grosvenor Hotel in Chester. Roland Smith led discussions to produce a corporate plan. Afterwards, he continued his interest in Timpson running some middle management courses at Wythenshawe. A year later he was invited to join the board. Shortly after his appointment my father stepped down as joint managing director. Geoffrey Noakes became deputy chairman and chief executive.

Smith introduced Geoffrey to "management by objectives" (MBO) Geoffrey fell in love with MBO. It appealed to his military mind. Clear objectives linked to rigid line management were seen as the way to improve Timpson profits.

It caused an even greater rift between Geoffrey and my father. By 1971, the two men were exchanging typewritten notes. In one note, Geoffrey says: "I do not propose to reply to the very personal remarks you made about me on Friday as I do not believe that this would be to the benefit of the company." In another, father says: "I have your letter of 9th September and again I wonder whether you realise how rude some of your letters read." The relationship between the two men was deteriorating rapidly.

Geoffrey used his love of line management and the new-found MBO tool to increase his power base. In one vitriolic exchange of letters, Geoffrey complained about father writing to congratulate some shops who had had a good week. He said it was wrong to compare turnover with last year because MBO required that everything be compared with budget. He also complained that father was cutting across the line management by writing directly to a shop manager.

The relationship got even worse. In 1972 Geoffrey decided that everybody should have a job description, including the chairman. He took it upon himself to write a job description for the chairman which emphasised my father's weaknesses.

Geoffrey saw little value in a family business or family management. He thought birthright was a bad way to choose a leader. He wanted to rebrand our shoe repair business to reduce our reliance on the Timpson name. He was stony faced at the Annual General Meeting in April 1972, when the senior partner of our auditors, Boyd Wrigley, stood up in response to their appointment and said: "I was pleased to see that another William Timpson has been christened, in many ways I think this explains the success of this company. For five generations they have been proud of the name William, proud of the company that bears that name and proud of the great reputation that company bears and has every reason to be proud." (The child he was referring to was William James Timpson).

Every half-year my father wrote a report to his fellow directors. It was a practice started by my grandfather in 1954 which father continued when he became chairman. In 1972 the report criticised Geoffrey's MBO approach. Geoffrey used this report (in discussions with the other directors) as evidence the chairman was undermining company policy.

Board room bust up

A month later, on a Thursday afternoon, I was called to the finance director's office. Three other directors were present. I was informed that Geoffrey Noakes and Roland Smith were in my father's office asking for his resignation. They proposed that father became an honorary president or consultant to the company but without (in either case) a seat on the board. I immediately went to see my father, who was both stunned and furious. The inevitable climax of the uneasy relationship had arrived. Geoffrey was making his bid to be chairman.

That night I went to see Geoffrey at home. He was clearly not going to change his stance. He and Roland Smith had lobbied the other directors. My father and I were outnumbered.

We had three options: to go along with their ultimatum (which would have left me as the next target); to join battle at a shareholders' meeting, risking the dangers of a public debate; or to use our shareholding to attract a bid. I had only one per cent of the equity but my father had five per cent and we believed family support would give us over 20 per cent to offer a possible predator.

The following week a board meeting was called to remove father as chairman. It was an unpleasant occasion. Father explained why he had no faith in Geoffrey Noakes or Roland Smith and that if he was removed as chairman his shares would be offered to a possible bidder. The board voted six to two against him. He received a letter from Geoffrey Noakes requiring him to vacate his office within seven days, to hand over all papers and to leave his company car in the office car park. He was instructed only to enter a Timpson shop as a customer. A notice was sent out to all employees: "This is to notify you that Mr W A Timpson has ceased to be Chairman and an employee of the Company. The Vice Chairman, Mr G W Noakes will deputise until a new Chairman has been appointed."

Takeover

The most likely buyers were Great Universal Stores, Sears or United Drapery Stores (UDS). We chose United Drapery Stores. Father met their chairman, Bernard Lyons, who, armed with acceptances from the family, called to see Geoffrey Noakes at Wythenshawe with a bid of £1 per share. But Sears entered the fray. There was a three-month battle but Sears withdrew when their bid was referred to the Monopolies Commission. In December 1972 UDS ended up the winner, buying William Timpson Limited for £28.6m.

During the four-month take-over battle the other directors seldom spoke to me. Although I had the support of most of our workforce it was an uncomfortable experience.

Twenty-six years later, when my father died, I realised how much the experience of the UDS take-over affected the rest of my business life. I was no longer the director of a family business with an assured future. Watching my father being undermined has stuck in my memory and shaped my management style.

Life with UDS

It was a great relief when the take-over was finally completed. I found I was part of another family business, although I was not now part of the family. UDS was run by the Lyons: the business included Alexandre Tailoring, John Collier, Richard Shops, John Myers and various department stores.

I spent the next six months as a spare part. I was attached to John Collier, and given the job of introducing footwear into 30 top stores. Footwear was not welcomed by the Collier staff and the lacklustre sales matched their enthusiasm. Within weeks I was spending most of my time golfing and gardening.

Running a business

After six months I went down to London to resign but never got the opportunity. To my total surprise, they offered me my first chance to manage a business: 60 shops, some called Suede Centre and the rest called Swears & Wells, selling suede, fur and leather clothing. It was experiencing a dramatic fall in turnover and making a significant loss.

The following week Bernard Lyons gave me some advice: "I want to speak to you before you see any people who sell you furs and leather," he told me. "Whatever bargaining you did in the shoe business, you must be a lot tougher in leather and furs. Whatever price they quote, get at least 40 per cent off. That is all I have to tell you." That was all the advice I received on how to run a business. I did, of course, bargain hard. The manufacturers played the game, they let me win at first but got more than their money back over the months ahead.

I followed my father's example and visited as many shops as I could.

The staff soon told me what was wrong. The previous management had adopted a dictatorial style and lost touch with their shop staff. Sales were falling and the company was demoralised. In the week before I arrived, sales were less than half the last year. The worst drop was in Oxford Street, London, where the two shops depended on foreign visitors, who would only buy if they were allowed to barter. The managers had been forbidden to give discounts. Having done my tour of the shops, I responded to what I heard. I let the managers in Oxford Street bargain with customers and I started a sale in the rest of the country. Within two weeks sales were back above last year's level. Then I had a stroke of luck. One of the shops in Birmingham caught fire.

Early success

I had experienced a fire five years before – in Wilmslow. The severely damaged shoe shop was closed for several days whilst the Wilmslow public waited for the sale of smoke-damaged footwear. The sale was so successful that lorry-loads of shoes were sneaked in the back door to satisfy the demand for fire salvage.

The Suede Centre fire in Birmingham was a repeat performance. The personnel director telephoned to break the tragic news. "The shop is a mess," she said. "How is the stock?" I asked. "A mess too," she said. "Is it saleable?" I asked. "Most of it really, but it all smells of smoke." "Is the shop trading?" I asked. "We could open tomorrow morning." "Don't," I said decisively. "Put up a notice saying fire sale starts next Friday." The shop was closed for a week but we took more money on that Friday than the shop had taken over the past two months. Suddenly, Swears & Wells and Suede Centre became a sales success.

I was fortunate to benefit from further tragedies such as flood damage in Argyle Street, Glasgow, and a bomb that all but destroyed our shop in Belfast. We had to wait four weeks before we could start the bomb damage sale and took eight days to sell every item of stock, including all the hangers.

Eighteen months after being thrown in the deep end, I was enjoying my routine, visiting some shops every week and all of them every four months. Despite my lack of any professional management, sales grew to £6m and the business made a respectable profit of £400,000.

Out of the blue, I received a telephone call from Stuart Lyons, a UDS director and chairman of my subsidiary company. He invited me to take on the role of managing director at William Timpson Limited in succession to Geoffrey Noakes. It was a magic moment. I can still recall exactly where I was sitting and how I was holding the telephone when I heard the news. Four weeks later I re-entered the Timpson head office as the company's new managing director.

Cut price king

Swears & Wells had given me a lot of confidence but I was still desperately short of experience. I was surprised at the difference between running 60 shops and 500. I started as I did at Swears & Wells by visiting the branches to listen to the people who served the customers. I should have spent a lot more time listening, but I was 32 years old and impetuous. I had been put into Timpson to do a job and I was anxious to get on and do it. Cut price promotions had worked well at Swears & Wells, so I tried them at Timpson.

During my first four months I organised a series of promotions: a big summer clearance, a 110th anniversary offer (110p off 110 styles) and a mammoth sale in July that used all my Swears & Wells experience. I closed all the shops for two days (Wednesday and Thursday) while we prepared for the sale and advertised on television that the biggest shoe sale ever would start on Friday at 10am. Unfortunately Bernard Lyons, the UDS chairman, was told that most of his shoe shops were closed. He rang me, so furious he could hardly speak. "This is complete madness," he roared. "Shops should always be open. Are you trying to ruin this business?"

I was in Sheffield at 8.30am, giving me plenty of time to walk around our five shops in the city centre before opening time. They were all ready to go, the windows blanked out by garish posters, but no one was showing any interest. I spent an hour going from shop to shop. I visited them all three times hoping each time I turned the corner to see a crowd queuing to spend money in the greatest shoe sale ever. No queues formed until 9.45 when suddenly Sheffield abandoned Woolworths and Marks & Spencer, gave up shopping in Boots or W H Smith, and went to Timpsons. I knew then that my ploy was going to be a success. In two days the shoe shops took more money than they had ever taken before in a whole week. Bernard Lyons rang to admit that he was wrong and congratulated me on the biggest percentage increase he had ever known. I had become a cut price specialist well before Gerald Ratner.

I had another chance to use my "sell 'em cheap" skills. In 1970 Timpson bought a 120-shop chain called Norvic. It was unprofitable when it was acquired and was still losing money in 1975. With Timpson Shoe and Shoe Repair shops also heading for a loss, it was decided to close Norvic and concentrate on Timpson. It was another opportunity to use the lessons of the Wilmslow fire sale. I held a closing down sale in each of the 100 Norvic shops. We established a routine, closing the shop on a Saturday evening with large notices plastered across the window announcing that the closing down sale would start the following Friday. This gave six days to prepare the stock and six days for the locals to pass by with increasing anticipation. It worked fantastically well. In the first two days of their closing down sales most shops achieved at least five – and in one case 15 times – the normal full week's turnover. Trade was so good that in the process of closing down, Norvic made a record profit.

Cut price retailing was not all good news. The July sale marked the end of my honeymoon period as managing director. The sale was so successful that we ran out of stock and the following six weeks were disastrous. I learned a hard lesson – there is much more to retailing than cutting prices.

Consumer champion

I had also discovered the importance of looking after customers. Customer care came naturally in my great grandfather's time. In the seventies things were different. The emphasis was on profitability, efficiency, keeping costs down and increasing margins. Good customer service came well down the list.

By then, Timpson had slipped down the league of footwear retailers. From being one of the market leaders in 1955, it now played second fiddle to the British Shoe Corporation. We needed to find a weakness in British Shoe which we could turn into a strength for Timpson.

Our chosen battleground was customer service. With over 20 per cent of the market, British Shoe did not have to care about customer complaints. They were taking a tough stance against the Office of Fair Trading who were trying to introduce a Code of Practice for footwear. We decided to make customer care an in-house speciality. I wrote a Timpson Code of Practice which was endorsed by the Office of Fair Trading who were keen to bring the rest of the industry to heel. Our Code of Practice brought the company favourable publicity but gave me a reputation within the industry for being a foolhardy loose cannon. I had nailed the company's colours to the customer care mast.

When I became managing director of Timpson, flushed with the success of Swears & Wells, I was dangerously over-confident. At the age of 32 I knew it all. On my own I would have fallen flat on my face but I had a lot of help especially from colleagues I had worked with before the takeover. Following three years of a tough dictatorial regime they welcomed the change. They wanted me to succeed but I didn't have the experience to win without their help. Help also came from Stuart Lyons who had appointed me to the job and generously gave time to help me do it.

Stuart wanted to use TV advertising following his success with John Collier's "The window to watch" campaign. The UDS agency Young & Rubicam produced a memorable advert to celebrate our 110th birthday. It literally sent customers singing the jingle into our shops and sales rose as a result. My dealings with Young & Rubicam were short-lived. The agency fell out with UDS and my one successful TV advertising campaign came to a premature end. It was only on the television for three weeks but I know people who can sing the jingle 25 years later.

Stuart Lyons also introduced me to public relations via Young & Rubicam's PR arm called Planned Public Relations (PPR). It was headed by Michael McAvoy. My first taste of PR did not match the success of the advertising. The objective was to establish my name in the shoe trade – but the announcement went sadly wrong. Press coverage was restricted to the trade magazine with my picture transposed with the director of the Footwear Industry Research Association. Following that hopeless start, Michael McAvoy has hardly put a foot wrong.

Within four months he did make a name for me by organising a conference in London to discuss the future of footwear. The conference was nominally organised by me, chaired by me and included all the industry experts. We got a full house and full coverage in the trade press. National publicity soon followed. Michael had helped create the concept of a consumer champion – I was Honest John, who unlike all the other unfriendly multiples was on the side of the customer.

Groupmanship

When I joined UDS, two Lyons were on the board. A year later, two more joined them. The style was familiar; it was like the Timpson family business before Roland Smith.

As a subsidiary chief executive in UDS, you were allowed to get on with it. No-one interfered. I had total control of our business but no influence on the group as a whole.

Controlling a subsidiary creates a different set of priorities from running your own business. You need to develop "groupmanship" – how to escape criticism and be allocated funds for investment. I was fortunate at UDS, as there was always another business doing worse than ours. In fact, many UDS companies did so badly, that they were closed down. In the space of seven years, I saw UDS bring an end to John Myers Mail Order, Grange Furnishing in Scotland, Alexandre the tailors, Claude Alexander, a number of department stores including Whiteleys of Bayswater and the fashion chain Van Allan (which the group had only purchased two years before its closure). With such a consistent record of failure, we were able to increase the size of our chain by taking on some of the closed shops. This was good for

Timpson while it lasted but it could not last for ever.

When the core retail chains of John Collier and Richard Shops also started to make losses, it was clear that UDS was about to lose its independence.

The buyout

In 1982 we were on the move. With three children in private education, we decided to buy a smaller house, leaving us with £20,000 in the bank and a £100,000 property with a £30,000 mortgage. I was a middle-of-the-range executive approaching middle age, settling for a comfortable but unambitious future. The Timpson business was performing better than most of the other UDS subsidiaries and, therefore, my job within the group was secure, but UDS itself was not so safe. Rumours had started in the City suggesting a take-over bid.

Dear James

The impossible does happen

One summer evening in 1982, Alex and I accepted an invitation to a charity dinner. Our party included several unfamiliar faces. Alex sat next to one of them – Roger Lane-Smith.

Roger was the senior partner of a small but high profile legal firm in Manchester. His headline client was Joan Collins but his heart was in the corporate side of the business. He was, and still is, a creative lawyer always on the look-out for the next opportunity. He spent the evening talking to Alex about my job and the possibilities of a management buyout. Alex, attracted by his enthusiasm, saw the chance of a complete change in our future fortunes. Roger made an appointment to see me the following week.

On Monday morning, Roger rang to confirm his appointment and on Tuesday he came to the office. Despite his air of confidence, I was sceptical. How could somebody with £20,000 in the bank contemplate buying a business which was probably worth over £30m?

My first concern was confidentiality. I had a secure position with UDS, but if the Lyons family discovered that I was plotting to buy the business, I could lose my job. But Alex put my mind at rest. "I'm just telling you it will work out," she said. She had an intuitive conviction that Roger held the key to our future. I didn't need much persuading – I wasn't designed for a safe but humdrum management job. An inward ambition was aroused by the excitement in prospect.

The decision was made easier by UDS itself – the group had such an uncertain future it no longer offered genuine job security.

A deal could work

I decided it was a risk worth taking and went with Roger on a furtive visit to see Candover, a newly-formed firm that specialised in buyouts. Before entering their office just off Fleet Street I looked round to check that I wasn't being observed by any member of the UDS board! I met Roger Brook, Candover's founder, and during the next hour started to understand the mechanics of a buyout. Roger Brook showed enough interest in Timpson to suggest a second meeting. But I couldn't make progress without involving our finance director, Peter Cookson. This was my first breach of confidentiality.

There was another shoe company in UDS – John Farmer – a 100 shoe shop chain run very successfully by brothers Patrick and Tim Farmer in Aldershot. I thought it unlikely that UDS would sell one shoe business without selling the other. A joint approach from Timpson and Farmer would be much more logical and could well provide a stronger proposition to venture capitalists. I decided to talk to Patrick and Tim. They were even more nervous than me and, despite showing some enthusiasm for the idea, declined my invitation to make a joint approach. I was not disappointed. In theory a joint approach had more chance of success but I had my doubts. Much would depend on whether our management style could work in harmony. It would be a lot easier to go it alone.

When I took Peter Cookson on my second visit to Candover, I felt firmly committed to the buyout cause. At first the figures seemed to present an impossible problem. Annual Timpson profits were running at about £2.5m a year, but the asset value was nearly £40m. The key was to use assets to fund the purchase.

The company still held a number of freehold properties purchased by my grandfather in the thirties. Roger Brook suggested I met Paul Orchard-Lisle, senior partner of Healey & Baker, to discuss what the portfolio was worth. After one hour with Paul Orchard-Lisle, I finally believed a buyout was possible. He identified £30m of property assets that could be sold on a sale and leaseback basis, with an initial rental charge of approximately £1.8m. We were already charging a market rent into our accounts before producing the current profit of £2.5m. Based on Paul's figures the rent charge would increase by £800,000 but still leave the company with a profit of £1.7m. We could fund a substantial purchase price and still make money.

Popping the question

We now had the shape of a deal but it would never be done unless I spoke to UDS, who had never sold a business and were unlikely to change the habit of a lifetime. I was nervous about putting the position to Stuart Lyons. He had shown considerable trust in me and I respected him for that. To turn round and suggest a buyout could be thought disloyal.

UDS was going through an even more torrid time than usual. There were regular rumours in the press about an imminent bid, which gave me the opportunity to talk about the future of the group and Timpson's role within it. I said that if UDS had any thoughts of selling the Timpson business, they should consider me as a serious buyer. I followed up our meeting with this letter:

"Dear Stuart,

I was pleased to have your assurance that there is no truth in current rumours regarding Timpson. I hope you appreciate the reasons for my concern. For the record I would like to reiterate that if there were a change and we became a candidate for asset realisation, I should hope to be kept informed and despite the substantial sum involved, be given the opportunity to raise the finance necessary to purchase the Timpson business.

I sincerely believe that my style of management is the best way to provide a good profit performance for Timpson shops and Timpson Shoe Repairs, something I am sure we will prove in the second half of the year.

Yours, John."

I had made my first approach and no harm had been done. But Stuart made it clear that Timpsons had a firm part in the future plans for UDS. There was no plan to sell our business. Six months after I had met Roger Lane-Smith, the buyout became a good idea that would never work.

Before the end of the year, UDS announced another set of poor results. In the face of increasing City pressure they changed their top management. Bernard Lyons resigned as chairman and was replaced by Sir Robert Clark, chairman of their merchant bank, Hill Samuel. Roger Lane-Smith saw the change of management as an opportunity to make a fresh approach. Over Christmas, I updated our business plan.

UDS bids

Everything changed in January 1983. Gerald Ronson made a bid for UDS, using a financial vehicle called Bassishaw. UDS management became hyperactive. In ten days I flew down to London five times for management meetings. It was clear that UDS would never be the same again. The Lyons family had lost control. The business was being run by Hill Samuel who were making all the major decisions in the take-over battle. The Hill Samuel defence relied on selling John Collier and Richard Shops to the Burton Group and replacing the Lyons family with a new management team. We hoped that Hill Samuel would include a Timpson buyout in their strategy. I decided to let Trevor Swete of Hill Samuel know of our plans.

Neither Bassishaw nor Hill Samuel got the chance to run UDS. Hanson Trust entered the battle and overbid Ronson to take control. Yet again I had to declare my hand and tell Hanson about our plans.

Life with Hanson

Five months with Hanson Trust was enough to tell me I could never be a corporate cog in a colossal company. All the fun was had by the 20 people who worked at their Brompton Road head office.

When UDS was taken over, no-one came to see me and no-one rang me up. I just received a fax telling me to cancel all capital expenditure. After a week I had my first Hanson visit, not from a member of their staff but from a consultant who spent three days preparing a report on Timpson. It was three weeks before I spoke to anybody from Hanson. We had a visit from Harvey Lipsith, (who later successfully led a management buyout for Allders Department Stores). Harvey was Hanson's accountant responsible for UDS. I did not enjoy the meeting. He made it clear that I was just another number in a business run by numbers.

Talking with Hanson

For three weeks there was no opportunity to propose a buyout. I had had no contact with a Hanson director until Tony Alexander, who managed their UK business, asked me to visit him at Brompton Road. Before going, I had a further meeting with Candover who agreed that I could use their name and suggest an offer for the business of £36m.

I had met Tony Alexander nearly 30 years before. We had been at the same prep school – Wadham House at Hale in Cheshire. It was helpful to have some common ground. It made it easier for me to raise the question of the buyout. I didn't expect him to give me an immediate answer. But he didn't say no. It was the first step.

Over the next few weeks, advised by Michael McAvoy, I tried to give Hanson the message that Timpson was a business worth selling. We wanted Hanson to believe that shoe retailing was very competitive, operating in shops with high rents and reliant on the vagaries of fashion. We also hoped to give the impression that Timpson was a well-run business heavily dependent on my own personal contribution. I had several visits from the Hanson team giving me ample opportunity to get my message across.

Roger Lane-Smith had his own Hanson contact. He had met Sir Gordon White (James Hanson's right-hand man), at a cocktail party in New York. As far as Roger was concerned, that introduction was enough to allow him to ring the USA and tell Sir Gordon about the Timpson buyout. Sir Gordon agreed to meet Roger on his next visit to London. Every day I waited for the meeting to be arranged and every day I was disappointed.

I was in Venice looking at shoe shops when the call came. Sir Gordon was coming over for Ascot Week and had agreed to see Roger and talk about Timpson.

Negotiating

The meeting with Sir Gordon White was cordial but inconclusive. We at least established that Timpson was for sale. Our offer of £35m was inadequate, Hanson wanted £46m.

The problem was capital gains. The book value of Timpson was £30m, anything over that figure would attract Capital Gains Tax (CGT) at the rate of 33 per cent. Sir Gordon White sent us away with the thought that if we could help them solve their CGT we could be in sight of a deal.

Within days, Peter Cookson found a solution. Through a complicated device he separated the property transactions from the purchase of the company, establishing a capital loss to set off against the gain. Solving the problem not only saved Hanson money but it also demonstrated our determination.

Conversations at Candover got more serious. We started to discuss the structure of our new business. I agreed to the appointment of Trevor Morgan as our prospective chairman. Trevor was known to Candover through one of their directors, Michael Stoddard. I had known Trevor for years; he had been the chief executive of Turners Footwear and represented them on the Multiple Shoe Retailers Association before selling the business and becoming a director of Hepworths. Trevor introduced George Davies to Hepworths and helped set up a new business called Next.

Candover offered us their standard buyout management deal. We (the Timpson management) would subscribe a substantial but afford-able sum (in our case £125,000) and in return would receive 12.5 per cent of the equity which, on a performance-related basis, could increase to 25 per cent. All the other equity would be held by Candover sup-ported institutions.

A second meeting was arranged with Hanson, to meet Tony Alexander and another director, Alan Hagdrup. Our latest figures showed that we could safely offer £40m. The absolute maximum we could pay was £42.5m. I went to Brompton Road with Roger and Stephen Curran of Candover. The meeting didn't last long. After con-firming that we had indeed solved their CGT problem, Tony Alexander declared that he was still looking for £44m compared with our offer of £38m. It took less than an hour to settle the price that changed my life. We moved to £40m, they moved to £42m. In the end we agreed a deal based on £42m with the last £2m being paid over the next three years. We had started the meeting at 5.30pm and before 6.30pm the deal had been agreed and whisky was produced to celebrate.

That night I was so excited I couldn't sleep. It was my first big deal and I thought that once the Heads of Terms had been agreed, it was all over bar the shouting, I didn't realise the deal had just begun.

Own goal

When I got home the following night, Peter Cookson rang to say we had got our sums wrong. His figures had assumed that we would not benefit from the inter-company balances between Timpson and UDS. The deal that we had made the night before gave us that benefit. We were £4m better off!

Peter Cookson got his team working through the weekend to con-firm the figures. By Sunday night it was clear that we were sitting in the pound seats. We had agreed a deal with Hanson that required £4m less funding than all the figures we had agreed with Candover.

I quickly saw the significance and seized the opportunity. On

Sunday night I agreed with Roger that we should aim for 80 per cent of the equity. On Monday morning I met David Briggs, the senior manager of our accountants Peat Marwick. He confirmed our figures. I then saw Alan Jones, the manager of NatWest in Manchester, who provided the quickest possible response: the deal was bankable.

Peter Cookson and I met Roger in his Manchester office to discuss what to do next. The whole deal had changed; we could now achieve a buyout without Candover's help. But it was a great advantage to continue the Candover contact. We didn't want to give Hanson the impression we had a comfortable ride financing the deal. Roger rang Stephen Curran at Candover. He explained how the figures had changed and said he was looking for 80 per cent for the management. At first Stephen offered 25 per cent. Then he moved to 50 per cent and then conceded. "I can see where you are coming from," he said.

Dividing up the 80 per cent was one of my most difficult tasks. There is never the right answer; I just produced an allocation I believed to be fair. But I was also thinking of the problems my father had suffered years earlier – I wanted to have control. I finished with 54 per cent, the four senior directors had five per cent each, Roger Lane-Smith got 2.5 per cent. The balance was split between two subsidiary directors, my sister and Michael McAvoy.

securing the funds

Despite NatWest support we still planned to raise £2.5m from Candover institutions for their 20 per cent. I compiled a slide show about the business. Our first presentation was made to Michael Stoddard of Electra; he gave Peter Cookson and myself a hard time. If his unfriendly and arrogant approach was meant to put us on our mettle, he succeeded.

We got a warmer welcome from the other Candover institutions; Murray Johnstone, Investors in Industry (3i), Robert Fleming and BP Pension Fund all agreed to take a stake. Despite his frosty reception, even Michael Stoddard invested on behalf of Electra.

We now had the funding to do the deal but most of the money still had to be raised through sale and leaseback deals on the Timpson properties. This is when I learned that in the property world, when someone says "yes" they mean "maybe." We had agreed to sell the bulk of the Timpson freeholds to Commercial Union and Scottish Amicable for £27m but the deals were subject to board approval. And before their board approved, a lot went wrong. Two properties had high alumina cement and dropped out of the deal. Several were in a poor state of repair and eight per cent of the price was held back to cover the cost of dilapidations. From a third tranche of properties we hoped to raise the further £3m required to complete our funding but deals with three different property companies failed to get board approval. For weeks the saga continued with the money that we were able to raise fluctuating from £30m to £27m and back to £30m.

Candover was keeping an eagle eye on events. They had the ready answer to any shortfall funding; they could increase the amount subscribed by their investors. But the management share would go down and I would lose control of the business. There was another balancing factor – cash flow within the business. While the buyout negotiations went on, the business traded well and created cash. Whenever we had a property setback, our trading cash flow came to the rescue.

Every day brought a new drama and five weeks after we had agreed Heads of Terms it seemed that we were no nearer to exchanging contracts.

Family holiday

I faced another problem. Twelve months before, I had booked a family holiday, a camper tour across the States, from Los Angeles to Miami. It was to be the first holiday with our newly arrived adopted son Oliver. Alex would not cancel the trip and I could not let her take four children in a camper across America on her own.

In blissful ignorance of the way deals work, I thought I had the perfect compromise. I booked a hotel on Galveston Island so that I could fly back half way through our holiday, sign the deal, and return to join the family! Things didn't turn out as planned. I rang the office each day to follow a game of snakes and ladders with property setbacks balanced by improvement in cash flow just keeping the Candover funding in place. Galveston Island was devastated by a hurricane the day before we were due to arrive. We were forced to continue our journey across America. Instead of breaking my holiday half way through, I cut it short. I left the family at a soulless hotel in Miami and flew home.

After two more weeks of insurmountable problems that somehow got resolved, the deal suddenly changed character.

Contracts exchanged

My biggest allies were the Hanson team. Throughout our negotiations they were always constructive and as keen as I was to get the deal done. One Tuesday in September, Tony Alexander gave everyone an ultimatum. "If the deal isn't done by Thursday afternoon, everyone can file their papers," he said.

Little problems suddenly disappeared and big problems were solved in minutes. The lawyers stopped raising points and worked through the night to resolve their difficulties. The Hanson deadline created a common purpose, with no-one wanting to waste three months' work.

It wasn't just a deal with Hanson. We also had to tie in the funding from Candover and the property deals with Commercial Union and Scottish Amicable. Scottish Amicable created the final drama. For legal reasons that deal had to be signed in Scotland not in London. At 3.25pm, five minutes before Hanson's deadline, we called their Scottish office but could only reach the switchboard – the extension was engaged. Finally, with the last minute drama that lawyers love so much, Roger was able to confirm that the deal had been signed. With three minutes to spare we exchanged contracts.

At £42m this was the second biggest buyout ever achieved in the UK and I had regained control of the family business.

William Timpson, who founded
the shoe retail business

The first Timpson shoe shop in Oldham Street, Manchester, opened in 1869

The first Timpson shoe repair factory; a central workshop that started in 1903

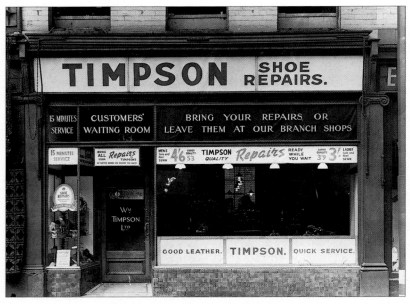

The shoe repair shop in Sheffield in 1939

Will Timpson

Noel Timpson

Anthony Timpson

Geoffrey Noakes

shoes and shoe shops in the fifties –
the shop was filled with shoe boxes,
every customer had a seat and the sales
assistant put the shoes on your feet

In 1958 shoe repairs were hidden at the back of a reception area

...or the repairs were carried out in the basement of a retail shop

In the early sixties heel bars grew rapidly, helped by the stiletto heel

...customers took their shoes off and sat down while the job was done

In the seventies shoe repairs started to decline and Timpson introduced merchandise into all shoe repair shops

Computers were introduced into Timpson in 1961
This early Univac computer had a 16k memory

The shoe factory at Kettering: opened 1923, closed 1972

Central office at Wythenshawe: opened 1964, sold to Oliver Group in 1987

The author in 1975, the year he became
Timpson Managing Director

Cartoon drawn to illustrate Anthony Timpson's sacking as Chairman
— he was forced to leave his Bristol car in the company car park

Roger Lane-Smith
Timpson company lawyer and non executive director
who first put the idea of a buyout to John Timpson

The buyout team from left to right: Michael Frank (General Manager
— Shoe Repairs), Bill Dawes (Shoe Retail Director), John Timpson, Jim Taylor
(Merchandise Buying Director), Peter Cookson (Finance Director)

Argyle Street, Glasgow 1980
The shoe repair shop on the left was originally a Suede Centre (Swears & Wells) and the shoe shop was Claude Alexander (part of John Collier)

Timpson Shoe Repairs in Ashton-Under-Lyne, 1982
Keys were still less than ten per cent of the business

In the seventies the shoe repair
business developed a large bag
and hosiery business

After 1985 all the space taken by merchandise was given to key cutting

The Shoetech in Worcester was acquired as part of a chain of 12 shops in 1987

This is the same branch in 1999

"Before and after" comparison of the shop in Slough
All the 110 Automagic branches acquired in 1995 have been converted to Timpson

Today Timpson has become a multi-service shop...

...keys are the biggest part of the business and watch repairs the fastest growing

A family photo taken for Alex's birthday in 1989
Back row: Oliver, James, Edward   Front row: John, Henry, Victoria

Alex and John Timpson, 1997

Back to earth

It was a dream come true. The company I thought had disappeared forever suddenly became a family business again. I was walking on air, hardly able to believe what had happened.

Dear James

Expect
the
unexpected

When I woke up from the dream, I found independent life was nothing like as good as expected. Our business plans showed that the company went from strength to strength, we successfully floated on the Stock Exchange and everybody – employees, investors, directors and myself – would enjoy the experience. It did not happen.

The buyout was very exciting but it put me under pressure. Having achieved the dream of buying back the family business, I had to make it successful. But that was pressure I brought on myself. Much more difficult was the need to satisfy the demands of outsiders. The other management shareholders, the venture capitalists and the clearing bank all expected to see success.

For twelve months following the buyout, the company traded fairly well but soon sales stagnated and profits started to fall. It was then that I most needed the tips that come from experience, which are illustrated in the rest of this book.

The buyout was a wonderful dream but for the company to then fail would be a personal nightmare. The more I faced that possibility, the more stressful life became.

Loss of confidence

High rents, increased competition and changes in fashion made trading difficult. Our high gearing put me under pressure and I made a few bad decisions that made matters worse. Throughout 1984 we were over-stocked – we bought too many boots. Good buying is critical to a fashion business, but even good buyers can have a bad season.

Under pressure to see our profits rise I was persuaded by Trevor Morgan to make sweeping changes. We split the roles of buying and merchandising – so that buyers selected the styles and merchandisers fixed the quantity and determined the shop distribution. That replaced flair with number crunching but sales did not improve.

My loss of confidence was so complete, that two years after the buyout I became chairman and handed over executive responsibility to outside recruits from the Burton Group.

The change in management style was dramatic and Timpson did not take kindly to the difference. The employees felt I had exchanged a wealth of experience for expensive executives who knew nothing about the shoe business. The new team worked very long hours but sales got even worse and the business was heading towards a loss. Just in time I learned the importance of getting the thinking straight. One day I took a cool hard look at the future of our shoe shops.

The shops faced a number of problems. At a time of inflation, shoe prices were not increasing – cheap imports were bringing prices down. For years there had been far too many specialist shoe shops on the high street, and now other shops were selling shoes, such as Marks & Spencer, Littlewoods and the clothing chains like Burtons and C & A. Training shoes brought competition from specialist sports shops. Fashion did not help. The wide variety of styles demanded by the public called for higher stocks. We had a poor stockturn and needed big shops to accommodate all the shoes. This meant high rents. We wanted prime positions and could not afford them.

Three years after the buyout I was facing failure. Fortunately, I was the first to realise that the whole of shoe retailing was heading for disaster. When I couldn't financially justify opening another shoe shop, it was clearly time to sell.

sell out

I put all these thoughts down on paper. At the top of the sheet I wrote "The future of Timpson Shops." I had two columns, one headed "Against" and the other headed "For." Once I had filled a column full of bad news, the simple question was: why should we continue?

FUTURE OF TIMPSON SHOPS

Against	For
• Cheap shoes	• Strong brand
• Trainers	• Family tradition
• B.S.C.	
• Mail order	
• High rents	
• Shopfitting cost	
• Cut price competition	
• Shoe fashion less predictable	
• M & S/BHS selling shoes	
• Concessions	
• Low stockturn	
• Wage inflation	
• High mark-downs	

Conclusion: We can't open another new shop!

The only reason to continue selling shoes was personal pride. It took three months to break my emotional ties sufficiently to take the decision and put the shoe shops up for sale. It took another eight months to sell them. It took me too long to accept the inevitable truth. I was selling the family silver which I had spent 15 years restoring to the family name. It took months to come to terms with the truth. If I had been more detached and more decisive, I would have got a higher price. I eventually decided to sell the shoe shops during a flight to New York with Peter Cookson. We devised a scheme that not only took us out of shoe retailing but retained control of our shoe repair shops.

Despite our problems we still had a profitable history and a net asset value of over £17m including property assets valued at £8m. The shoe repair business made a profit of £450,000. We reorganised the asset register – up to then the shoe repair and shoe shop properties were intertwined. We put all property assets not directly associated with shoe shops into a pot labelled shoe repairs. This established a shoe repair portfolio worth £3m. We put the shoe shops up for sale on condition that we kept the shoe repair business at a nominal price of £3m. We knew the assets could be quickly realised to pay the price.

We were encouraged by an initial guide price of £20-25m given to us by the retail guru and stockbroker Gerald Horner. But we went about the sale in the wrong way. After several false dawns, trade rumour suggested the name of Olivers. George Oliver was a 350 shop shoe multiple based in Leicester with its stores mainly in the midlands, south-west England and Wales – we were a near perfect fit. It was another family business. Chaired by Ian Oliver, it had recently brought in an aggressive managing director, Graham Taylor, from Sketchley and Asda. His appointment suggested a keenness for rapid growth – probably through acquisition. We quickly agreed terms at £15m.

Both businesses faced the same problems. One solution was to sell, the other to expand and get economies of scale. The purchase bought Olivers breathing space and it took us out of shoe retailing altogether. It was a good deal for both of us.

I knew I couldn't afford the deal to fall through. We had lost the confidence of our shop staff. Trading was getting worse by the week, sales were down on last year. I was terrified that Olivers would ask for our latest sales figures, but they never did. The figures on which they based their purchase were three months out of date. I spent five weeks of legal process, waiting to be asked "how did you do last week?" The question never came and after a final all-night lawyers' drama, the deal was signed.

Everyone thought Olivers had got a bargain. After all, I had purchased the business for £42m only four years previously and now I had sold it for £15m. The headline figures hid the truth. Olivers bought the shares which we had purchased for £250,000.The venture capitalists achieved a high rate of return and my fellow management shareholders each received £750,000.

The deal was done in a daze. It was like selling the house you have lived in since childhood. I was not only selling a business; a lot of people I knew well went with it. I had let them down. Many would lose their jobs because I had failed to find a way to make our shoe shops profitable.

Looking back it was the best decision I ever made. To dispel any lingering doubts, I only have to look at the shoe multiples who continued to battle on in the High Street. The best known names like Clarks, Stylo and Stead & Simpson have continued to find trading very difficult. Olivers had a traumatic time but the extra Timpson branches helped them to survive. The wisdom of my decision is shown by the dramatic demise of British Shoe, which had well over 20 per cent of the market when I sold the shops. Today BSC has disappeared. Some people realised it was a good decision to get out of footwear retailing. But no-one knew how smart it was to keep the shoe repairs.

My life changed completely. The deal gave me financial security and a less stressful business – £5m after tax and a 65 per cent shareholding in a debt-free shoe repair business – but I also had to tell the Timpson Shop employees I had sold their business.

Specialist cobbler

I did not want to retire at 44 and Alex certainly did not want me hanging round the house. As much as I enjoy golf, tennis, squash, snooker (and in more recent years real tennis), I prefer sport as a pastime rather than the main event. I still wanted to run a business and Timpson Shoe Repairs gave me that opportunity.

We acquired Timpson Shoe Repairs for a personal investment of £120,000. The purchase price was £3m and this bought a property portfolio worth £3m. Timpson Shoe Repairs was making profits of £450,000. We were able to fund the purchase price with an overdraft facility provided by NatWest. We now had no venture capitalists to worry about. We just had to keep the bank manager happy.

Clogs to clogs

It took six months to recover from the trauma of selling the shoe shops. When I woke up, I had not only changed the business but I had changed my lifestyle. For the first time, I had cash in the bank and could move to a large house with a small mortgage. I started to play tennis and golf during the week and still had time for a regular day off with Alex. The shorter my working week, the better the business seemed to do. A workaholic chief executive doesn't necessarily make a business more profitable.

The business only had four shareholders: myself with the majority stake, Peter Cookson, Mike Williams (the property director) and Roger Lane-Smith.

The pressures of shoe retailing had left little time for anything else. I could now get closely involved in shoe repairs. Although I couldn't repair a shoe, I found the business fascinating. We were soon looking for ways to expand. Within months we made our first acquisition: Shoetech, a 12 branch chain of shoe repair shops based in the south and midlands but owned by two entrepreneurs living in Jersey. We bought the company for shares giving the owners – John Stratford and Chris Fowler – 18 per cent of our equity and seats on the board.

Our long term aim was to float so we saw a paper purchase as the cheapest way to grow – keeping the company in credit at the bank. We intended to be another niche retailer following in the footsteps of Sock Shop, Tie Rack and Body Shop who had recently come to the market at P/E ratios between 35 and 50. The Shoetech deal was completed in October 1987. Four days later, the stock market collapsed. We had a lucky escape. We had appointed a stock broker but never wrote the prospectus. We were the niche retailer that never came to the market.

shareholder strife

Alex stopped my ambitions to float. She told me I was mad. When everyone else was rushing to the market, Alex told me to keep clear. She saw the benefits of a private business and the threat of demanding shareholders. Once my intentions became clear, the Jersey-based share-holders turned against me. Despite an improvement in profits, they said I was incompetent and wrote a long letter, listing my faults.

They had a justified grievance. When we bought their business we agreed to a float. I had broken that promise. The only solution was to buy out their shareholding. Their 12 shops cost over £1m at £80,000 per shop; it made Shoetech our most expensive purchase ever. All 12 shops survive and have repaid the £1m nearly twice over.

I then encountered criticism from closer to home. Mike Williams and Peter Cookson were minority shareholders and wanted the protection of a shareholders' agreement. They had a good point so I agreed that they could sell me their shareholding on a P/E of ten at any time during the next five years after that I had the option to buy their shares on the same multiple.

The business did well for three years. We acquired three business-es, grew to 225 shops and bought a 26 per cent stake in our next largest competitor, Automagic. Everything was fine until depression hit the high street and slim heels went out of fashion. In 1991 profits fell from £1.8m to £1.3m and I found I was being increasingly criticised by my fellow directors. I resisted their calls for a cost cutting campaign, being convinced from visiting branches that our competitors' trade was even worse.

One Friday afternoon, Peter Cookson came to my office. He said he was going to immediately invoke our agreement in respect of half his 20 per cent holding. The formula based on the record profits of the pre-vious year made half his stake worth £1m.

Mike Williams saw me the following Monday. He wanted to cash in his shares. One weekend had swallowed up all my personal assets and put me on the other side of the negotiating table from my two main directors and shareholders.

I chose the most expensive solution. I offered to buy the whole 35 per cent of the shares I did not own. I had to find £3.5m within three weeks. We raided company cash flow, sold all my investments, used most of my spare cash and still needed to take a £1m mortgage on our house. I ended five years of personal financial security but it was well worth it. I now own the business 100 per cent.

There was no public announcement and I said nothing to the people in the company but the business had changed. As sole owner, I started to manage in a different way. It was much more my business where staff and customers were seen as the main asset and I took a longer-term view of our future fortunes.

In search of magic

In 1987 we were the second-biggest shoe repairer in the UK – the largest was Mr Minit, part of a multinational chain. In third position was Automagic with 120 shops. Between 1987 and 1990 I had regular talks with Mike Strom, the Chairman of Automagic. He would only contemplate a merger which left him in management control. Our talking days ended when Timpson acquired 26 per cent of the Automagic equity. We hoped the share stake would lead to a total bid but Mike Strom retained a 47 per cent personal stake and, despite a poor trading record, was able to block any approach we made. Strom's non-executive directors were aware that the business was in a fatal decline. In 1992, they agreed to sell us 35 Automagic branches. Mike Strom blocked the transaction. In 1995, another package was agreed, again for 35 branches, but on the day that contracts were due to be exchanged, Barclays called in the receivers to Automagic.

Dear James

You need a fair share of luck

Dealing with the receiver

At a stroke we lost the advantage of our 26 per cent shareholding and we were just one of 400 companies that responded when the receivers put Automagic up for sale. We sought advice. We were told that receivers sell most companies for a song and we offered £1.8m. Our advice was incorrect. There was a lot of interest in Automagic. The receivers asked for a serious offer. We revised our price to £2.8m. The receivers asked us to bid for a third time, saying several companies had made similarly sized offers. We were given three days to come up with our best price. It was clear that the receiver wasn't bluffing.

Our best shot

We thought that Automagic was worth £3.8m but the bank would not give us backing for such a bid, even though I made a major sacrifice.

Three years after acquiring the 35 per cent shareholding I didn't own, I had, much to Alex's relief, paid off the £1m mortgage. Totally against her wishes, I now planned to reinstate the £1m mortgage to give us the finance to have a decent shot at Automagic.

This was probably the most difficult and certainly the most courageous decision I have made in business. I say courageous because I did not have Alex's support. I have relied on her intuitive judgement on every other occasion and she has always been right. For once we disagreed. I was devastated that she would not listen to my argument – I knew the potential of Automagic would transform our business but she could only think of the mortgage. Without the mortgage the only way to fund the deal would be to give up equity. I put my neck well and truly on the block.

Final bids were required for 5pm on Wednesday afternoon and by 2pm it was clear that the bank would not approve the £3.8m we wanted to offer. We submitted a bid of £3.35m and crossed our fingers .

The receiver promised to call early on Thursday morning. I had a sleepless night and arrived in my office all alone at 8am waiting for the call. It was good news and bad news. Our bid was pitched at the right level but two other parties had made a similar offer. During the conversation it became clear that one of the other bidders was our major competitor, Mr Minit. Knowing that Mr Minit had almost unlimited cash resources, I rang Kenn Begley, the Minit chief executive, with a proposition.

I proposed a half. I suggested a joint bid and if we were successful, to toss a coin. Whoever won the toss would pick the first shop and we would alternatively select shops until the last Automagic branch had been allocated. Kenn Begley needed the advice of his chairman.

Within 20 minutes my offer was rejected. He said they were determined to acquire Automagic and one day hoped to buy our business as well. I pointed out that, with a son already in the business, we would not be available for another 30 years. Our conversation was at an end and the next 24 hours would decide who owned Automagic.

The longest day

The receiver put together some further information to help the final bidders. Our team – finance director Martin Tragen, Mike Williams, Roger Lane-Smith and myself had to go to London to view the information pack and fix our final price. With our limited resources we thought that our best hope was to force Minit to pay a high price for the business. I was likely to be a bad loser.

Roger and Mike set off first. Martin and I stayed behind for two more hours to try and secure stronger bank support. Roger got to the receiver before the opposition and secured a vital factor in the deal. They agreed that there would be no Dutch auction – the sale would be settled by a sealed bid submitted by 7pm that evening.

We spent five hours poring over new figures which confirmed a substantial redundancy liability at the Automagic head office. By 6.30 pm we had still not settled on the price. We had to offer at least £3.8m but didn't have a strong indication of bank support at that level. At 6.50 pm Martin went out on a limb. He felt sure that we could fund a bid of £4m. Before we faxed through our offer, I added £12,500. I had heard that Richard Branson always added a little bit extra to avoid being tied with the opposition at an exact round price amount. We faxed through £4,012,500 at exactly 7pm. Five minutes later we got a response. We had put in the highest bid.

The receivers wanted us to go straight away and sign up the paperwork but Roger stalled. The letter from our bank was not strong enough to stand scrutiny. Roger spent three hours pulling out reasons for our delay until we faxed through our bank's letter. The receiver gave us an ultimatum. The other party was still in his office ready to sign the deal. If we could not produce better evidence of bank support by 10am the following day, we were out of contention.

It was 10pm before we got to a restaurant for a meal dominated by the mobile telephone. A series of desperate calls went out to find the

£750,000 that would bridge our funding gap. No real progress had been made by midnight. We went to bed, not to sleep but to dream of how close we had been to securing the deal.

Threadbare through lack of sleep, we arrived at Roger's London office early the following morning for a further round of calls. The office clock seemed to move faster than normal. The 10am deadline quickly approached.

Cliffhanger

The air of gloom started to lift at 9.15 am when we got our first encouraging call from Brian Ferguson at NatWest in Stockport. By 9.45 am we had his letter backing our deal. We rang the receiver to confirm we had the money and we were immediately called over to their office to start the final paperwork. Roger stayed behind in his office but 45 minutes later was on the telephone. "I have had a call from Mr Minit," he told me. "I think you ought to ring them and listen to what they have to say." He gave me the number of a room at the Savoy. I got through to Kenn Begley. "It appears we are in the middle of an auction," he said. "Do you remember the deal you offered me yesterday? I think we should get together and talk about it now." I told him I would think about it and ring back. I never did. For the next hour we made rapid progress but suddenly there was a phone call. The room cleared leaving the Timpson contingent to worry about the mystery caller. This final Minit intervention was clearly not enough to stop our negotiations. The room refilled. Two hours later I sealed the contract with a nervous squiggly signature.

Making it work

Over the weekend we put the administration in place and by Tuesday every Automagic branch had received a visit from their new area manager. Three weeks later, the Automagic head office at Harpenden was closed down and all Automagic stock deliveries and wages came from Manchester.

The relief that followed the deal was soon followed by further anxiety. The act of receivership brings shop leases to a close. We had purchased the business but had still to acquire the properties. Mike Williams had the task of renegotiating 110 separate leases covering the whole of the Automagic chain. Two weeks after the deal I discovered that Mr Minit had written to some landlords offering to acquire leases at a substantially increased rent. The danger hit me like a thunderbolt. I thought the worst: I could lose the best performing branches and my £1m mortgage. Fortunately, in this area property law sees justice is done. We renegotiated every lease and in many cases (taking advantage of a weak property market) reduced the rent.

The day-to-day integration of Automagic was swift but it took six months to sell the freehold warehouse at Harpenden for £400,000, a welcome inflow of cash but well below the hoped-for figure. It took even longer to improve the turnover.

The workforce were demoralised. Several years of ineffective management had made them suspicious. They had no faith in management promises of new investment. With no increase in wages for three years, they had taken matters into their own hands. Standards of customer service and housekeeping were poor and staff dishonesty was rife. We didn't win round the workforce until we started to invest. We developed the Automagic key business with considerable success. Once they saw we knew what we were doing, things changed. Sales increased by over 20 per cent for three years running and, by 1998, 17 of our top 20 turnover branches had come from the Automagic acquisition. The deal had changed the shape of Timpson and we were now the market leader.

Changing market

Within nine months of our deal, a major change happened to the other big player Mr Minit. It was founded in 1956 by American entrepreneur Hillsden Ryan, when he started repairing shoes in the Bon Marche store in Brussels. In effect, he invented the Heel Bar and over the next 30 years expanded the concept to over 25 countries creating a chain of over 4,000 shops. Lack of management succession in the eighties caused the business to falter and in 1996, Minit was acquired for around £50m by UBS (Union Bank of Switzerland).

Initially I thought of this as an opportunity rather than a threat and went to visit the new Minit management. It was a frosty and fruitless meeting. I had arrived hoping that I might be able to purchase some of Minit's UK stores. I left knowing that I had a competitor with unlimited money to invest but little knowledge of the market.

Sitting at a café outside the UBS office with Martin Tragen, I formulated the strategy which has guided Timpson for the last three years. Faced with such a well-heeled competitor, I was determined that we would become the best at what we do in the UK and the best company to work for. Since then we have invested over £1m on training and our wage rates have risen by 35 per cent.

The Automagic acquisition changed our business but it didn't change the market. Demand for shoe repairs has continued to fall. We needed another source of income to compensate for the decline of our core business. We found it in watch repairs. Starting with an experiment in four shops in 1996, we now have 250 shops offering a watch repair service with a total turnover of over £3m a year.

Over the last four years, our trading cash flow has been invested in existing units. All but 30 of the 320 shops have been completely refurbished, changing the old fashioned shoe repairer image into a modern service shop. I hope that we now have shops that my great grandfather who founded the company would be proud of.

Good business

For 12 years Timpson Shoe Repairs has given me everything anyone could look for in a business.

Our core market is constantly declining. Spending on shoe repairs has gone down every year for the past 25 years and given us our major challenge. Despite that handicap, we have prospered by cutting keys and introducing both engraving and watch repairs, but most important of all by developing the people who serve our customers.

CHAPTER 6

How to use this book

During 25 years running a business, I have seen plenty of good times but I have had many bad years as well. You, James, have only seen the business growing rapidly. It will be difficult for you to contemplate anything other than an unbroken future of success. But there will be setbacks. There will be bad years. There may even be times when you despair that things will ever get better. That is when this book will become most useful to you.

Dear James

I hope this will help

We both know that golf can be extremely frustrating. Just when you are starting to play well and it feels easy, it suddenly becomes difficult again. When you start playing badly, you can't ever remember what you did when you played well. That is where this book helps. It contains things which have worked for me. Most have been learned in the past few years. I am still learning. I have never been able to understand how impossibly naive I could be only five years ago. I thought this when I was 30 and I still think it today at the age of 57.

I hope that these notes will be useful. Treat them as tips from your predecessor. A list of ideas that have worked, they constitute the best advice I can give you – 25 years of experience. It is only a guide; put your own personality across, add your own ideas, because no-one can run a business by a textbook.

I have learned as much from failure as success. The ideas in this book often come from lessons learned when I got things wrong. Even when I know what to do, I have not always followed my own advice! Please take note of what I say rather than what I have done. But be your own man and read this book purely as a guide.

I appreciate that it looks odd because it is written in pictures as well as words. I have bought several management books over the years, particularly at airports when setting off on holiday. Most of them don't get read beyond page 30. Today people read pictures rather than words. They read the *Sun* and *Hello* and they look at the television. I hope this book will be an easy read.

It contains lots of tips, many ideas and several important messages. Most important of all it is the people who work in the business who make the ideas come to life. Remember that 95 per cent of the people in our business are better at key cutting than we are. You need their help – your job is to help them to run the business for you.

Family first

The business plays a very important part in my life. It is my number one hobby. You seem to have a similar view, but don't forget what you are doing all this for. For over 30 years my best critic and adviser has been your mother. She really understands where our true priorities lie. You married a similar talent. Listen to what your wife Roisin says about the business, she is both close enough to what is happening and far enough away from the detail to give the advice you need.

If you inherit my role you will take on considerable responsibilities. Your guidance will determine the future of the business and the prospects of the people we employ. It is fun, it is rewarding and it is terribly important to remember where your priorities lie.

The only thing more important than your family business, is your family.

Being a chief executive

CHAPTER 7

Your job

Don't believe what you read in the newspapers. Running a business is not about big deals and being driven around by a chauffeur. You don't sit behind a desk making snap decisions and you shouldn't spend your life in meetings.

> Dear James
>
> Whatever you do, don't run the day to day business!

Text books give useful guidelines but there are no rules for an entrepreneur. Business schools don't tell you everything about being a chief executive; they provide the theory but not the practice.

Family business training

Read as many management books as you can, but take 80 per cent of your lessons from experience. A family business has two great advantages – a lifetime knowledge of the industry and the fact that you risk your own money!

When I was asked to run Swears & Wells at the age of 28, no-one had told me how to run a company. I just arrived at the Liverpool office on a Monday morning and started looking at figures, talking to people and visiting the shops. Luckily the family firm had taught me that running a business is about ideas, common sense and getting the support of employees. Being thrown in at the deep end was just as good as going to a business school.

Managers trained by big companies sometimes assume that an independent family business must be run by a bunch of amateurs. From time-to-time, I have been concerned that our business lacks "professional management." In 1985, when our retail shoe business was going through a bad time, I recruited people from the Burton Group, the most successful retail company at that time. It was a disaster. The new recruits worked harder than anyone else in the business before or since. They used all the techniques that had been successful for Burton but it didn't work for Timpson.

Set the style

You can't run a business without a lot of help from employees. Your job is to lead them. You set the style of the business. People want to know who they work for; once they recognise you are the boss, they will be guided by your expectations. Many of the successful businesses reflect the personality of their leader. Body Shop and Anita Roddick, Virgin and Richard Branson, KwikFit and Tom Farmer, Dixons and Stanley Kalms – none of these companies would have had such success without a clear style set by their chief executive. Your enthusiasm will be infectious. If you have a clear direction the company will know where it is going.

YOUR LEADERSHIP WILL SET THE STYLE FOR THE BUSINESS

Get the thinking straight

Your job is to define the main problems and find solutions that work. Every business has lots of possible strategies to choose from. You don't have to discover the perfect solution. There will be many that work. Just find one and stick with it.

It is your job to do the thinking for the business. You must make the big decisions. You must choose the direction to go and decide when changes should be made. You also have to think how to make change happen.

It is no good having a great idea that doesn't become a reality. One of your jobs is to clear obstacles out of the way so that your ideas can work. You will constantly face a resistance to change.

I wanted to introduce watch repairs in 1990. It seemed then just the right service to add to our portfolio. We couldn't find a qualified

watch repairer, so it didn't happen. It took us seven years to realise we would have to train our own staff. In 1998 the Horological Institute sorted out our problem. Their training course convinced our staff that they could become qualified watch repairers and my idea of the watch repair service became a reality. "Getting the thinking straight" is what most companies call their business plan.

The right people

A chief executive should not run the day-to-day business – it's not your job to do the detail. You can't be in 300 shops at once, so you have to rely on your staff to run the business. They will always be better at repairing shoes than you will. Your job is to pick the right people.

I like staff that are successful! Promote the winners, not the good administrator, the good talker, or the people who look smart but don't perform. The best managers are in the shops that take the most money.

We haven't brought outsiders into our management team for 13 years. Throughout my career, superstars of the business have been home-grown. Be careful how many people you bring in from outside. Consistently successful businesses are places where change happens gradually. Businesses thrive on stability. If in doubt, stay with the devil you know and make your appointments from within the company.

When I was a footwear buyer, I worked with two of the most respected buyers in the industry, Tom Howell, who bought children's shoes, and Tom Hardman, who bought ladies' shoes. Both started with the business as soon as they left school. It is unfashionable to stay with one company throughout your career, but it still seems to happen with us.

All our area managers started working in shoe repair shops, as did our three regional managers. Our technical managers, Mike Donoghue and Jim Jardine, also joined straight from school and have both completed more than 25 years.

As the business gets bigger, we may bring in more graduates. But their brains are not the main qualification. We look for personality and the ability to make things happen.

Look after people

Keep your business and social life as far away from each other as possible. I rarely socialise with senior colleagues, not because I don't like them but because I think it is best to keep the two lives apart.

But your interest in employees should extend beyond the workplace. You need to know them as complete people and you can't do that without having knowledge of their families and their hobbies. Don't interfere with their lives outside work, but be there to help. At times of sickness, bereavement, or financial and family problems, you may be just the person to turn to.

The most important way you can look after employees is to help them make more money. Aim to increase their pay packets. Our branch bonus scheme has helped the business grow over the last few years. We pay a weekly bonus of 15 per cent on turnover beyond a floating target figure. The target is set at 4.35 times the total wage paid in

the branch. There is no upper limit to the bonus an individual can earn. The current weekly record bonus is £654.

It is a simple system that at a stroke rewards both performance and productivity. We regularly check with our staff to see if they want the system changed. The answer is always…No!

If you can honestly say "My job is to find ways to increase your pay," you will find everyone on your side.

Set standards

Our shoe repair business was originally a network of factories hidden from the public, providing a service for our shoe shops. When we put the shoe repair machinery on view during the seventies, the operatives came out of their workshops and took the first step to becoming retailers, but their style was based on the factories of 1950 rather than the high street of 1970.

In 1979, while spending a full week visiting our shoe repair shops, I suddenly realised the business lacked retailing standards. The shops looked like factories. The shelves were dirty, half the staff had not shaved and there was an overflowing ashtray on the counter. I introduced a new set of rules. No smoking in the shop, no cups of tea on the counter, daily dusting of displays, and the loo disinfected regularly. The most important change I made was to insist the men wore a tie. Ties became the symbol of our new retailing standards. Cleanliness and good house-keeping became part of the Timpson image.

The look of our shoe repair outlets has changed but this has had no influence on the rest of the industry. Most independent shops are just as scruffy as those that I saw on my visits in 1979. Even our ex-employees return to the dirt and filled ashtrays within six months.

Make sure the company is not dominated by administrators. Left on their own, administrators concentrate on saving money and drawing up rules that keep power concentrated at Head Office. But we want a business that delegates authority to those who serve our customers.

To turn this vision into reality, aim to be the best at what you do. Set the standards yourself. If you don't care whether standards are maintained, no-one else will.

Communicate

Everyone has the right to know what is going on and they need to hear about the company from the boss. A chief executive should listen to everybody and tell them everything. People like to know who they are working for and they want to meet him face-to-face. You can't expect employees to trust a chief executive that they only recognise from a signature at the bottom of a memo.

Your job is to listen, set the standards, get the thinking straight and tell everybody about it. Give everyone the authority to get on and run the business for you.

Get the thinking straight

Dear James

Write a new script every six months !

When I was at university studying Industrial Economics, I couldn't understand why my tutor posed such basic questions as: "What business are you in?" "What are you good at?" and "What things are most important in the business?" The answers seemed obvious. In our family company, we were in the shoe business. We were good at selling shoes and it was important to have the right shoes in the right shops.

I now ask the same questions I first heard at university. With no direct day-to-day responsibility, I can stand back and think about the future. You can be too close to your own business, not able to see the wood for the trees. Often the right answer is staring you in the face. Most good business plans are based on a heavy dose of common sense. They come with an inspirational flash of the obvious. You don't need genius, just a clear mind, but to the outsider you might well appear to be a man of vision!

Change of key

For years we have been fighting against the decline of shoe repairs that started in 1967. We had kept the business in profit by the addition of more merchandise. Shoe care was supplemented by hosiery, leather goods, canvas bags and straw shopping baskets, until merchandise represented nearly 40 per cent of our turnover.

Merchandise brought its problems. Lower margins, high markdowns, and the hassle of stock control. We had to introduce extra staff into each shop to cope with displays, the ordering and extra administration. Key cutting, on the other hand, produced an even better margin than shoe repairs and was more suited to the hands of a traditional cobbler. After a useful start, key cutting reached a plateau at ten per cent of total sales. Our most significant flash of the obvious came in 1985 when we finally found our answer to the decline of shoe repairs.

The trend away from slim heel fashion in the mid-eighties brought a further downturn in the demand for shoe repairs and made us have another serious think. During a short discussion with managing director Kit Green, I latched on to the obvious idea that £1 of key cutting turnover was worth a lot more than £1 of merchandise. If we could swap merchandise business for keys, we would improve our profitability. We decided to do an experiment. We altered the layout of our shops in Leicester and Gloucester, replacing the bags with an enormous board full of keys. The effect was dramatic. We doubled the key cutting sales and produced an overall increase in branch turnover and profit. Encouraged by success, we converted ten more shops and got the same results. Wherever we put the big key board, key cutting sales doubled. Unaware of what we were doing, we had a stroke of luck. To fill our new, very large key board, we had to substantially increase our range of keys. Eighty-five per cent of our key cutting business is done using only ten per cent of the key blanks. Twenty-five per cent of the sales came from one key blank. The classic accountant's approach is to restrict the range and keep stock down. Our big key board forced us to do the opposite. Our big selection of key blanks developed a much bigger business. We became the key cutting experts on the high street.

Buoyed by our success, we made the key boards bigger still and the bigger the selection of keys, the bigger our key business. Key cutting turnover has increased ten times since we first had the idea – we now have over 15 per cent of the UK key market.

Out and about

This critical key cutting strategy was one of the few ideas found whilst sitting in the office. Ideas don't usually come to people sat behind a desk. Inspiration appears when you least expect it. Planning conference delegates can sit around for hours without a single good thought between them. In the seventies it was fashionable for management teams to disappear on a "forward planning retreat" at a sun- drenched resort where everyone was given the space for new ideas. These expeditions can be positively dangerous. They often occur in response to poor trading and can make matters even worse. Most inspiration lies within the business. You find it by going round branches. You are unlikely to spot the winning wheeze by flying everybody to a beach 1,000 miles from your nearest shop.

(The stampede into estate agency by building societies and banks in the eighties could have been the result of a forward planning conference. Everyone is together thinking about the future and they are under pressure to produce the golden idea. The acquisition of estate agencies must have seemed like a classic ploy, satisfying every buzzword of the decade. Diversification, synergy and extending the franchise all in one go. It was a disaster, because estate agencies need people who know about houses not folk steeped in finance.)

In a meeting

I dislike meetings but we have developed a forum which often gets our thinking straight. We gather together the experts, a collection of people whose knowledge we respect.

We collected together a group of branch managers who had the best watch repair turnovers and asked them how they did it. It is amazing how much you find out by opening the debate and listening to people talk amongst themselves. That meeting probably put 20 per cent on our watch repair sales.

Six people make the right size group but choose people who know what they are talking about. Don't select candidates on seniority. The management structure doesn't indicate where the expertise resides. Discussion often goes in an unexpected direction. Once we formed a group to discuss the future of computer engraving. We learned a lot about computers but the real benefit was much more fundamental. They told us our pricing structure was wrong. Engraving is a time consuming business and our prices were so low that many branch staff felt

IDEAS SPOTTED ON SHOP VISITS

JOHN LYONS
jewellery & watch repairs

WATCH REPAIRS

IDEAS FROM THE HIGH STREET

"DIXON" FLAG

OSWESTRY BOARD

SHOES OVER MACHINERY

they could earn a better bonus by concentrating on key cutting and shoe repairs. They were turning engraving business away. Following that meeting we increased engraving prices by 20 per cent and sales went up 25 per cent.

Visiting shops

The best ideas are in the branches. That's why I visit our shops at least one and usually two days a week. Other executives use lap tops but my most useful tools are a camera and a notepad. One day around our shops can fill eight pages of my pad. Never rely on your memory when you find a new idea. If you don't write notes, the best ideas are gone by the end of the day.

Shop visits have had a profound effect on our business. In 1990, I saw that one of our best shoe repairers, John Higgs, in Cheadle, was displaying a whole line of leather shoes on a rack above the machinery. He was repairing more leather soled shoes than anyone else in the business and his shop was in a small suburb of Manchester. Within a year,

every branch had a similar display. In the next eight years our leather business doubled.

Shortly after we bought Automagic, I met two people who set us on the road towards watch repairing. There was a small sublet next to our shop in Stevenage run by John Lyons, an experienced watch repairer. He agreed to teach us the trade. Shortly after meeting John, I was in West Bromwich, where I met Glenn Edwards. Glenn had just joined us from a competitor. I discovered that his real love was watch repairing and he persuaded me to take watch repairs seriously. Glenn now runs our watch repair workshop in Wolverhampton, where he is the company's recognised expert. We now have a fast developing watch repair business which, within three years of meeting John and Glenn, has grown from nothing to over £3m per year.

Holiday reading

I pick up a lot of tips from books about business but I am more interested in practice than theory. The best business books are written by people who have run their own business.

Recommended holiday reading includes the books about McDonalds, Body Shop, Starbucks and any other business that lets you in on the secrets of their success. I have used ideas from *Nuts*, a book about Southwest Airlines; *The Nordstrom Way*, charting the success of Nordstrom department stores; *Ben & Jerry's Double Dip*, the story of the "values-led" ice cream company; and Julian Richer's *The Richer Way*. (Our "introduce a friend scheme" for recruitment, our "hardship fund" that helps employees in financial need and the rewards we give to staff who score highly on our mystery shopping visits are ideas taken from Richer's book.) The illustrated gardening books by A G Hessayon gave me the idea for our pictorial training manuals. Thanks to Dr Hessayon, we have a rare commodity – a set of training manuals that people actually read and understand.

Don't switch off

Good ideas are found in the most unexpected places. Look at the whole of the high street not just our own shops. We used to have a sandwich board outside each of our branches, but gradually a succession of jobsworth characters from the local authorities put a stop to them. We found an alternative 20 years ago when Dixons (which was then mainly a photographic shop) had a promotional flag, flying above head height where no local authority could touch them. We pinched the idea and have used it ever since. We still call it our Dixon flag.

We have a habit of naming our ideas after the source of inspiration. Another method to foil the local authority is now called the Oswestry board. This display hooks on the wall between our shop and the next door neighbour. I first saw the idea outside a gift shop in Oswestry.

Leaflets have a useful role to play but can cause a lot of clutter. The solution was found in Early Learning who used a lectern to display their catalogue. Twenty per cent of our house sign business now comes from leaflets picked off the lectern by customers.

You never know when the next idea is going to pop out, but always keep your notebook handy.

Keep ideas on file

Don't expect everyone to welcome your good ideas with open arms. New ideas put people on the defensive. They resist change and part of the defence is to produce a string of reasons to demonstrate that your ideas won't work.

A prime example of resistance to change occurred in the Norvic shop in Windsor in 1975. We were starting a closing down sale and the manager made a last ditch attempt to hang on to his traditional values. Our closing-down sale had been so successful elsewhere that a queue usually formed before we opened. We could expect ten times the normal week's business in the first two days of the sale. To cope with the crowds, all the shoes were put out on racks. The chairs and fitting stools were hidden behind the scenes. Our Windsor manager was not happy, as he could not contemplate selling shoes without providing a proper service using a shoe horn, sitting on the fitting stool and lacing up the shoes for the customer. "They won't like that in Windsor," he claimed. "It's worked everywhere else," we responded. "But they can't try on the shoes without being able to sit down," he said with concern. "The chairs will just get in the way," we explained. Then he came back with the final crushing argument: "But what about the one-legged folk"? His area manager ignored him, cleared the chairs and filled the shop full of shoe racks. Windsor was very enthusiastic about our closing down sale. By 9.30 a large queue had formed under the shadow of Windsor Castle. The first person in the queue was a man with one leg.

Don't throw any ideas away as you never know when they might come in useful. Keep a list of all your brain waves, even those that everybody else thinks are ridiculous.

Several years ago I was trying to dream up ways to improve our key cutting. We were already the UK's market leader but we still needed to improve our expertise and thus further enhance our reputation. The answer seemed obvious – turn the business from a key cutter to a locksmith. I wanted to turn part of the shop into a locksmith bench – containing security locks, rare keys and specialist locksmith tools.

No-one liked the idea. They tried it out because I was the chairman but it was a half-hearted experiment doomed to failure. Within six months the locksmith bench had been forgotten and was buried in a file labelled "Ideas."

In the last 12 months the business has learned to love the locksmith trade. It is now seen as a natural development of our key cutting service. We have developed a specialist training course known as our "Locksmith Academy." We have a mobile locksmith business with nine vans covering Manchester and Liverpool aiming for a national coverage with seven years. And we are changing the look of our shops – 30 shops have our latest design that includes a locksmith bench.

The big think

Every six months have your own private planning session. Dig out all your lists and re-sort between major and minor. Put everything into headings that represent the few things that are really important, with all minor items being part of a major subject. Now sit down and think. Ask yourself: "What is the most important thing I can do to improve the business"? You want as few big ideas as possible, ideally one big concept which contains all your good ideas.

"Every Key Every Time" was the phrase that linked all the new ideas to do with key cutting. "Benchgrade 2000" is doing the same job for shoe repairs. We have used the introduction of computers to focus our attention on all the new ideas that can help our engraving business.

Most ideas provide the answer to a problem. A vital part of your thinking process is to define the problem. That isn't always as simple as it seems.

It has taken us years to develop engraving, because we didn't really understand what was holding back the turnover. We knew there was a healthy market and we made several attempts to improve our displays. We produced special leaflets and improved the quality of our machinery but still something was holding us back. Our shop staff lacked enthusiasm for engraving. They didn't believe they could earn enough extra bonus to justify the effort involved, that was the real problem. We had to find a way of persuading our staff that engraving was something worth the trouble – we are still searching for a solution!

It doesn't matter how much time you spend planning or how hard you think about problems, if you can't get everyone's agreement, the ideas will fail. If everyone likes your idea, get on with it before they find reasons why it won't work.

History helps

Most business books and autobiographies are full of success and short on failure. Bad decisions disappear from the memory, leaving us to reflect on the good old days. When the book is written, a piece of luck can become a brilliant management decision and a disastrous mistake totally forgotten.

Our biggest disaster was "Keycall." In 1994, we discovered new

Dear James

HOW TO WRITE A BUSINESS PLAN

LIST EVERYTHING YOU CAN THINK OF

REARRANGE YOUR LIST INTO HEADINGS

THINK!

PRODUCE A DRAFT PLAN

TALK IT THROUGH WITH SOME COLLEAGUES

THINK!

PRODUCE THE FINAL PLAN

computer technology that let us cut keys without having the original – all we needed was the code number. A South African developed the idea of a car key rescue service and we decided to help him progress the concept in a joint venture. Using direct marketing to find our customers, we thought we had a modern product taking full advantage of today's technology. We spent over £100,000 developing "Keycall." We advertised in a Sunday newspaper. Despite the help of market research, and a high powered direct marketing expert, we persuaded only 15 customers to sign up to "Keycall" and that included myself, my wife Alex and one of my aunts. I still don't know why it didn't work. The public are happy to insure against losing their credit cards but the same did not apply to keys. It cost me a lot of money but taught me some lessons:

1. It is very difficult to create a brand new business.
2. Don't dive into a new venture with both feet – test the concept in a small way first.
3. Market research is no substitute for testing the market.
4. You have a better chance of making money by investing in the business you know.

Sometimes you get a good idea that doesn't work out through no fault of your own. In 1997 we spent four months negotiating to buy the retail part of Sketchley. We saw it as a similar business to Automagic, with a good shop portfolio but suffering through poor management. Sketchley wanted a high price and even after negotiating a sensible figure, we couldn't find a bank to agree with our valuation. I still think we would have made a sensational success of the Sketchley business. It just wasn't meant to be.

In 1990, we had plans to develop a contract side to our business. Several opportunities existed to sell our services direct to large customers, including selling house signs to garden centres, badges to other retailers and shoe repairs to the Ministry of Defence. Six years later we had done little about it. The idea is still a good one. We now have a team determined to develop the con-

tract trade and the signs are good.

Some of the best ideas are worth repeating. Our "Service Challenge" competitions have always improved the service we give our customers. That basic idea is over 20 years old and is still being used on a regular basis.

You can't stop thinking about the business. Each plan seems perfect when you produce it but you never really get the thinking straight. You will soon want to do things slightly differently. An imperfect plan is much better than no plan at all. It gives the business a sense of purpose, even if you have to straighten out your thinking again in six months' time.

Make easy decisions

I wish I had read this chapter 20 years ago instead of writing it today. I would have saved a lot of time worrying about things that didn't matter and agonising over decisions I never made. Avoid difficult decisions – just make the obvious decisions where you know the answer.

> Dear James
>
> If in doubt,
> sleep on it !

Being pestered

A stream of people will pop in your office, hoping to thrust their decisions upon you. Cars create the biggest problem. Despite your carefully considered company car policy, some people always want a better one. Better than the one they had last time, better than the person in the next office and better than their next door neighbour. They quote savings on depreciation, better miles per gallon, and lower servicing cost to justify the most expensive vehicle they think you will allow. This is another decision you should not take.

Shop staff want snap decisions. "Can we close on Good Friday?" "Can you upgrade my key cutting machinery?" "Can I advertise on the back of Sainsbury receipts?" "My area manager says I can't take four weeks off to see my daughter in South Africa. Is that fair?"

Avoid all these decisions. Don't undermine people with the real authority to decide.

Delegation

You cannot manage a business without delegating. Give your team the authority to make decisions. Don't take their decisions for them. It is a

DON'T MAKE OTHER PEOPLES DECISIONS FOR THEM

ADVISE   PERSUADE   PESTER   BUT LEAVE THE DECISION TO THEM

frustrating process, especially when you can see something that ought to be done.

First, try advice. "Here is an idea that might help"; "One thing you could do to make things better"; "Have you thought of?" If gentle advice doesn't work, try more persistent persuasion. "Once you have decided to appoint George, the rest of the team will fall into place"; "I am sure you already know the right answer to this one."

Finally, if the right decision is still being avoided, be even more persistent. "I need a decision to put to the board"; "When are you going to announce the new price list, we need it before Christmas"; "I bet you a pound you won't do it by Friday!" Whatever you do, don't take the decision. Save yourself for the major problems.

Big decisions

Big decisions that have a significant effect on the future very seldom happen. Only eight decisions have made a difference to my career,

My first major decision was to ask Alex to marry me. She has provided thought and encouragement behind the major decisions that followed. I proposed 12 months after we first met.

Staying with UDS following the Timpson takeover shows that ducking a decision often works. I decided to "stay put" and matters took a fortunate course.

My biggest decision was the management buyout. It takes courage to turn to your boss and bid for the business - things will never be the same again. It took three months to pluck up the courage.

Our decision to concentrate on key cutting provided the platform for our success over the past ten years. The idea to go for keys came from a half-hour conversation but it took ten years to develop the concept.

Selling the shoe shops in 1987 was an example of clear logic overcoming emotional prejudice. Once I took a detached view of the business, it became clear that the odds were stacked against shoe retailing. It still took me six months to come to terms with the evidence before putting the shops up for sale.

Following the sale of the shoe shops, my original idea was to run a small business leaving plenty of time for golf, tennis and holidays. It took four months before we made our first acquisition. In the process, I added service retailing to my list of hobbies.

Buying all the shares in 1991 was an excellent decision that was thrust upon me. It was really made three years earlier when Alex told me never to float the company.

Buying Automagic was the only decision we made in a hurry. The receiver sold the business within three weeks and we had 12 hours to make our final bid. We had been looking at Automagic for seven years and had been their major shareholder for five years.

I have made eight important decisions in 38 years and only one of them had to be made in a hurry.

Spotting the decision

It is easy to look back, but how do you spot a major decision in advance? You never do! Once you know you are facing a major decision, it isn't a major decision any more.

You can avoid most decisions through hard work. The more you know about the business, the less decisions you have to make. If you know everything that is going on, the right path will be obvious. You will make correct decisions by instinct.

There are three ways to avoid decisions:

1. Never take a decision if you don't know the answer.
2. Delegate as many decisions as possible.
3. Have a complete knowledge of the business so decisions become instinctive.

Where you are needed

Although my advice is to duck decisions, you can't avoid them altogether. My method of avoiding decisions will help reduce stress, but don't be deceived, your job is to give guidance to the business and to decide the route the company is going to go. Your guiding hand is going to be important in the following areas:

1. Making an acquisition or selling part of the business
Big deals take a lot of time and involve so much detail that it is easy to forget what you are doing the deal for. You can always change your mind until the last piece of paper has been signed.

2. Major capital expenditure projects.
In our business big capital expenditure projects, such as a branch refit programme or the introduction of computer engraving, don't involve one big order but cover several small orders in lots of branches over many months. Just because the project has board approval doesn't mean it can't be changed.

3. Changes in the company's product.
A change to the product can have a profound effect on the rest of the business. The introduction of watch repairs tipped the company's image from being dirty and artisan to clean and skilful.

4. Small changes that make a big difference.
Small decisions have a butterfly effect on the business. Insisting branch staff wore ties made a significant difference to the housekeeping and helped our claim to be the "Quality Service People."

Clear your mind

Whenever you need to convince yourself what to do, make a list. Write down the reasons for and against.

The most important list I made was written in 1986 when we were still shoe retailers. I asked myself the question: "Do you think our shoe retail business will survive?" I quickly wrote down a long list of reasons why shoe shops hadn't got a chance.

1. Too many shoe shops on the high street.
2. Too many other shops selling shoes.
3. Low price shoes due to imports.
4. Poor stockturn and high levels of stock.
5. High markdowns.
6. Shoe retailing requires big retail shops.
7. Big increase in rents and upwards only rent reviews.
8. Higher wage rates.
9. Increasingly difficult to predict shoe fashions.

At that point, I tried to find a reason to be optimistic about the future. I couldn't find anything other than my own determination for the family business to succeed. Once I had completed my list, there was no decision to be made. I could not justify opening another new shop. If a business stops growing, it starts to decay. There was no doubt we had to sell the shoe shops. That list changed my life – it led to one of the best decisions I have ever made. I now always put the pros and cons on paper before making up my mind.

Two minds are better than one

Avoid decisions whenever possible. Most decisions don't need to be made or they make themselves. Others should be delegated to someone else. If, in the end, you do have to make a decision, never do it on your own. You can't make a decision work without help from other people, so it is a good idea to involve them in the decision itself. If you have the company's support, the idea will work.

You won't be short of advice on why good ideas won't work. People don't like change and will vote for the status quo. Here are some of the reasons why we couldn't introduce a watch repair business:

1. Customers won't associate us with watch repairs.
2. There is too much competition on the high street.
3. We haven't got the skilled staff.
4. The shops are too dirty to take in watch repairs.
5. There is nowhere to secure the watches overnight.
6. We will never be able to compete with the jewellers.

Despite all these very good reasons, watch repairs have been a huge success. But we had to win over the critics who came up with the reasons why it wouldn't work. Watch repairs were introduced gradually. As each trial was successful, the new service became more a part of the business. Many critics now claim to have played a large part in the development of this very successful service.

However good your idea, if you meet strong opposition, shelve it! Any good business will have loads of ideas. Choose the ones that most people agree with. It makes for an easy life and creates a successful business.

Take your time

Don't rush into decisions and don't let anyone else create false deadlines. You can sleep on most decisions for weeks before you have to decide. New facts often emerge.

It is a good idea to be half-hearted. Test things out in a small way rather than going in with both feet. A trial period shows whether the idea works and can indicate how to do things better. If you wait, business opinion may change. If you have an excellent idea that has been rejected, keep planting the seeds until someone else comes up with the idea for you. Often it's the biggest critic who adopts your idea as their own. In an independent business, where the shareholders also run the company, we can make decisions very quickly. But there is no point in being decisive if you get the wrong answer.

Other people expect you to say "yes" or "no," but you can always say "wait and see." Don't worry if others call you a ditherer. Doing nothing is often as courageous as changing your mind!

Develop the business by making lots of small changes and as few big decisions as possible.

CHAPTER 10

Board meetings

Dear James

Board meetings give you an essential discipline

I hate meetings and I like being unconventional. We don't have outside shareholders, so why bother to have board meetings every month?

The disipline

We all need order in our lives. A precedent was set when the seventh day was declared a day of rest. I have developed that idea. On top of four holidays a year, I play golf every Saturday morning, two Real Tennis league games every month, I play tennis once a week, I try to visit each branch once a year and every six months I go to the dentist.

The monthly board meeting is part of my personal discipline. It ensures that once every four weeks, we look at the whole business.

To make board meetings work you need some rules.

1. All capital expenditure and major projects must be approved by the board.
2. Every senior manager must write a report for the board papers.
3. The board can discuss anything and everything.
4. The board should never make a new decision, it can only ratify decisions that have already been recommended.
5. The board will never take a vote.

Routine

To help the discipline of board meetings, follow a fixed timetable. I choose the third Monday in every month, the earliest time when the previous month's figures are available.

Insist on comprehensive reports from all senior managers. This usually creates a problem. It is difficult to get board papers written on time.

Minutes provide the glue that sticks the meeting process together. We don't have a secretary. Directors volunteer for the role of minute taker. It is an extra task but can be a position of power. The minutes have a considerable influence on the following meeting. Our minutes have developed a style of brevity without losing the main content.

The longest and most detailed minutes I have seen were produced for a small organisation – the British Shoe Repair Council, a body I helped establish to represent the Shoe Repair Industry. The BSRC minutes went into minute detail about everything from the Cobbler's Cup competition to the Annual Shoe Repairers' conference. The only significant event the BSRC organised was a House of Commons Lunch which created the headline: "Cobblers to the Commons."

Board meetings can be used to provide a range of excuses:

1. They can create a deadline, as in: "I need it for the board meeting."
2. They can provide a good excuse for delay, as in: "I will put it to the board, but they have not got a meeting until July."
3. The board can create a higher authority, as in "I like the idea but it will have to go to the board."

December 2000
18 Monday   7.30 Dentist
10.00 Board Meeting
2.15 Real Tennis
19 Tuesday
Yorkshire Shop Visits
20 Wednesday
Holiday

Our board meeting schedule also reminds me of my dental appointments. My dentist, Mr Torlop, starts work at 7.15am. He sees me before our board meetings in June and December.

Preparation

You must read all the papers. First, read the reports making a note of any points you want to raise, then check the minutes of the last meeting. Identify any items not covered in the papers. Go through all the papers twice, the second time listing items which require detailed discussion. It will take you four hours to prepare a proper plan to guide you through your board meeting.

The meeting itself should take less than four hours. Don't stop for lunch, have coffee and sandwiches while the meeting takes place.

Even if you face the most important decision ever, spend the first ten minutes going through the minutes of the last meeting – but keep it to ten minutes. In the late seventies I was a member of a NEDO (National Economic Development Organisation) Committee on Footwear. Sometimes we discussed the minutes of the last meeting for two hours. We met every three months and always had the same debate. Union representatives complained about jobs, manufacturers complained about imports, and both the unions and the manufacturers complained about the retailers. The civil servants said how good it was to have a dialogue but nothing happened as a result.

I got so fed up with the feeling of *deja vu* as each meeting's discussions followed the previous meeting's minutes, that I decided something should be done. I wrote "The Retail Commitment," in which retailers promised to deal with imports and help jobs. It was designed to stop the unions and manufacturers complaining. It brought a good response. For the next three meetings no one complained, and there was some positive talk of improving the industry. But after a year we returned to the same old discussion and the first two hours of each meeting were spent discussing the same old minutes.

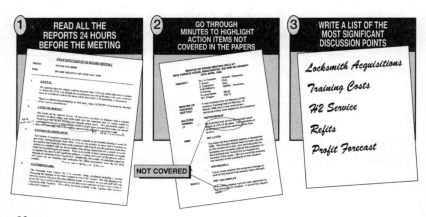

Avoid the detail

Cover all the important points in the first hour. My company lawyer and non-executive director, Roger Lane-Smith, has a busy life and a low boredom threshold. If I allow the directors to talk trivia, he leaves. Discussion on the sales of padlocks, the stock of brown shoe laces, or the price of the soft drinks in our canteen will cause Roger to pack up his papers.

As chairman, you must lead the discussion but give everybody a chance to have their say. In particular, help the minute taker by indicating the outcome of each discussion.

Who's on your team?

In 1969, I became a director for all the wrong reasons. The business was having a bad time. Poor half-year profits had been announced and the full year's results would not be much better. A change in the boardroom showed shareholders that something was being done. I was one of four new directors picked for political balance. In retrospect none of us should have been appointed. I became the ladies' shoe merchandise director. I was too young but I was the son of the chairman. The men's shoe merchandiser also joined the baord as his father was the director in charge of personnel. The new property director was the right-hand man of Geoffrey Noakes, who didn't want to be outflanked by a Timpson father and son. Finally, the computer manager was put on the board because it seemed a terribly modern thing to do.

Now I don't have to bother about politics. I can have directors who make a real contribution.

Don't have more than five executive directors. The board is not there to run the day-to-day business. If that's what you want, set up a separate management board. There must be someone who can talk on each of the main areas of the business. Your managing director, property manager and financial controller must be on the board. Other appointments depend on your trust of an individual's opinion.

Don't always pick people who will agree with you; don't forget you don't have to agree with them. You don't let them vote and with 100 per cent of the equity you always have the final say.

Non-executives

A private business isn't forced to have non-executives, as there are no outside shareholders to protect, but I want non-executives because they look after me.

Pick people you totally trust. They must be interested in the business but much more importantly, they have to be on your side. Pick people you can go to whenever you need advice and whose advice you value. Private businesses can get insular. We live in our own little world, dealing in a specialised market with home-grown management. Non-executives broaden our perspective. Appoint your non-executives to a salary committee, they will help you make the lonely decisions where executive director help is not available. Senior appointments have a major influence on success but your executive directors are too closely involved to help. You need someone to talk to who will also help with senior salaries and bonus schemes.

Following our buyout, Trevor Morgan was appointed non-executive chairman by the buyout organisers Candover, who also appointed their chief executive, Stephen Curran, to the board.

I had met Trevor Morgan regularly through the Multiple Shoe Retailers' Association. He was an extremely successful chief executive of Turner's, a 150-strong shoe chain, which he ultimately sold to

Hepworths. Trevor became a Hepworth's board director and played a key role in recruiting George Davies. Trevor knew a lot about shoes and I had a great respect for his achievements, but we had very different styles. We got on well but it was an uneasy relationship; we never allowed our individual talents to complement each other.

When Trevor retired as chairman, I had to look for a successor. A stockbroker recommended someone who he considered an ideal candidate with retail experience. We met for dinner and although I was not impressed, I invited him to spend a day going round the business. We were complete opposites. I tend to be guided by unmeasured flair, he was a finance director who looked for cold calculations. The day included lunch with Alex, who gave the immediate thumbs down.

I now have the perfect non-executive. Patrick Farmer was a colleague at UDS. We both ran family shoe businesses within UDS. After the Hanson takeover, Patrick's business became part of Clarks where he made a great success, not only of John Farmer but also Ravel and Peter Lord. He finished his Clarks career on the main board, responsible for Clarks overseas. Patrick was a much better shoe retailer than me. I was lucky to find such a knowledgeable retailer who had got the time and enthusiasm to work with me. Patrick remains a firm friend but that doesn't stop him being frank and telling me what I need to know.

Final thought

The board plays a vital role without making decisions or taking a vote. Board meetings give a snapshot of the business every month. They keep you informed, remind you of problems and they make you think. This provides vital discipline to the chairman of an independent business.

Property

Although 18 per cent of our turnover is spent on rent and rates, for my first 22 years in business, I knew nothing about property.

The special department

People in the property department seldom spoke to us. They spent their days talking to other property people. They never left the office but knew the detail of every high street, travelling round the country guided by maps of every town centre.

After I left school, I had training as a shop assistant and a shoe repairer. I spent six weeks in the shoe factory. I worked with area managers, accountants and helped with the installation of our new computer, but I never spent a minute in the property department. My first property deal was, like most other people, when we bought our first house. Buying a home gives the feeling that every property transaction is traumatic. As a result, the property department had my sympathy. For years I pictured them working in stressful isolation, taking on the biggest burdens of the business without any help from the rest of us.

I had no involvement in property until 1982. I have since discovered some of the secret rituals of property dealing. I can now reveal that property management is not as stressful as buying your own house. Most good deals are down to plain common sense, but you need to be wary of a very strange set of rules.

UDS property

My first property decision was a complete farce. When I became the Timpson managing director in 1975, all property matters were handled in London by the UDS property department. Most weeks UDS would send us a list of possible new sites for inspection. We had to give them a detailed appraisal. It was a futile exercise. Capital for new shops could only be obtained by special request to the UDS finance departments and permission was seldom granted. Late in 1975 we were asked to appraise a site in Parliament Street, Hanley, and were surprised, but delighted to receive approval from UDS finance department for the new shop to go ahead.

A week later, the property department said that they had made a mistake – they had sent details of the wrong shop. Our appraisal was for 43 Parliament Street, and the shop they now had on offer was 41 Parliament Street, at a slightly lower rent. We resubmitted our proposal using the same turnover but producing a slightly higher profit because of the lower rent. Imagine our surprise when the second application was turned down – UDS thought our turnover estimate was too high! After howls of protest we got them to change their mind and are still trading profitably in No 41 Parliament Street, Hanley.

Freehold portfolios

The UDS property department wielded a lot of power. Most multiple retailers in the seventies had a strong balance sheet bristling with prime properties. Today's retailers are valued by profits, the strength of their brand and the quality of their sites. In 1975, the analysts looked first at the value of the properties. UDS, Sears and indeed Timpson all had a precious property portfolio.

Property power

The UDS property department could overthrow any decision made by a subsidiary. We suffered in Scunthorpe. In 1978, a large number of our shoe repair factories were located in the backroom, upstairs or basement of a shoe shop. When we moved on to the high street, we had much more success. Such a move was contemplated at Scunthorpe. UDS came up trumps, they found the ideal site, and after four visits from the Timpson team, an appraisal was submitted and agreed.

There was a Timpson routine for new shops. A detailed schedule covered the four weeks prior to opening. The development manager, Alan Chatterton, arrived the day before the opening with a checklist and tape to ensure everything was ready. Alan's visit was a dress rehearsal to prepare for the arrival of general manager, Michael Frank, complete with clipboard for the final approval. Michael Frank was expected at Scunthorpe station at 11am, giving Alan ample time to complete the finishing touches. Not long after 9am, Alan got a call from the property department. "When are you fitting out the shop?" "We have done it," replied Alan. "When is it opening?" "Today," replied Alan. "That's unfortunate," said the man from UDS, "We have an offer we can't refuse. We complete a sale of the shop in ten days time." Alan went to the station armed with this bizarre news. Undaunted, Mike Frank carried out his inspection to ensure that nothing was out of place until the shop closed ten days later.

Corporate cuckoos

During ten years with UDS, site visits and new shop appraisals became more and more futile. With profits falling, all the cash was needed for dividends, with nothing left for capital expenditure. UDS briefly had extra cash in the bank in 1980, following an issue of new shares, but all the money was quickly blown on a chain called Van Allan, which cost £20m, never made money and was closed down two years later.

With no money for expansion, we started to play a different game. As long as one company in UDS was performing worse than us, no-one got on our back. UDS had a portfolio of loss-making businesses, so it wasn't difficult to keep clear of the relegation zone. UDS never sold any assets. If a business performed extremely badly, they simply closed it down. As each successive UDS business closed, the remaining parts of the group formed a queue to acquire the plum properties that had become vacant. There was a certain element of luck. If you were on holiday when a company closed, you might miss out altogether. On the other hand, if you had a meeting at UDS on the day a closure was announced, five to ten prime sites could be presented on a plate.

I was quite good at this game of "Corporate Cuckoos." When Grange Furnishing closed, I got two excellent shops in Saltcoats and Kirkintilloch. The closure of Alexandre the Tailors brought ten new Timpson shops, including superb sites at Glasgow and Gloucester. The Van Allan disaster was good news for Timpson, providing four excellent sites including a very good shop in Luton. In 1976, I handed over the responsibility for Swears & Wells to Jack Maxwell, managing director of Richard Shops. Within 12 months, the business had gone into a loss and six months later it closed down with Timpson Shoe Repairs getting shops in Glasgow, Aberdeen and Wrexham.

Wrexham provided my first experience of true property management. The Suede Centre shop occupied a prime site on Hope Street. The property included a small staff room down a passageway. Although not much bigger than a broom cupboard, I turned it into a shoe repair shop – in 1999 it made a profit of £45,000.

sale and leaseback

The management buyout taught me a lot about property. My tutor was Paul Orchard-Lisle of Healey & Baker. In two one-hour meetings, Paul explained sale and leaseback deals. For the first time I had come face-to-face with funding rates, market rent, Zone A and the strength of one's covenant. I was starting to learn the secret language of a property department.

For most multiple retailers I was contemplating the unthinkable – selling freehold property. Shortly after the buyout, I had lunch with Arnold Ziff, chairman of Stylo. He was horrified. Stylo hung onto its freeholds and thought the property portfolio was much more important than trading profit.

We would never have achieved the buyout without selling properties. Timpson was already paying a rent to UDS on all its freehold properties. Profit in the year before the buyout was £2.5m. Although we would have to pay an extra £800,000 to secure the £30m from the sale and leasebacks, the profit was still £1.7m. It all seemed so simple. By turning freeholds into short leases we obtained a large sum of money to buy back the business. The pitfalls appeared later.

Profiting from property

Property was at the centre of the sale of the shoe shops four years later. We sold the business to Olivers for £15m. With just over 50 per cent of the shares, my personal gain was £7.5m (£5m after tax). But the most significant part of the transaction was the purchase of the shoe repair shops. Peter Cookson, Mike Williams and myself planned the deal well ahead. Timpson Shoe Repairs had a profit of £450,000. That suggested a fair price for the business was £3m.

Despite the sale and leaseback deals done to acquire the Timpson business, we were still left with a number of freehold properties. The portfolio dedicated to shoe repairs was worth approximately £.1.5m. A small number of freehold properties were occupied by third parties. All these non-trading properties, together with the shoe repair portfolio, were transferred into a separate company which had property assets of about £3m, equal to the future purchase price of the business. These properties provided the money to buy the shoe repair business. Several of the freehold shops did not trade profitably. The branches at

Hamilton, Dundee and Barrow were loss makers; the freeholds of these three branches raised £550,000. The shoe repair shop in Leigh was physically joined to a Timpson shoe shop. The freehold of the whole property was transferred to the new business with Olivers taking a lease with a break clause after six months. When the six months came up, both shops were closed and the freehold sold for £503,000. A long leasehold property in Lincoln was let to a card shop at a profit rent of £80,000, a significant contribution to the profitability of our new business. In all, property sales raised £2m. With help from the bank we could pay Olivers £3m for the repair business with no involvement from venture capitalists.

Watch the small print

Each year we make a profit out of property, usually when we are in someone's way and we can extract some nuisance value.

In Brighton we were next door to Body Shop who wanted to expand. We were the only place they could go. Their first offer for our lease was £20,000. We refused but as the shop was unprofitable we finally accepted an offer of £100,000. In Bracknell we occupied a small kiosk underneath an escalator in the middle of the precinct. The landlords wanted to move the escalator. To get us to move, we were offered the full cost of removal and a much better shop at the same rent, plus a 15 year lease without rent review.

In High Street, Sheffield, we stood in the way of a major development. We moved down the road, but only when our rent was reduced from £31,000 to £1,000 per year without any review for 20 years.

Dealing with the receiver

When Automagic went into receivership, all its leases reverted back to the landlord. We therefore had to agree a new lease for all the 110 Automagic properties. This was good news and bad news. We ran the risk that some of the important leases may not be assigned to us at all. Our feeling of uncertainty was made worse when we saw copies of letters sent by Mr Minit to the landlords of all the plum properties. Minit was offering higher rents to persuade the landlord to boot us out. Fortunately, property law protected us from this tactic and leases were successfully renegotiated on all the Automagic properties that we wanted.

Buying from a receiver was good news, because we could renegotiate a number of the leases. In 1995, property values were suffering and we agreed a number of rent free periods and rent reductions. Our Salisbury rent fell from £50,000 to £30,000. We now sub-let part of the shop for £10,000, giving a net occupancy cost of £20,000.

Strong language

Once I received a letter from a property company telling me to "flit and remove myself" from a successful shop in Greenock. I was furious. When I met up with Mike Williams the following day, he seemed unconcerned. It was normal correspondence between one property person and another. They were establishing their right to renegotiate at the end of a lease.

Property is an amoral business. There are no gentleman's agreements – you stand by the letter of the law. If you don't watch the small print, you are in trouble. The property expert waits patiently for someone to make a mistake, so they can jump in, take advantage of a break clause, or the unfortunate tenant who has applied to renew a lease one day too late.

Property is not a game for amateurs - leave it to the experts. Let the specialist worry about upwards only rent reviews and full repairing leases – your job is to get the trading right.

Should we open?

Don't think of opening a shop unless you have seen the site at least twice and get another two people to do the same.

Computers can do the same job. They work out the likely number of customers based on socio-economic groups and spending power. I prefer to walk the high street. Computers reduce everything down to fine detail. Instead of using the back of an envelope, you can plug all the information into your PC and out comes the answer. For years we have used a complicated appraisal system for new shops. We forecast sales for the next five years, and estimate all costs in detail. The computer then churns out a five year forecast, calculating the return on investment using sophisticated discounted cash flow methods. The final set of figures looks so scientific it is easy to forget that they totally depend on the accuracy of your sales forecast.

I use two simpler methods. The easiest (for our business) is to guess the weekly turnover, multiply that figure by ten and if it is greater than the annual rent, you will make money!

If that seems too simplistic, I have another approach. Method two is to decide which of our existing branches most closely reflects the proposed new unit. Take the branch accounts for the similar unit, substitute the rent for the acquisition and that gives you the forecast profit.

In the end, I rely on instinct. After 35 years of walking up and down the high street, you tend to know whether a unit is going to work. It is easy to sign a lease that commits you for 25 years, but things can go terribly wrong.

Go and see new shops at least twice before you sign anything

Never open a unit unless you are totally confident. My worst shop opening was in Kingston. We paid a premium of £30,000. Shortly after we occupied the shop there was a review and the rent rose from £18,000 a year to £30,000. In our first year we lost £25,000. By the time we realised our mistake, the property market had weakened and we would have had to pay a reverse premium of £30,000 to get rid of the shop. We traded on. We have lost £60,000 over ten years but I am pleased to say that Kingston now makes a profit.

Don't overpay

There is a shop in the centre of Liverpool that I was offered 11 years ago – I turned it down. Every time I walk past that shop I think of my mistake. It would have been a goldmine – a competitor is now making a fortune instead of us. There are other shops in Swindon, High Wycombe, Winchester and Croydon that I regret not taking but they don't cause me lost sleep. To miss five good opportunities in 12 years is nothing to worry about.

In 1989 I nearly succumbed to the property boom when I was offered a group of six Visionhire shops (just bought by Granada) for a premium of £150,000. They were all in prime sites and I could only see success. If that deal had gone ahead I really would have lost some sleep – the rental values were far too high and the proposed premium was outrageous. We would have lost a lot of money.

We make money out of trading – repairing shoes and cutting keys – but we can't make a profit if too much goes to the landlord. Don't pay over the odds for property – high rents increase the risk and make life unnecessarily difficult.

You can't compete against the latest fast growing retailer. The current high flyers are coffee bars and mobile phone shops – in the past rents have been hiked by jeans retailers, Sock Shop, the Burton Group and many others. They have one thing in common – the desire to rapidly "roll out"' a concept.

The growth retailer has a requirement list covering the best shopping locations in the UK, and hires an agent to find them. The agent gets the sites – at a price. The high rents will be a millstone round the neck of the multiple for years ahead – and when their concept ceases to be flavour of the month high rents could kill the company. Even if you fall in love with a property, never pay more than it is worth.

Closing time

We close between five and ten branches a year whether we like it or not. End of leases, relocations and development can at first appear unwelcome but in retrospect keep the business up-to-date. Occasionally we decide to close a shop simply because it is making a loss. Don't be in a rush to close units, you will find plenty of people in the business keener on closure than you are. Area managers see closure as a way to solve their most difficult branch problems.

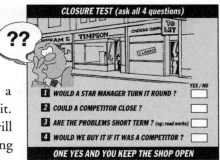

It takes five years to establish a shop and only five minutes to close it. Beware of throwing away goodwill with one rash decision. Resist closing shops but listen to common sense. Follow the clear financial signs and don't be sentimental. The first shop I closed was the first shop my great grandfather opened when he started the business in Oldham Street, Manchester. Two years later, I also closed the shop where I started work in Railway Street, Altrincham.

Before you commit yourself to a closure, ask four questions:

1. Would a star manager turn the business round?
2. If a competitor closed, would that transform the business ?
3. Is the difficulty short-term, such as road works or a change to the car parking?
4. If we acquired a multiple competitor and this shop was part of that business, would we keep it ?

If the answer to one of these questions is yes, there is doubt in your mind and you should keep the shop open.

Stick to shopkeeping

Don't be overawed by the problems of property, you will in the end, gain more from property dealing than you will lose.

As long as you know your business, you will be able to make the right property decisions. Leave the legal language to your property department. Your job is to know the shops and run them properly.

CHAPTER 12

Acquisitions

Dear James

You make the big money out of doing deals

You can't make money without being good at running your day-to-day business, but acquisitions can provide the opportunity to substantially increase the amount of money you make.

Easy way to grow

It's tortuous expanding simply by opening new shops. Acquisitions are a lot easier and a lot more profitable. Automagic increased our chain from 210 to 320 shops overnight and within two years our turnover doubled. Since 1980 we have acquired about 120 shops through other small acquisitions. Chains of between 12 and 35 branches which have all made an improvement to branch contribution without any addition to central overheads.

You spot the right acquisitions by knowing the industry very well. You achieve that by visiting the shops. Most retailers say that they spend at least a day a week going round their branches. Some do but a lot don't. Some chief executives of well-known high street names don't know where their shops are.

We have been very lucky with acquisitions. So far every purchase has matched our profit expectations.

You need luck. But it's a bit like Gary Player and his golf; the more you get to know the industry, the luckier you seem to get with acquisitions.

Look for subsiduaries

The best deals are often done when buying a small part of a big company. Contrary to expectations, it's the small business that drives the harder bargain.

Our most profitable deal was an acquisition from the British Shoe Corporation. At the time British Shoe had 2,000 shoe shops, 22 per cent of the shoe retail market and 35 small shoe repair factories that made a loss. No-one cared about shoe repairs and no one knew much about it. They just wanted to get rid of it. Luckily, I knew Philip Hammersley, the man given the job of selling. We bought 35 shops for £175,000, including our flagship in Selfridges, London. Most of the shops were in British Shoe properties so we entered into a rental agreement. As a result, British Shoe got out of shoe repair and still received an annual rent of £350,000 per year. We, in turn, rapidly increased the sales and made a £360,000 profit, a payback of less than six months. Both of us were better off, a classic win-win situation. I visited all the outlets twice before the deal was concluded and probably knew more about the business than the existing management. That knowledge helped us secure an excellent deal.

Glamour business

Doing deals is good fun, it's the glamour part of the job. Accountants love them, it is their equivalent of playing in a cup final or riding in the Grand National. Lawyers thrive on deals and merchant banks depend on them.

But be warned. Deals might give a big buzz but they don't always work. Van Allan was a disaster for UDS; it lost £20m in two years. The purchase of Supasnaps blew Sketchley off course. Instead of solving problems in their dry cleaning business, they bought another chain full of problems.

I am suspicious of the current deals funded by merchant banks and venture capitalists with plenty of money but short of management. Every business needs its entrepreneur to inspire success. Financial engineering and close supervision of the management accounts are not by themselves enough to rescue an ailing business.

When you hear of the City having a lot of money looking for a deal, there will be every chance that some of that money will be spent unwisely, especially if the businesses are given to "professional managers," who lack the flair to turn a business round.

Before getting involved in negotiations, ask yourself seven questions:

1. Does it fit in with our strategy?

The buzz of a deal is so attractive that it is tempting to get involved in projects irrelevant to your chosen strategy. We British still think that we can conquer the world. In 1988 I visited shoe repairers in France, Germany, Holland, Ireland and the United States and I decided that the best way to run our sort of business was to stay at home. We are the ultimate people business. Success depends on the 800 people who serve our customers, scattered through 315 branches in the UK. We know how to motivate Englishmen, Scotsmen and Welshmen, but I wouldn't know how to start enthusing the Germans!

We get regular approaches from abroad, people who see our shops and think we have a concept that would be successful elsewhere. I am sure they are right but, having decided that expansion overseas is not for us, when we get an approach, the answer is no.

2. Are you certain to increase profits?

There is no point in doing a deal if you are not going to increase profit and it is best to do deals where success is a certainty.

Whenever we buy a business, we want the shops but not the head office. That way branch contribution goes straight to our bottom line.

When we bought Automagic, £500,000 rapidly disappeared from the overheads. Profits had to go up.

3. Do you know how to run it?

Don't base an acquisition purely on figures - you must have a business plan. Get the thinking straight for the new business before you negotiate. Have a picture in your mind of the first 12 months before you make an offer.

Armed with a business plan, you can approach the new company with an open mind. After any acquisition is completed, talk to the people in the business. They will help you with the detail needed to strengthen your strategy.

4. Do you know who is going to run it?

However good your plan, its success will depend on people. Keep an open mind about the people you acquire. You are bound to find lots of talent. One third of our area managers have come from acquisitions made in the last seven years. But however good people may be in the new business, the chief executive and the financial controller must be your own.

Success will depend on establishing your style of management. Something which you take for granted but is difficult to explain to others. The only way to get the culture right is to put your own man in charge.

5. Do you know what you are doing it for?

I have already mentioned the buzz that people get from acquisitions and the excitement produced in the hearts of accountants and lawyers, but you must ask the question: "Will it make your life easier and will you be better off?" A bigger business is often easier to run and your existing business has to grow. So an acquisition may make life better by providing an easy and relatively risk-free route to growth. But you must be certain it's worth the hassle.

6. Is the risk low?

I still remember from university a definition of profit: "the reward for taking risks." It is misleading. Risk should be avoided whenever possible. Profits are usually made from racing certainties. Never risk the existing business.

PRE ACQUISITION CHECKLIST

DOES IT FIT OUR STRATEGY ?

ARE YOU SURE PROFITS WILL INCREASE ?

DO YOU KNOW HOW TO RUN IT ?

DO YOU KNOW WHO WILL RUN IT ?

IS THE RISK LOW ?

DO YOU KNOW WHY YOU ARE BUYING IT ?

IS THE CORE BUSINESS RUNNING OK ?

7. Am I running the current business OK?

Acquisitions will take more time than you imagine. Don't even think of starting without having a good accountant, a good lawyer and a lot of patience.

If I go a week without visiting our branches, I feel out of touch. Absence may be a good thing (we usually trade well when I go on holiday), but the longer you are away, the more you find out about your senior management. You must be confident in your management team before getting involved in an acquisition.

Only proceed with an acquisition if the answer to every one of my seven questions is yes!

Phases of a deal

Buying a business takes longer than you think. It is not as simple as the weekly shopping or buying a car or even a house. It is an assault course with a predictable pattern. Many of the stages seem unnecessary, but the accountants and lawyers will not agree and once negotiations start, they play the leading parts. You only appear on stage from time to time as an extra.

Don't be nervous about asking whether a business is for sale. If you don't ask you will never do any deals.

But be nice about it. I have received approaches about Timpson from arrogant figure-minded administrators, who live in public companies and don't understand an independent entrepreneur. They think there is a price I can't refuse. They cannot understand that to me the business is priceless, and even if it wasn't, their superior attitude would make me sell to anyone else but them.

You usually approach your target at the wrong time but strike up a pleasant dialogue to sow the seed for later.

The first encouraging sign is the confidentiality letter. It's also a signal that lawyers are involved, and someone is now paying their fee.

Your finance director will then ask his opposite number to supply volumes of information. He will ask for so much it will take at least ten days to get a response. If you don't have it already, ask for a list of their branches to be sent ahead of the account's information so that you can get on and look at their shops.

Take lots of pictures and write down your first impressions. When the numbers arrive, the computer takes over, but you must determine whether to go ahead. Don't be deceived by random numbers. Understand all the assumptions in producing the forecasts. Remember you can prove anything with figures.

Put yourself into the other person's position. What are they thinking about, what's important to them, what will make them happy? It takes two to make a deal. It won't happen unless you both agree.

Don't try and be too clever. When we bought the Timpson business from Hanson in 1983, Burton was also negotiating with Hanson to buy Richard Shops and John Collier. Burton's chief executive Ralph Halpern was taking a tough line. Every time Hanson thought they had a deal, Halpern found a reason to drop the price. He did it once too often and Hanson refused to negotiate any further. They sold Richards Shops to Storehouse and John Collier to the management.

When you finally agree heads of terms, don't be deceived. There is still a long way to go. You have given the signal to the lawyers to chop down a few trees, crank up the word processor and bury you in paper.

It takes 2 to make a deal

Put yourself in the other persons shoes

Lawyers find it easy to make enemies out of the best of friends. Some solicitors see life as a point scoring exercise. As well as battling on your behalf, they want to finish one up on the opposing legal firm. Clarify fees at an early stage or legal costs will be the last item discussed before contracts are exchanged and that could be expensive.

Set a deadline. There are always legal points left to discuss and, with meetings being billed at an hourly rate, the longer the deal, the larger the bill. The reason for the deadline doesn't matter – as long as one exists.

Hanson said our announcement had to coincide with their half-year results. Tony Alexander rang all the parties and told them to exchange in two days or file their papers and forget their fees. The deadline with Olivers was set by their lead lawyer, called Mr Windmill. He was going on holiday and dramatically signed the last document at

6.00 am, three hours before his flight left Heathrow.

Expect to work through the night or at weekends - it is popular with lawyers. They don't think they have done a decent deal without unsociable hours to complain about.

Back to business

When the accountants have finished producing random numbers and the lawyers have finished discussing points of principle, you will be left to run the business, delighted that the whole process has come to an end.

You then realise how much of your thinking time the deal has taken. The adrenalin can flow for months and then suddenly, when it is over, you recognise the pressure. You will never want to do a deal again, but acquisitions are the way to grow and it won't be long before you look for the next deal.

ACQUISITION SURVIVAL TIPS

TIP 1	DON'T BE SHY! ASK YOUR TARGET IF HE WANTS TO SELL.
TIP 2	SIGN THE CONFIDENTIALITY LETTER - DON'T PAY FOR LEGAL ADVICE.
TIP 3	DON'T BELIEVE ANY OF THE FORECASTS - THEY ARE ALL RANDOM NUMBERS GENERATED BY A COMPUTER
TIP 4	RESPECT YOUR OPPOSITE NUMBER
TIP 5	FIND OUT HOW MUCH THE LAWYERS ARE BEING PAID - AND WHO IS PAYING
TIP 6	GO WITH YOUR GUT INSTINCT

CHAPTER 13

Financial advice

We tell our bank manager everything. He sees our budgets, forecasts, and monthly figures, with detailed comments from Martin Tragen, our financial director. We make sure the bank gets no surprises.

Dear James

Watch the cash!

Banks have good reason to be suspicious. Too many company accounts hide the truth. There have been several examples of individuals frenetically collecting shops, but those in the know could see that these businesses were not working. The banks lent money to them and continued to support them until the problems finally became public.

Failed retail businesses make life more difficult for the rest of us — they make bankers more cautious. It is not surprising that lenders are suspicious of new business plans when past customers have let them down.

A difficult customer

Our 100 per cent equity holding makes life more difficult. There is no equity stake to compensate for the banker's risk. I don't find it easy to get a loan. In 1991 when I bought all the shares I did not own, and in 1995 when we bought Automagic, I had to mortgage our house for £1m. When the possibility of buying Sketchley came along in 1997, I didn't even ask Alex whether I could mortgage the house for the third time!

Banks don't delegate. Big decisions are referred to head office. I can't get any bank to guarantee that decisions will be made by somebody who knows me and knows my business. When a critical moment comes, the loan is made by a faceless financier.

We are not a bank's idea of a good investment. We are too big for local decision and too small to talk to people in London. We seem to ask for money when retailing is unfashionable and the bank is worried about the high street. They think service retailing is particularly risky.

Our balance sheet doesn't help, we have few assets, only a few freeholds, not much stock, and capital expenditure which we write off as soon as possible. Our biggest problem is our independence. We will never look at a deal that involves equity.

Having whinged about banks, I can reveal that we have been with the same branch of NatWest for 17 years. We tell them everything and they give practical support in return. I am a happy customer who now only looks for projects that can be financed through our local branch.

For a long and happy relationship with your bank manager, don't give him any surprises. Provide a constant stream of news and keep an eagle eye on your daily bank balance.

Count the cash

The bank balance is our best barometer. Before producing profit figures, accountants adjust for depreciation, contingencies, extraordinary items and sometimes use acquisition accounting. In contrast, the bank balance is a plain untampered fact.

We have a great advantage. Most of our sales are in cash. We have low working capital with little stock fluctuation from month to month.

Our major expenses are wages which are paid weekly or monthly, and rents which are paid quarterly. Fluctuations in our bank balance almost entirely reflect profit, capital expenditure and dividends.

Although shoe repairing is a simple cash business, some independent competitors get in financial trouble. They develop a false sense of security in their first year of operation, failing to anticipate their future liability for tax and

VAT, and they don't keep money aside to cope with the machinery breakdowns.

I look at the cash figure every day. We designed a simple report nine years ago and have used it ever since. The secret is to compare today's bank balance with the same day last year. The annual pattern of our payments and receipts doesn't vary. A comparison with 12 months ago eliminates all seasonal differences.

The change in the cash should reflect profits less capital expenditure. Most days I look at the cash report for 15 to 30 seconds and then throw it away. I ask two questions. "Why has it changed since yesterday?" and "Why the change since last year?" Usually, I know the answer. If I don't, I see Martin.

Budget with care

Businesses have an annual budget ritual – a series of meetings, deadlines, drafts and re-drafts, leading to final board approval.

Some companies put great store behind their budget. It is the bible against which the business should be judged and provides a map for the next 12 months. I have a more cynical view. The main value of our budget is to provide the point of contact between Martin and our bank manager.

Two cautionary tales illustrate the dangers of budget dependency.

In 1971, our shoe repair business took to budgeting in a big way. They were keen to give branches a sense of direction. If each shop had its own target, which in turn equated to the total company budget, there would be every chance targets would be achieved. With this thought in mind, the sales budget was set for each department for every week of the year. Head office set a company target, and every shop went through the same exercise. It took three months to get all the figures to balance. 175 expensive calculators were bought. Some branches had to recalculate their

figures six times before the company had achieved a 15 per cent sales increase. The board approached the new financial year with an air of confidence. The budget seemed to ensure a 15 per cent sales increase was just round the corner. At a time of ten per cent inflation, this meant a substantial increase in profits. Excited anticipation quickly gave way to disbelief when the first week of the new financial year failed to meet the company target. The customers took no notice of the budget and continued the spending pattern of the previous year!

In 1974 the Timpson directors thought figures would solve their problem. Sales had been severely down and, with only two months to go, profits were well behind budget and last year. The accountants and the administrators put their heads together and came up with a strategy – increase the margin. A fortnight was spent studying the statistic for each shoe style, increasing prices where possible. Within a week of the price increases, sales got even worse but head office stuck to its strategy. With a further fall in sales even more margin was needed to achieve the profit target. Prices had to rise again. After seven weeks of progressively more disappointing sales and higher and higher prices, the board saw their folly. Early in 1975 they opened three shoe discount warehouses to clear the surplus stock.

Profits come from good ideas, the right strategy and getting the thinking straight. Budgets put a value on your decisions and quantify the risk. They do no more than continue the current trend or extrapolate someone's dreams. Budgets had more purpose during years of high inflation. When prices were rising by over 20 per cent, we needed a budget to provide a proper reference point. But with inflation down to three per cent, it is better to compare with last year. Never allow anyone to just compare against budget – they must always show last year's figures. Last year is the comparison that most people respect. Companies don't show budget in their annual accounts. Beating last year is the prime target.

Using the figures

Despite being a budgetary cynic, I approve of budgets, but I don't get involved in detail or attend a budget meeting, I have spent too much time attending intense conferences about theoretical decisions.

I attended a bizarre budget meeting in 1981 when five of us spent two days discussing every property to construct a capital expenditure proposal to UDS, at a time when UDS had no money to invest.

No one can escape the final budgetary approval meeting. The danger is in the detail. Concentrate on the front page and ask three simple questions: "Are you happy with the profit?" "Are you confident about the sales?" and "Are the costs near to last year?" If the answer to these three questions is yes, look no further. If the answer is no, adjust the figures according to these simple rules.

1. Put the sales budget at a figure you believe you will achieve.
2. Set the profit at the minimum figure that will make you happy.
3. If necessary reduce the costs, but never let them go below last year without a good explanation.

As the year unfolds and budgets give way to management accounts, the whole thing gets more serious. Each month ask two questions: Are these figures what I expected? Am I spending money that I shouldn't be spending? Don't look at the detail of the management accounts. Keep your eye on the big picture. If you find you are discussing the cost of food in the canteen, it is time to close the meeting.

Prophets of doom

There is not much chance of complacency if you have got an accountant in the office. They have a happy knack of spreading gloom and despondency. The accountant's job is to point out the bad news. Their vocabulary is full of words like "shortfall," "overspend" and "slippage."

The finance department might be the prophets of doom but you would be in a pretty poor state without them. Despite two A-levels at maths, I fell at the first hurdle of accountancy. To make matters worse,

I am computer illiterate!

A good accountant is essential. You need someone you can totally trust to add up your numbers. Don't be tempted to work out figures for yourself. Your job is to ask the right questions, leave the accountants to produce the financial answer.

"Will this shop make money?" "Will I get a return out of that machine?" "Is it worth thinking of acquiring that business?" The finance department always has a ready answer. But the question you must ask most of all is: "What's the cash looking like?" With a good position at the bank you can sleep without any worries.

Stay independent

Having experienced a publicly quoted family company, a subsidiary of a group, part of a conglomerate, a management buyout, a business owned by the boardroom and finally total control, I can tell you that total independence has all the advantages.

> Dear James
>
> Read this before you sell a single share !

A priceless position

The business is not just our livelihood, it is our number one hobby. I wouldn't accept money in exchange for never playing golf again and I won't sell the business. Being independent lets me pursue my main hobby in the way I wish. I can do it my way, use my style of management, give charitable donations to causes I wish to support, take holidays when I want them and in the end, know that right or wrong, it was my fault. Compared to most businesses, we don't waste time on politics and make quick decisions. This is a selfish view. I want independence because it suits me, but it also seems to work for the benefit of our customers and staff. With your own business, you are committed to the company for life, so staff and customer loyalty become very important. It helps employees to know their boss and know he will still be the boss in five years' time.

Don't be greedy

Last year the business created £4m of cash, to split between dividends and capital expenditure. Invest in the future, don't take any more than necessary out of the business. I am consistently unsuccessful on the

stock market but the money invested in Timpson has produced a superb return. The sum of £137,500 invested in 1983 provides all the income I need and ownership of the business.

I strongly recommend putting all your eggs in one basket. Independence puts a useful control on our rate of growth. It is easy to be tempted by expansion but we are limited by our cash flow. Serious money won't come from a bank without an equity involvement. Equity is the most expensive form of finance. Both Body Shop and McDonalds sold over 35 per cent of their equity in their early days for a small amount of money. In five years we have doubled our turnover and quadrupled our profits and this has been achieved from our own cash resources. James, you are now 28. If we double the number of shops every five years between now and when you retire at 65, you would finish up with 80,000 shops, a useless statistic which demonstrates the possibilities of steady growth.

Outright share ownership will limit the number of opportunities we can take. Treat the restriction as an advantage. You can't pursue everything. You have to choose. Choose wisely, and you will concentrate on the best routes for expansion.

Unhelpful advice

You will be advised to lose your independence. Mostly by people with plenty to gain when you have got it all to lose. Stockbrokers, venture capitalists and their team of advisers make little out of independent businesses – they only start to earn money when you give up equity.

The most persistent advice will come from the tax planners. I don't want to live in Jersey, nor do I intend to make tax-efficient sacrifices to pass wealth on to another generation.

I am pleased that recent changes in tax makes my stand for independence even more justified. Large company shareholdings such as ours can be passed from one generation to another without tax being paid. The government clearly feels personal ownership is good for business.

Happiness is 100 per cent

Large quoted companies do an excellent job. The economy needs multi billion pound corporations to provide us with oil, computers, super-markets, banks and pharmaceutical research.

Fortunately for us, the best shoe repair and key cutting chain in the UK can still be independent.

You may be tempted that 51 per cent still keeps control. In theory that is true, but it is not total control. As soon as you have another shareholder, they want to protect their minority interest. The gap between 100 per cent and 99.9 per cent is enormous.

Whoever the shareholders may be – bankers, venture capitalists, private individuals, directors or employees – they want to know what's in it for them. They look to you to maximise their dividends and their share price.

Only turn to outside shareholders when you desperately need them to survive. That should be a move of last resort. At other times the only benefit outside equity brings is the opportunity to expand quicker than your cash flow allows. But shareholders will bring the politics of jealousy and greed. Choose your own charitable donations, decide your own salary and most important of all, set your own business strategy. My advice is unequivocal: "DON'T SELL A SINGLE SHARE."

Amazing Our Customers

How retailing got a bad name

Being nice to customers seems such an obvious retail policy, it is amazing that everyone on the high street doesn't do it as a matter of course.

Good old days

Shopping has changed a lot since 1960 when I started work as a sales assistant. In those days we had big windows full of shoes and no display inside the shop. The shop was full of chairs and shoe boxes, every wall lined with fixtures carrying stock. There was no self-service, not even for shoe polish and socks, and no computers, as each customer received a hand-written receipt.

The company had just introduced paper bags to wrap up slippers but we were forbidden to use slipper bags for other footwear. Each shop had a wrapping counter with a big roll of paper, a ball of string and a razor blade. This was before Cellotape, and we were not allowed to use scissors. It was impossible to wrap shoes without putting them in the box, that is why households in the sixties had plenty of shoe boxes. I needed four weeks' training to get the hang of parcel wrapping!

The method might seem old-fashioned, but it gave good customer service. You couldn't sell a shoe without talking to the customer. You had to know your stock, which styles were in the window and where the shoe boxes were stored in the shop. You had to know about shoes to be able to talk to the customer while you sat on your fitting stool, using a shoe horn to fit the footwear.

You also needed a good memory. We had to offer every customer three styles of shoe, and at busy times served three customers at once. It was easy to get confused on a busy Saturday, between the tall man who wanted black lace shoes size nine, and the short man who was after working boots size seven, with your third chair being occupied by the brown shoe size seven customer with corduroy trousers.

I never remember us being short of staff. Twelve people worked in the Altrincham shop where I started and some of our city shops had 40. The shops were a lot busier because in 1960 you could only buy footwear in shoe shops. There was no competition from Marks & Spencer, Tesco or JJB Sport. Wage rates were low – my starting pay was £6 7/6d a week.

The whole high street has changed dramatically. In 1960 Marks & Spencer did not sell food, most branches of Boots the Chemist had a lending library. Every shopping centre had its multiple tailor. Burtons, Hepworths and John Colliers sold 50 per cent of the men's suits in the United Kingdom and 95 per cent of the suits were made to measure. All the ground floor of these shops was devoted to window displays and pattern books laid out on tables, showing the range of cloths from which the suits were made. They employed good salesmen who knew how to talk to customers. When the ready-made market took over, the look of the multiple outfitter completely changed and the highest levels of service disappeared from the high street.

Retail engineering

Everything changed by the early seventies. Designer-led shops became "a theatre" to project the merchandise. Self-service took over. Checkouts were installed and staff stationed by the till. Computerisation increased head office control. With better information, the head office team took charge of stock control and decided how displays should be laid out. It was called retail engineering, bringing efficiency to the high street.

These new management tools became doubly important when inflation hit the wage rates. Wage control in 1973 created the biggest percentage increase retail wages have ever seen. The government introduced a £6 increase for all levels of pay. It ended any thoughts of having enough staff to look after all your customers.

The accountants took over and led a tight control on staff wage levels. There was a decline in both the quality and quantity of staff and customer service suffered. By 1975 bad service had become the norm and consumerism was born.

Consumer champion

When I became managing director of Timpson in 1975, shoe shops had a particularly bad reputation. Complaints about faulty footwear were running at five per cent. British Shoe Corporation, who had over 20 per cent of the market, had an arrogant disdain for customer care.

We were desperately keen to find a way to compete with the dominant BSC. Their shops occupied prime sites and their buyers bought the best range on the high street. A visit to our shops confirmed the worst. We were just as bad. I decided to use better service as the way to compete.

My Chairman, Stuart Lyons, arranged a visit to the newly formed Office of Fair Trading, where we met the Director General, John Methven, who was trying to agree a Footwear Code of Practice. The OFT negotiated with the Footwear Distributors' Federation, which represented both independents and multiples, but negotiations were dominated by British Shoe. The Footwear Code was one of the first five codes produced by the OFT and shoe retailers did not like being a guinea pig. They fought every clause to stop the OFT producing a better deal for the consumer.

We were the first retailers to see John Methven voluntarily. He was delighted at our positive attitude. We left a cordial meeting with a draft Code recently proposed to the Footwear Distributors. It was written in civil service language, long sentences with little meaning. Two nights later I rewrote the draft in plain English and added some ideas of my own.

We took my version back to the OFT and said we had decided to produce our own Code of Practice to set standards for Timpson. We got a warm response; this was just what the OFT needed to bring other shoe retailers to heel. We launched the Timpson Code of Practice at a joint press conference, John Methven supported our initiative and I was interviewed by Woman's Hour and Jimmy Young. In one move I became a consumer champion. We have used customer care as a positive marketing tool ever since.

Good service is good business

In our shops, a good manager makes a big difference. Success depends on their quality, and their honesty. Good managers are keen to increase turnover and the best are very good with customers. If a shop is performing badly, look at the quality of customer care.

I get irritated with the modern day signs of poor service. The high street has cut prices and saved time but lost the personal touch. You can do all your shopping without saying a word to anybody and even shop via a PC. One day, personal service will undergo a major revival but, in the meantime, the public has to endure my pet hates – queues at the till, checkout points left unmanned, no-one to help you find something, till technology that keeps you waiting if your purchase isn't on the computer, staff without authority to do anything out of the ordinary without the permission of their manager.

The title sales assistant suggests they are there to help and yet a lot of them don't. ("If it is not on display we haven't got it"; or, when you offer a £20 note, "haven't you got anything smaller?" and "this till's closing now, love.") Good sales assistants enjoy providing the sort of service that most people don't expect. They give change for the telephone or a parking meter. They will even accept a credit card from someone only buying a tin of shoe polish. They reopen the shop for a customer hammering on the door after closing time. They let a desperate customer use the staff lavatory. If necessary, they deliver to the customer's home. Happily these things happen, I certainly hope they happen in our shops, because this sort of service brings in the extra business.

Finding ways to improve customer service is much more interesting than retail engineering which concentrates on cutting costs. Staff enjoy working in a shop that promotes good customer care. If they are pleasant to customers, they find customers are pleasant back. Most of all, good service shops make good money.

Good service means good business. Our problem is to provide it in over 300 shops throughout England, Scotland and Wales on every day to every customer. That is the challenge of multiple retailing.

THINGS THAT AMAZE

129

Define good service

Dear James

Describe ways to amaze customers

When I was first appointed managing director, I spent two weeks going to as many shops as possible. I was appalled. The shops were scruffy and the staff didn't take much notice of customers. In shop after shop I took note of the shortcomings: customers walking out without being spoken to, sales assistants chewing gum and shoes not sold – simply because they couldn't be bothered to find the stock.

I called in all the area managers and told them about my experience. It was an emotional meeting, especially when I said how sad I felt that such poor service took place in shops with my surname over the door. I had a simple message: "Go and make sure our customers are served better."

During the next few weeks, I saw no improvement. The area managers claimed they were doing everything possible to give staff my message. It took months before I realised that all I had done was define the problem. I had not found a solution.

You must define good service in detail. It's no good telling people to do better unless you say what better means. Eventually, I got the message and using my experience as a sales assistant, I wrote what became the Timpson Code of Service.

Code of service

My 1975 Code of Service looks odd now but it was a revolution in its day. Shop staff were not accustomed to receiving guidance on how to serve customers. There were plenty of rules from head office about running a shop. They covered every aspect of administration, strict procedures from stock-taking to the cash register. Timpson administration was detailed in a thick book of standing orders so everyone knew how to toe the line. There were no helpful hints on customer care.

I wrote Ten Golden Rules (today I would call them guidelines). It was a simple list of good customer care in shoe retailing, welcoming the customer, smiling, offering a choice of styles, introducing shoe polish and finishing the sale with a "thank you." Our staff were not only told to be nice to customers but how to do it.

It worked. Not only did customers get a better service, but the staff found their job more fun and sales increased. Our competitors emphasised self-service and better merchandising. They thought my approach was old-fashioned and bound to fail.

We enjoyed ten years of fairly buoyant trading while gaining a reputation for being good with customers. When I brought in new management to face the market pressures in 1985, we lost the plot. Good service only happens if the chief executive leads the crusade. My new team had other things on their mind. The Code of Service was filed in a cupboard. Within six months standards were declining and two years later the shops were just as bad as I found in 1975. Managing customer care is like gardening; you must keep weeding and cutting the grass.

Customer care manual

I introduced a complaints procedure for shoe repairs in 1977, called the "Fair Deal Plan." But I didn't write any code of service for the shoe repair shops until 1996. Simple golden rules suitable for 1975 wouldn't work in 1996. I didn't want to mimic the American system of service. I now cringe when I see a "mission statement" by the till with a picture of the chief executive. I am unimpressed by great big staff badges declaring "we care" or "here to help" and insincere phrases like "you're welcome" and "have a nice day."

Before writing our customer care manual, I wanted to find out what good service really meant in our branches. The best people to tell me were the staff themselves. I went to see lots of our people who were good with customers. Once put at ease they talked me through each type of sale. They told me what they did to impress.

We didn't talk in general terms (such as a warm welcome, smiling and saying thank you), we talked about specifics: how to greet customers as soon as they came into the shop; how to set prices for an unusual job; how to handle customers with a complaint.

I gathered a vast collection of good service ideas which were being used in our shops. I now knew what our customer care manual should contain. My next problem was how to get the message across. I went on holiday for a week on the Isle of Lewis armed with my notes – seven days of peace and quiet to clear the mind and create the customer care manual.

I wasn't searching for a set of rules, I wanted to give guidelines. The manual was written for committed people to help them serve customers better. But these tips were not just meant to provide an ordinary service. I was trying to create something special. Once I realised the goal was to amaze our customers, the whole thing came to life.

Our technical manuals are written in pictures rather than words. The customer care manual needed the same pictorial treatment. We used cartoons with speech bubbles.

I returned from the Isle of Lewis with all the basic thinking done and the first rough draft. It took another six months before I was happy with the finished product. Each page not only had to say the right things, it had to look appealing, with the right sort of illustrations. As each draft was produced I went back to our shop staff to check that the ideas would work in practice. As I talked to the staff, I discovered more new ideas to include in the manual. Eight months after my holiday, the customer care manual was launched to all Timpson staff through a video and a series of seminars.

The end product is a comprehensive attempt to define what good service means in practice. It had an immediate effect. As soon as we launched it, our mystery shopping reports showed a dramatic improvement. We now had a way of communicating good customer practice. But my customer care manual won't work for ever. It must be updated on a regular basis. As the high street changes, so do customers. In another decade, you will need a different manual to redefine good service for the year 2010.

Pages from our customer care guidelines

Teaching good service

Dear James

You will be as good as your Area Managers

Writing a manual defines good service but it does not ensure the message gets home. Find as many interesting ways as you can to spread your good service philosophy and make sure everyone knows how to achieve it.

Explain why service matters

Never suggest your customer care manual is a set of rules. Encourage everybody to think of it as a guide to help do the job better. Sell the idea that customer care matters. Most people who join us want to be shoe repairers, key cutters, engravers or watch repairers, but serving a customer is another skill which is just as important.

The company must give customer care the highest priority. It is good news for customers and good news for our employees. Explain why good customer care makes shop life more enjoyable. Cheerful staff get a pleasant response and good service makes shops busy. When business is brisk, time goes quickly, and each working day is more enjoyable. The extra trade brings in more bonus and everyone's pay packet is bigger at the end of the week. With good customer care, everybody wins – the customer, the company and everyone who works in the shop. The customer care manual will make everyone's life better. It is not a set of rules but a guide to better business.

Don't just rely on the manual. To spread the company's philosophy, supplement the manual with the spoken word. This is an ideal job for a video. Our customer care video brought the manual to life using cartoons to describe each customer care tip. The video doesn't just teach better service, it also explains why good service matters. This is a personal message so I myself start and end the film by explaining why I believe in good customer care.

It is ten times easier to teach customer care to someone who believes it is important. Get the message across by showing your staff life from the customer's side of the counter. We regularly survey the high street and ask our own staff to carry out the research. Before attending our customer care course, every participant is given £10 to go shopping. They complete a shopping experience questionnaire which they bring to their course.

Customer care training

Everyone in our shops attends customer care courses. It is an expensive exercise. The courses are run by an experienced trainer, and no more than four people attend. When we introduced the customer care manual, 200 separate training sessions were held for 800 staff. Every new employee attends the course during their apprenticeship. At least 75 one-day courses happen every year. With only four people on a course everybody talks. The biggest barrier to good customer care is the reluctance to communicate. We use role play to get the introverts to contribute. We start the day with a report on their shopping survey. That sets the scene by looking at life through the eyes of a customer.

The basis of the day is the video. At the end of each section of video, the trainer uses slides to illustrate the significant messages. Then role play turns the message into practice. Each course ends with a discussion on what to do when candidates get back to their branches. Everyone leaves with a list of personal targets to improve the way they relate to customers.

Throughout the course we emphasise that good customer care makes shop life more fun. Those that put the ideas into practice go back to a more enjoyable job!

Everyone should attend a new customer care training day every year – even people from head office! Our branch staff spend about 225 days each year serving customers. It is well worth taking one day to remind them how important customer care can be.

Our follow-up courses concentrate on the critical areas that set the good shops apart from the mediocre. People that amaze customers are good at handling complaints and rise to the challenge of unusual requests and difficult customers. Most of all, they are supremely good at talking to customers.

Keep reminding everyone why customer care is so important and confirm it works in practice. Talk about our past success – show a collection of complimentary letters, results of mystery shopping and quote our own staff who have seen the benefit of good customer care.

For the training to work, staff must believe in customer care. Demonstrate it is in their interest to serve customers. It will make their life more enjoyable and increase their bonus.

Don't use rules, provide guidelines. Keep showing how customer care can develop our business. If you stop talking about service, standards will fall. You must never stop teaching good customer care.

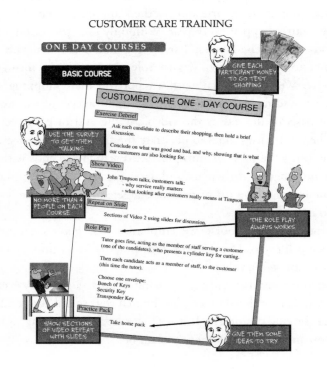

CUSTOMER CARE TRAINING

ONE DAY COURSES

BASIC COURSE

GIVE EACH PARTICIPANT MONEY TO GO TEST SHOPPING

CUSTOMER CARE ONE - DAY COURSE

Exercise Debrief

Ask each candidate to describe their shopping, then hold a brief discussion.

Conclude on what was good and bad, and why, showing that is what our customers are also looking for.

USE THE SURVEY TO GET THEM TALKING

Show Video

John Timpson talks, customers talk:
- why service really matters
- what looking after customers really means at Timpson

NO MORE THAN 4 PEOPLE ON EACH COURSE

Repeat on Slide

Sections of Video 2 using slides for discussion.

THE ROLE PLAY ALWAYS WORKS

Role Play

Tutor goes first, acting as the member of staff serving a customer (one of the candidates), who presents a cylinder key for cutting.

Then each candidate acts as a member of staff, to the customer (this time the tutor).

Choose one envelope:
Bunch of Keys
Security Key
Transponder Key

Practice Pack

SHOW SECTIONS OF VIDEO REPEAT WITH SLIDES

Take home pack

GIVE THEM SOME IDEAS TO TRY

Complaints are welcome

In 1975 customer complaints were a major problem. Higher imports and the introduction of platform soles dramatically increased the incidence of faulty footwear. Timpson shoe shops were as bad as the others – five per cent of all shoes sold came back as complaints, ten per cent of ladies' fashion shoes were returned. For some styles the return rate was one in five but the company continued to sell the shoes. Most multiple shoe retailers, particularly British Shoe Corporation, reacted with a tough complaints policy. Staff were encouraged to reject complaints and were given a target. In some companies a high level of complaints affected staff bonuses.

Dear James

Offer complaint customers more than they ever expected

On the customer's side

Within weeks of becoming managing director, I published my Timpson Promise. I put my picture and signature in all our shop windows: "If you have good reason to be dissatisfied with your shoes we will give you your money back!" We advertised the Timpson Promise on television.

Our multiple competitors thought I was mad. British Shoe Corporation's managing director said it was like giving petrol to an arsonist. It certainly caused us some short-term difficulties. We returned all the high complaint styles to the manufacturers, even though that took some of the best sellers out of our shops. We lost sales but our complaints policy quickly gave us the reputation that we cared for customers. Within six months our complaint rate was well down and our sales were going up.

It was not just customers who approved of our complaints policy; after a few misgivings our approach was strongly backed by shop staff. We had taken away their complaint problem. For years they had been told to keep complaints down and been criticised if refunds rose above the target. Suddenly they could settle every complaint in favour of the customer whatever the level of refund. Some resented our policy, especially if they thought the customer was taking them for a ride.

For 25 years I have been told my approach is open to abuse. They forecast a rip-off by a large number of customers keen to take us to the cleaners. My Timpson Promise didn't produce a substantial increase in unjustified complaints, even though I promoted it on television. I now give our shoe repairs an unconditional guarantee: "If you aren't happy, we do the job again or give you your money back." Despite the prophets of doom, the unconditional guarantee produces very few claims. A generous deal to customers always does more good than harm.

A generous complaints policy must be good for business. Most complaints are genuine and we should be grateful to customers who tell us of a problem. They give us a chance to put things right, and make us aware of shortcomings. They also give us a wonderful opportunity to amaze them with our standard of customer care. Some of the highest compliments we receive result from a well handled complaint.

The most serious problems arise from routine complaints that are badly handled. Most people are remarkably tolerant, they recognise no business can be perfect and that things go wrong, but even the mildest people get steamed up when a justified criticism is ignored.

Wherever possible, settle complaints immediately. Give your shop staff the authority to deal with every customer face to face. I give everyone authority to do whatever they think will make a complaining customer happy and they can spend up to £500 to achieve it.

My "no quibble" policy can make staff feel that they are being ripped off. I try to create an atmosphere where our staff are generous to even the most nit-picking of customers. We even accept complaints about jobs that have been done by our competitors! No-one is ever criticised for being too generous. We regularly praise those who move complaining customers to write complimentary letters.

Difficult customers

Some customers don't want their complaint to be settled, they get more pleasure by continuing the grievance and becoming Mr Angry. These are the most difficult people to deal with. We suggest staff should ask: "What will make you happy? What can I do to settle this complaint to your satisfaction?" But those questions won't work with Mr Angry. He gets his pleasure out of complaining, not by having complaints settled.

Give them direct access to my office. Whatever the staff try to do in the shop, the customer won't be happy. There is no point in passing them to an area manager or the sales director, they want to talk to the boss. We only have two stages to our complaints procedure: if it is not settled in the shop, customers write to me.

Some customers are never ever satisfied. A few years ago a customer rang up head office and got straight through to my desk. He was complaining about key cutting at a shop. It was the day before a Bank Holiday and all our in-house experts were out of the office. I decided the chairman should get out from behind his desk and resolve the matter immediately. With enthusiasm I set off to the scene of the problem. On the way, I picked up a member of staff from our local shop. I knew I had a real problem. The one person available to help me had only been with us two months and didn't know much more about cutting a key than I did. But I was committed to help the customer. We tried filing down one key but failed to make it work, so I said I would go to our shop to cut a replacement. After I dropped our young and ineffective assistant back at our branch, I took the customer's original key to our local competitor! It didn't matter by that stage that I had the keys cut by a rival – at least I could go back and give our customer a set of

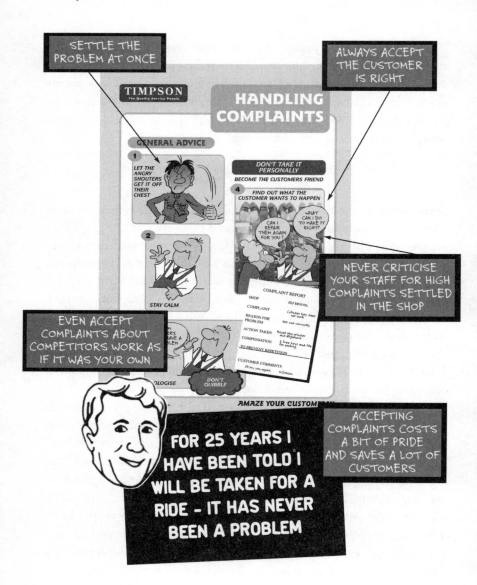

FOR 25 YEARS I HAVE BEEN TOLD I WILL BE TAKEN FOR A RIDE - IT HAS NEVER BEEN A PROBLEM

keys that worked. I expected some special praise. The customer was bound to have been impressed with a chairman who spent two hours sorting out a customer complaint. No such luck! He gave me a lecture on the importance of staff training and said that next time he would have his keys cut down the road!

I met another difficult customer during a visit to our shop in Buchanan Street, Glasgow. A lady came in complaining bitterly we had refused to supply her with the shoe laces she wanted. She had called half an hour earlier and our manager, faced with six other customers and a delivery of 16 cartons, explained politely that the laces were in the new delivery, and he would find them when the shop was free of customers. The woman stormed out of the shop saying she would be back in half an hour when she expected the laces to be ready. It had been a hectic day and the incident got up the manager's nose. When the woman returned, he said that he had been busy getting ready for a visit from his boss who had only just arrived. "I'll talk to him then," said the woman. So I was summoned to deal with the complaint. I followed my own advice: "What can I do to make you happy?" I asked the woman. "Fire the manager. He is useless." I told her I wasn't prepared to do that, but I was happy to give her the laces free, or a large discount voucher, or anything that would satisfy her complaint. "Everyone has got a lousy attitude in this shop," she said. "Who owns this business?" "I do," I meekly replied. "In that case," she said, "there is no point in complaining to head office." She stomped out of the shop. I am told she is still a regular customer. She comes in almost every week and every three months, when things are going badly at home, she complains very bitterly indeed.

Letters to head office

Although letters of complaint are usually addressed to Mr Timpson, get someone else to answer them for you. You have not got the time, the experience or indeed the patience to handle difficult complaints and are not always in the office to deal with your post.

Speed is essential. Reply to every letter on the day it is received. Either give immediate compensation or promise to investigate the complaint within ten days. If you investigate, send your next letter no more than seven days after the first – well within the ten days you promised. If you find the customer is totally in the wrong, explain your conclusions in the letter, but still give the customer a full refund. It doesn't matter what you think; if they bother to complain, they must be dissatisfied. Don't just give full compensation; add just a little bit extra to give the customer more than they ever expected.

Even our incredibly generous complaint policy won't satisfy everybody. I draw the line at giving in to outlandish or fraudulent claims. We found the "lost" shoes for one customer lying on the shelves of a competitor. One customer claimed that we had ruined shoes that cost £400. When we checked in the shops, they were less than £100. Even we cannot deal with Mr Unreasonable!

You must delegate the job of complaints letters but don't forget that they are replying to letters sent to you personally. The letters matter. They must not come off a word processor. Each one should be individual, with "Dear Sir" and the signature hand-written.

We handle several complaints by telephone. Each key we cut carries a guarantee tag which encourages customers with a problem to call our central advice line. A hotline for customers gives an opportunity to settle complaints very quickly – as long as the hotline works!

Soon nearly all our complaints will be handled over the telephone but not until we are certain our telephone system allows the customer to talk to someone who can help within 30 seconds. I mistrust new fangled telephone technology. We won't make the customer tap loads of buttons – or be stacked in a queue while they listen to Vivaldi. We don't want a complaints system that gives cause for complaint.

Even if a complaint is settled over the telephone we will still write to say sorry and offer a discount voucher in compensation.

Learning from complaints

Customer complaints save a lot of money in market research. Complaints indicate where the company has failed. If we listen we will learn how to improve our service to future customers.

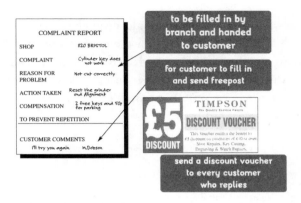

We learn from our complaints, and customers are impressed that we take notice of their advice. Every time we receive a complaint our staff write a report. They detail the nature of the complaint, the reason why it happened, what compensation they have given and what is being done to prevent the complaint happening again. A copy is given to the customer, asking for their comments to be sent by freepost to our head office. In return, we send the customer a £5 discount voucher to say "thank you" for helping us improve our service.

We try to stop staff sweeping complaints under the carpet. To encourage them to handle complaints, we pay a £2 bonus for every properly completed complaint report. Rather than criticise staff for complaints in their shops, we pay them extra money for handling them!

The same complaint report is completed when customers write direct to head office. On our report we also ask why the complaint came direct to us instead of going to the branch. Sometimes customers avoid the shop because they mistrust the staff attitude. Staff attitude is the only type of complaint that can lead to a warning letter. We don't criticise anyone for making mistakes. In a busy shop there are bound to be problems. Some keys won't work and some of the shoes get mislaid, but there is no excuse for being rude.

Don't be half-hearted in your complaints policy. The way you handle complaints says a lot about how you handle the rest of your customers. Go out of your way and turn a potential tragedy into a triumph. Offer customers more than they ever expected and there is a chance you will amaze them. We should always be grateful to customers who take the trouble to tell us about their complaint. Each year I say thank you to everybody who's complained by letter by sending them a Christmas card which contains a bar of chocolate and a voucher to encourage them to give our shops another try. Some customers have sent me a Christmas card back!

HOW TO TURN A COMPLAINT INTO A TRIUMPH

1. OFFER MORE THAN THEY EVER EXPECT

Extra keys for nothing

Discount Voucher

Tin of free polish

2. GO OUT OF YOUR WAY TO SORT OUT A PROBLEM

3. SEND A CHRISTMAS CARD TO EVERYONE WHO WRITES TO COMPLAIN

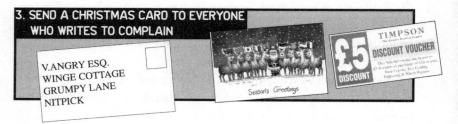

V.ANGRY ESQ.
WINGE COTTAGE
GRUMPY LANE
NITPICK

Season's Greetings

Our service can always improve

Not long ago, I asked a journalist to write an article about our customer care programme. The idea was to produce a report that we could use at our one-day training sessions, demonstrating to our staff that the customer care programme really did work although there was still room for improvement. I hoped to have the article published.

Dear James

You will never have perfect customer service

Room for improvement

I expected the article to say that Timpsons had done a lot to improve customer care, changing the attitude of staff and customers alike. I expected our customer care manual, the associated training courses and the personal interest that I had taken in customer care to be held up as an example for other companies to follow. I knew that the journalist would reveal the company, warts and all, quoting examples where the service in our shops could be improved.

I paid her £500 a day. She quizzed me about our policy, attended a training course and then set off for the high street to inspect our service and shop at our competitors.

I was shocked by the result. Instead of writing an article, she sent me her shopping survey which showed that our shops were the worst on the high street. She scored every shop out of 50 and some of our branches got less than ten! She did, admittedly, have one bad experience, but she was on the lookout for bad things in our shops while she was keen to recognise good elsewhere. It was a subjective and highly critical report which she recommended as a staff training tool to bring our standards up to those of our competitors.

I thought I had wasted my money. I could not present a report to our staff saying that their standards were poor when it was untrue. It taught me a lesson – there is always room for improvement.

Journalists have a natural affinity for bad news. Biased consumer surveys based on a small sample are often used by newspapers to expose sensational stories on the high street. Any newspaper hearing our stance on customer care could easily prove that we are not as good as we say we are.

Despite the dangers of tabloid journalism I am still happy to throw open our business to outside criticism. I seek publicity for all that we have done on customer standards because most journalists report it as it really is. We know our standards have improved because we measure them.

Measuring performance

We carry out a regular programme of mystery shopper visits. Every branch is checked by a mystery shopper five times a year and sometimes we also check out our competitors.

Some visits concentrate on the quality of a particular service. In this way we can see the quality of shoe repairs or check whether the keys we cut actually work.

On every visit we measure customer service. Each mystery shopper has a detailed check list based on our customer care manual. The check list tells them what to look out for, but the scoring system is based on their subjective judgement. We ask them ten questions which cover the main parts of the shopping experience.

Detailed scoring systems just don't work. For example we once awarded points to every branch that mentioned the customer by name. So as long as they mentioned a name, they got the points even if they-said: "And you, Mrs Smith, can piss off!"

Keeping our test shopper a mystery can prove difficult. Once we wanted to test our watch repair service. Our staff didn't recognise the mystery shoppers but they had seen the watches before – they were the

TO JOHN TIMPSON
YOUR STAFF HAVE AMAZED ME !!!

STAFF NAMES BRIAN
SHOP
WHY I WAS AMAZED I TOOK MY SHOES ELSEWHERE
... WAS TOLD THEM COULDN'T BE SOLED OR
... AS THE SOLE IS A MAN MADE HARD
... BRIAN DID IT !!
... D. DAVIES

TELEPHONE

TO JOHN TIMPSON
YOUR STAFF HAVE AMAZED ME !!!

STAFF NAMES
SHOP 661
WHY I WAS AMAZED When I entered the shop
both men were busy with other customers, but
they immediately acknowledged me and one
said he would be with me in a few minutes. Both were
cheerful and helpful
NAME C. Egerton
ADDRESS   TELEPHONE

TO JOHN TIMPSON
YOUR STAFF HAVE AMAZED ME !!!

... MES BARRY
SHOP ARBROATH
WHY I WAS AMAZED I WAS SHOPPING AT THE
ABBEYGATE When I locked my keys in my
CAR. BARRY CAME DOWN AND OPENED THE
CAR IN A FEW MINUTES. (FREE GRATIS)
NAME LANCE MORGAN
ADDRESS   P.S. I will shop at
Timpsons

TELEPHONE

TO JOHN TIMPSON
YOUR STAFF HAVE AMAZED ME !!!

STAFF NAMES Danny
SHOP BECKTON 749
WHY I WAS AMAZED I presented them with 9
pair of dancing clogs needing repair at very
short notice & they did the job as well as a
specialist clog maker. Two hours dancing over
cobbled streets (photos to prove)
showed how good
the work was
NAME Janet Pringle
ADDRESS   TELEPHONE

TO JOHN TIMPSON
YOUR STAFF HAVE AMAZED ME !!!

... MES RAY
... HENLEY
... WAS AMAZED I HAD A KEY STUCK IN MY LOCK
... CAME TO MY HOUSE AFTER WORK AND TOOK THE
LOCK AWAY FITTED THE KEY TO THE LOCK TO AK. LOCK BROUGHT
IT BACK THE NEXT DAY. FITTED IT, NOW WORKING GREAT!
NAME MRS BARKER
ADDRESS   TELEPHONE

TO JOHN TIMPSON
YOUR STAFF HAVE AMAZED ME !!!

STAFF NAMES (Not known) But Two Great Lads.
SHOP VICTORIA CENTRE
WHY I WAS AMAZED At What they did for me
in regards to my shoes. I thought they
couldn't be mended but they did a good job
and are like New. (GREAT)
NAME Mrs P. Barton
ADDRESS   TELEPHONE

CUSTOMER POSTCARD

CARRIER BAG

TIMPSON
The Quality Service People
Est. 1903

£25 BONUS FOR EVERY 20 COMPLIMENTS

FRAMED PRESS CUTTINGS

FRAME CUSTOMER COMPLAINTS

same ones we had used on a training course a few weeks earlier.

Although many staff claim they can spot a mystery shopper, most don't. It happened once to me.

One Saturday in Cambridge, I found one of our shops facing a crisis. It was short staffed due to illness. The shop was disorganised and the staff didn't have the experience to deal with a very busy shop. I thought that this was a wonderful opportunity to see what happens when things go wrong. I wanted to see how we coped with a queue and how long customers would wait before they walked out.

After a few minutes' observation, I went to our other shop in the centre of Cambridge and got another member of staff to come and help. But, while I was observing the chaos, I didn't realise that one of those customers was a mystery shopper. I was mentioned in his accurate and uncomplimentary report as the older man who looked to be part of the management but didn't do anything to help the customers!

We use the report in two ways. Every shop – good or bad – receives a copy. They see how well they were rated and what let them down. The very best (those that score over 95 per cent) get a special award – £25 to everyone in the shop when this level of service was recorded. Following each report we ask the manager to make observations on the comments and what action they are taking to rectify any problems. We do this five times a year. It is a reminder why customers matter so much.

Service challenge

Whenever possible, reward good customer care rather than criticise bad service. We run customer service-related competitions under various titles like our "Amaze Me" month and the "Service Challenge Competition." This makes customer care the centre of attention.

Once every two or three years we have a major drive on service standards – four to eight weeks doing everything possible to improve customer care. Before the promotion starts we repeat our one-day courses around the country. We put graphics into the shop that tell customers how well they can expect to be served. A poster that talks about good service causes branch staff to respond by being nicer to customers.

At the centre of every customer care promotion is a competition. Some points are given by mystery shoppers but most marks are based on complimentary comments. Throughout the competitions we urge our staff to hand out freepost comment cards to every customer – 5,000 customers every week take the trouble to fill in the reply card and put them in a letter box. Each postcard is assessed and the cards returned to the shop to show the staff what their customers are saying. Nearly all the postcards (98 per cent) are compliments – we put them on display for our customers to read.

Who better to judge service than customers themselves? We don't just give out comment cards when we are having a competition, they are available all the time. For three years our packaging carried information about the customer survey. Most of the time we don't use freepost, comments are of even more value if customers buy a stamp. But we give an incentive: every compliment is rewarded with a £5 voucher. We also give prizes to shops with the most complimentary cards sent in their support. We want to make sure that customer service makes everybody a winner.

Customer care must be in the forefront of the company's mind. You can't find too many ways to praise good service. Every "well done" increases the chance of good service happening again.

As well as service competitions and the prizes for postcards, we find many other good reasons for rewarding excellent service. We give £50 for the "Compliment of the Month" and special awards for amazing service ideas sent to our suggestion scheme. The best reward is a special mention in the local newspaper. Journalists can write about good news as well as bad. If a paper prints an article about one of our shops, we frame a copy and put it on display for all their customers to see. This not only increases the pride in their work but is also good for business.

Service will play a critical part in the company's future success. Keep looking for new ways to amaze your customers.

Managing people

Look after your people

Dear James

Look after the
people who look
after your
customers

At first, I thought the job was all about meetings and telling everyone else what to do. I thought the secret of success was to make the right decisions. Good management is not like that. No manager can be in total charge of a business.

It is obvious really, none of us can be in more than one place at once and yet we have over 300 branches stretching from Inverness down to Plymouth and from Norwich across to Swansea. Ideas won't work unless they are embraced by the people who work for you. Staff only follow leadership if they believe in what they are being told to do.

False economy

Look at some financial facts. Last year our turnover was approximately £44m, £6m of that went in VAT and we made a profit of £2.7m. The remaining £35m represents the cost of running the business.

There are three major cost items. Raw materials, (the leather soles and key blanks) adds up to £4m. Our bill for rent and rates comes to about £7m. Wages and salaries, at £17m, are nearly half the total cost of running the business.

How you regard this figure depends whether you are an entrepreneur or an accountant. The accountant would see a major cost saving opportunity: "Cut back on staff, save on the wage bill and make a major contribution to profits." The entrepreneur takes a different view. Seeing staff as his most important business asset, he would look after the good staff and invest in the best people.

When a business goes through a difficult patch, the accountant's argument becomes very attractive. I have observed the cost cutting process on several occasions. No stone is left unturned – car expenses, training department, window cleaners, Christmas parties and the head office usage of lavatory paper are all put under the financial microscope and added together to provide cost savings to rescue the company.

I have rarely seen cost saving bring real success. Turnover is not a fixed figure. All too often cost cutting measures reduce the turnover and produce a further downturn in profits, leading to yet another round of cost saving! This process can continue for two or three years until the enterprise finally disappears

Rather than cutting back on staffing costs, look after your staff and have the best people in the industry. Aim to be the best company to work for. The better your people, the better the business. Look after those who in turn look after your customers.

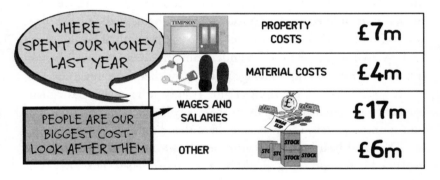

A salutary lesson

Every week, I see examples of talented staff running our branches. I have seen a spectacular turnaround in many shops due to the individual efforts of star managers. Our acquisition of Automagic illustrates how people can influence success.

In 1995 Automagic was a run down business. Turnover had not increased for four years and the company was running at a loss. Every possible cost was being cut to stay solvent and the management was inevitably blind to the major problem because the problem was the management itself. They issued orders but didn't listen. This is shown by their aversion to key cutting. The branch staff knew that shoe repairs was declining and that a developing key business was essential for future prosperity. Despite a head office ban on key cutting displays, managers still made displays of their own. They hid them in the back of the shop if they thought a director was likely to call.

By the time we acquired Automagic, staff levels had been cut so far that shops could not open every day. Few staff had received a salary increase for three years. The branch telephones had been adjusted to accept incoming calls only. There was no budget to repair faulty machinery. There were severe restrictions on the level of material stock. Business was being turned away simply because the branch did not have the tools or materials to do the job. All these restrictions, designed to save costs and improve profits, had a disastrous effect on turnover. The branch staff suffered in their pocket not only because their basic wage was frozen, but the loss of turnover severely affected their bonus. Some took the matter into their own hands, maintaining their lifestyle by taking money from the till. Pilferage caused a further drop in turnover.

It was not easy to put things right. Twenty years of autocratic management had convinced employees that every business was like that. For four months we failed to persuade them that anything would change.

They had heard so many promises of jam tomorrow, that when I explained how good things could be, they didn't believe me. They continued to pinch money from the till and sat back to see what would happen.

Turning point

We tackled the biggest problem area first, central London. I have never seen a group of staff so much at odds with their management. Shops in prime sites were trading at a loss. The main problem was pilferage. Some staff were taking up to £250 a week from the till and Mafia-style pressure caused new recruits to do the same. With so much money going into the staff's hands, turnover was disappointing. No new money had been invested in shopfitting or machinery. Potentially the best shops in Britain produced some of the worst results in the company. The local staff had taken over. They ran the shops for their own benefit and to the detriment of the company. I believe in delegation but not the way it was being done in London!

We formed a "hit squad." It was a team of two firm fans of the Timpson philosophy who had a proven track record of increasing turnover. They spent three weeks in each London branch to prove how much turnover every shop should achieve. The hit squad arrived with very little warning. The resident branch staff were informed late on a Thursday afternoon that they were about to spend three weeks in another branch (our financial week ends on a Thursday night). The hit squad arrived on Friday morning. We had immediate and dramatic results. Turnover went up by at least 40 per cent and in some cases even doubled. At a stroke we proved the branches were under-performing. With the right attitude, they could be extremely profitable.

We demonstrated our faith by giving London the priority for new investment. Within eight months of the take-over, central London was completely re-equipped.

But the hit squad was only a partial success. When the regular staff returned to their branch, turnover improved on last year but failed to match the targets set during three weeks of the special treatment. The Mafia still operated in London. The regular thieving from the till had become a necessity to support expensive personal habits. They thought we didn't have the determination to cut out systematic thieving.

We introduced two more hit squads. Some staff improved their ways while others threw in the towel and moved to the opposition. Within 12 months London turnover had increased by 40 per cent and after two years it had nearly doubled. That success was only partly due to eliminating dishonesty. The main gains came from a change in the staff attitude. Business had been transformed and the only change we had made was the way we looked after the people.

People make the difference

Shop staff make a big impression on customers. If I meet a friend who has been to one of our shops, or if I bump into a customer round the dinner table, they are keen to tell me about key cutting and shoe repair problems and their shopping experience. Within the first sentence they talk about the staff who served them.

It is the attitude of the staff that gives customers the lasting impression of our business.

We give everyone the authority to serve customers as they know best. The main job of area managers and head office is to help the staff who serve our customers. That simple principle defines our management style.

I do not want a set of rules. We don't want to serve every customer in exactly the same way and we discourage phrases like "you are welcome" and "have a good day." Our rules should be restricted to cash security (the money has got to go in the till!) and personal discipline (look smart and be on time). Everything else to do with the running of the business is purely a guideline. Anyone with a better way to serve customers should be allowed to get on and use it – as long as it improves the turnover.

Total delegation is a simple management style, and it works. But it is difficult to get all your management team to play their part. Managers like to issue orders and keep information to themselves. I want managers to delegate authority and tell everyone what is going on.

This management style is critical to success. It will only work if every manager respects the talent that exists in the branches and really does look after the people who look after the customers.

CHAPTER 21

Fair pay

If you are really serious about looking after people, look after their pay packets. Don't expect anybody to be happy just because we have up-to-date machinery, well laid out shops and a growing business. Everyone wants to know what is in it for them and the most important measurement is their pay.

Dear James

Make sure everyone shares in your success

Don't be mean

Don't try and save wage costs by holding back wage increases. Being mean with your employees just won't work.

The business needs loyalty and enthusiasm; if you pay people less than they are worth, you get what you deserve. Automagic had a pay freeze that lasted several years. Profits declined throughout this period.

Often the most profitable business in an industry has the highest rates of pay. This is no coincidence. Not only can successful companies afford to pay workers better, but better pay in itself helps create the success. The only way wage cuts can produce more profit is by reducing the number of people. Don't hold back on the level of people's pay.

We made a substantial saving in our wage bill during 1988.

Kit Green and myself inherited a branch staffing system established in the sixties. Every shop had a minimum staffing level of a manager, an experienced shoe repairer, a counter girl and a young trainee. In the small shops this team of four spent a lot of time with nothing to do. The wage cost of small branches was as high as 50 per cent. The level of trade didn't warrant this well-established minimum staffing. Over 12 months we reduced numbers by over 30 per cent. There were no redundancies; we just didn't replace people who left. Despite the lower staffing, turnover went up. We increased the basic levels of pay and our bonus scheme gave much larger payouts. Although the total wage bill had been reduced, everyone had more in their pay packets at the end of each week. The business made more profit and it gave our customers a better service.

Weekly bonus

We have proof that payment by results really works. Our bonus scheme has hardly changed since it was introduced 20 years ago. The people in our shops wouldn't let me change it. It works well for them and it works very well for the company.

The success of our bonus scheme can be put down to:

1. We pay out the bonus every week, based on last week's figures.
2. There is no limit to the amount of money people can earn.
3. Exactly the same system applies to every branch in the business.

To calculate our bonus, we add up the wages paid to everyone in a branch during the week in question. The total wage number (including NI payments), is multiplied by 4.35 to give the target turnover. Any sales beyond the weekly target attracts a 15 per cent bonus. Anyone who is off work for more than a day for any reason is excluded from the bonus for that week. We do not have a major absentee problem.

TOTAL OF ALL WAGES
PAID IN THE BRANCH
X 4.35
= BRANCH TARGET
ACTUAL SALES - TARGET
X 15%
= BONUS PAID

THERE IS NO LIMIT TO THE AMOUNT YOU CAN EARN UNDER THE BONUS SCHEME

BONUS

The total bonus is allocated between staff on a points basis. The manager gets six points, full-timers five points and part-timers are awarded points according to the number of hours they work. Trainees gain points towards their bonus as they improve their skills.

We give further rewards to the most experienced staff. Everyone has a regular assessment of their skill level. For each of our main services, shoe repairs, key cutting, engraving and watch repairs, they are rated from level 1 (basic skills) through to level 4 (the expert). Bonus earnings are increased by a percentage relating to individual skill level. The system is designed to reward the best people and make sure that everybody is keen to receive training to improve their skills.

Our people find the bonus easy to understand and appreciate the immediate rewards of a scheme based on a weekly calculation. It is very important that the bonus is paid within seven days.

Minimum guaranteed pay

The major drawback of high bonus earnings is uncertainty. Basic pay is assured but bonus depends on future turnover. It is not easy for new employees to see how high our annual pay-packets can become. Existing staff find the bonus a problem when they are applying for a mortgage. We reduce the uncertainty with a system of minimum guaranteed pay. For existing employees we guarantee 90 per cent of their previous year's earnings. Everyone, including new employees, is also guaranteed a minimum related to their individual responsibility and skill level. At the end of each year the basic and bonus for each individual are added together and compared with their guaranteed minimum, any shortfall is made up immediately.

A flexible structure

We don't have a company pay structure. We provide guidelines to our area managers who have the authority to pay according to regional variations and individual talent.

We don't believe that a company pay structure should stand in the way of an area manager's ability to recruit the right people. Nor do we believe that the weakest member of the team should be paid as much as the most talented.

With such a flexible system the inevitable grapevine causes a problem but we don't resent anyone who makes a case for their own pay to be increased. This makes the area manager justify decisions on individual pay and roots out injustice when it occurs.

No pay review

We don't have an annual pay review. Every individual has their pay reviewed on the anniversary of the date they joined the company. This helps us to look more closely at each individual's worth and avoids an annual pay free for all when everyone gets the same increase regardless of performance.

No system will satisfy the whingers. Some people have never commented on their pay for 25 years, others complain every year. In some companies whinging works.

I know who is going to look glum faced when they hear about their new salary, so there is no incentive for me to be generous. Why pay them more than they are worth when they are going to complain again in 12 months' time. It is important to look carefully at the pay of those that never complain. They never question their value to the company so you must do it for them.

A few people write a formal letter to thank me for their pay increase, but the letters seldom come from the whingers!

Jealousy and status

It's not just pay that causes a problem. Job titles, the make of motor car and the size of an office sometimes seem to cause as much unrest as satisfaction.

Jealousy thrives in a central office, where lots of people work under the same roof. People believe that their department has the most vital role in the business, and that others are less efficient than they are.

You will never stamp out "green eye" and you can't ignore the problems caused by a disgruntled executive. Have a reputation for being open and fair. Agree to discuss any individual's pay problem. If you know your business you will know the value of everybody who works for you.

The profit bonus

Our weekly branch bonus works so well that any other bonus scheme is bound to feel inferior.

It is easy to devise a system that rewards people who have a direct effect on the weekly sales of each branch. Designing a profit incentive for head office executives is much more of a challenge.

In a private business the profit bonus for senior executives isn't just a question of incentives. Its a matter of conscience. If the business does well, I do very well and receive a substantial dividend. Although this is a fair reward for the money I have invested and the risks I have taken, I couldn't get a good result without the help of my team and they should share in the success.

My idea of a significant bonus falls well short of the rewards being received by some of the directors of public companies. Bonus should never be more than twice the basic salary. My dividend can be more but I have no conscience about that figure; I have mortgaged my house and invested several million pounds in the business. I am now receiving a return on my investment.

Profit-based incentive schemes are never fair and not much of an incentive but I haven't thought of a better reward for senior executives at the end of a successful year. Sophisticated schemes don't work. Use the same formula for everybody.

There is no need to set the details of the scheme until you have seen at least two months of the financial year in question.

Each year you have to change the rules because as the company gets bigger or smaller and the profit grows or falls, the targets must change. Before deciding on a new target, have a clear idea on how much bonus you want your senior executives to earn. I suggest 20 per cent of basic salary. Then decide what you think the profit will be if things go according to your plan. That profit figure you should give your executives your 20 per cent. Now you can produce a sliding scale. Even if profits drop by ten per cent, I think everyone should earn a small bonus. So that's your starting point. Anything ten per cent below last year's profit doesn't qualify for bonus. Organise a bonus scale which takes you through the 30 per cent target to a maximum of between 50 and 100 per cent of salary.

A profit-related incentive scheme won't cause your senior managers to increase sales or reduce costs. Frankly, it will make little difference to their performance, but at the end of the year you will give some reward in line with success and you will take your dividend with a clear conscience.

Are they worth it?

Look at the cost of your top 40 people. Don't just include the wages, add in their expenses and the cost of their car. You may be amazed how much it costs to employ each of your managers.

Don't look at the salary figures as an opportunity to increase profit. We are in the people business. Forty-five per cent of our costs relate to wages and salaries. It's the people who work in the business that earn our reputation and make our profit.

Some people will be over-valued. That's not their fault, it's ours. At some time in the past we have given them a salary increase that over-valued their talent.

You can't run the business on your own. Good employees give extremely good value. Look after the good people that are making your business a success.

DON'T TAKE PEOPLE FOR GRANTED

Upside-down management

Recently I went to a pet supermarket to buy a large amount of dog food. I needed a trolley but it could only be released by inserting a coin in the slot. I only had notes, so I went to ask the cashier whether she would change £5. "Sorry love," she said, "we are not allowed into the till." I waited five minutes for the supervisor to change my note so I could buy their dog food. I will never go back to that shop again.

Dear James

Your job is to help everyone else

It happens all the time. Life is full of red tape – people who can't do something or have to ask their supervisor. In retail you can't give customers good service by relying on a set of rules.

In our business we are forced to delegate. There is no choice with 800 staff spread between 315 shops. People talk about empowerment. It's the modern word for delegation and I don't like it. Empowerment implies that senior management give something up, that they are handing down a special gift giving employees the chance to make decisions.

We call it "upside-down management." I believe that most of our important jobs are done in the shops. We make money by repairing shoes, cutting keys and looking after customers. It follows, therefore, that the real management of our business is done by the people who work in the branches - everyone else is there to help them.

Sticking to the rules

Up to the eighties, we were run on military lines. There was a clear set of rules called the "Standing Orders for Shoe Repair Factories" (SOSRF). This was the bible followed by area managers who had the power to insist that everybody stuck to the letter of the law. The culture of military precision was so strong that it still lingers on in the minds of some longer serving employees.

Within the past 12 months, I was in a shop which had a particularly unattractive display of shoe care. "What do you think of the display?" I asked the manager. "Well I just do as I am told," was his reply, implying he had an area manager who took all the decisions. I pressed the point: "What do you want to do ?" He listed all the display changes he would make. Later that day I asked the area manager to stand back and let his manager do what he wanted. At first, he said that the shop wasn't taking enough money and insisted the manager did things his way. But I explained that if he stopped the shop manager showing initiative, he wasn't in a position to criticise his sales performance. It worked. The displays were changed, and the atmosphere in the shop improved immediately. The manager suddenly realised he had to perform and he did; sales rose by 20 per cent.

Most people expect to work in a culture where success is determined by the ability to stick to a set of rules. When I visited an Automagic branch shortly after taking over, I saw a home-made display of brushes on the service counter. I thought it was an idea that could increase extra sales, so I took a picture of it – the manager looked aghast. "I will take it away," he said thinking that my picture was taken because he had broken the rules.

Changing the culture

We worked very hard to change our culture. To get the message across I turned our upside-down management style into a pictorial chart. It shows branch staff at the top and myself at the bottom. It demonstrates that everyone really does have authority; we list the decisions they can take.

Our shops order their own stock, (we don't rely on computers). They can spend up to £500 to settle complaints without reference to their area manager. Shop staff can change our price list. If they think our prices are too high or too low, they can write their own price list. If it increases turnover, that's fine by us.

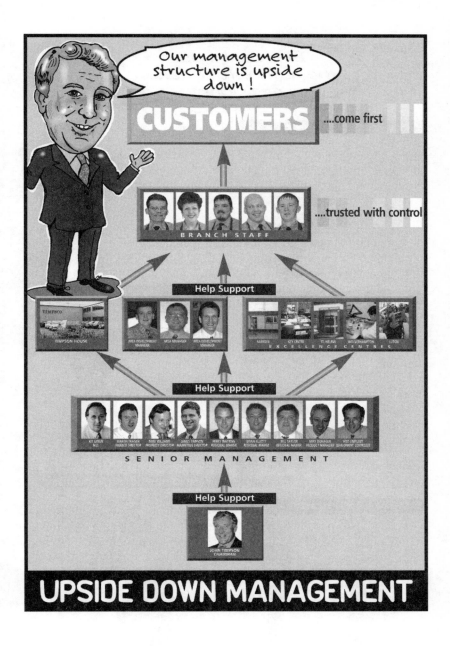

Everyone has the authority to take decisions

Pick your own price list

Order the stock you need

Authority to give discounts

£500 available to settle a complaint

Free to go after extra business

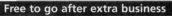

Our latest shop design incorporates a message signed by me: "Everybody in this shop has my authority to do whatever they want to amaze our customers."

Everyone attends a one-day training course about upside-down management and it is described in a video which has been sent by post to everbody's home.

Despite all this effort, it is difficult to get upside-down management working properly; people are used to working to rule and resist change.

The chief executive must set an example. Upside-down management says that you are there to help, so whenever I get a request, I have to respond. Usually it is a question of unblocking the system. "My key machine isn't working but head office says I can't have another one because my turnover is too low." Or: "A local branch of the Cystic Fibrosis Trust needs some trophies for a golf competition. Am I allowed to donate them?" I nearly always agree; it's the sensible thing to do. They know the business better than anybody and every time I support the branch management, I am helping our upside-down management work. But it is easy for me, as I have nothing to prove, I have no reason to exercise a macho management muscle to achieve any ambition. It is much more difficult for middle management.

We have lots of shops and one main office. I try to ensure it is called Timpson House but most people called it the head office. Everyone's ambition was to be promoted to head office. It used to be where all the decisions were made; My upside-down management gives the office a completely different role. They are now sending less memos and receiving more calls. Instead of laying down the law, we act as a helpline. It means a complete change of attitude and that takes time.

Young management teams sweep into businesses thinking they can change a culture in weeks; you can't, it takes years. I have been plugging my upside-down management for nearly three years and every month I meet a shop manager who has done something because "they told me at head office."

Area managers find upside-down management particularly difficult. All our area managers have been promoted from within the company, having been a branch manager for several years. The job is not what they expected. They soon discover that you can't be in 20 shops at once and that people don't always do as they are told. We explain that with upside-down management they can achieve success by giving advice not giving orders, creating the culture rather than making instant decisions. They expect, having served their time as branch managers, to become "the boss." Instead we ask them to provide a service to their shop managers. It takes a lot of getting used to.

Signs of success

Three years down the track upside-down management is working. When I visit shops I now hear phrases like "it's nice to be left to get on with it", "head office does what it promises" and "it's good to know help is at hand."

We are giving space for people to achieve success, like Bob Northover in Taunton who has taught us much more than we could ever teach him about developing a contract business. He uses his new-found freedom to introduce lots of new ideas, such as the discount vouchers he has given to the local pet shop who send their customers round for dog tags, and the contract he started with the local bowling alley which has developed into a nationwide business already worth £100,000 a year.

When cutting a difficult key, many shops now have the confidence to suggest the customer doesn't pay until they have been home to check the key works. That's real customer service.

Complimentary letters from customers are nearly always a response to staff who have used their initiative. People notice shops that don't have to stick to the rules.

We have got a long way to go before everyone in our business recognises the benefits of upside-down management, but we know it works. It gives our customers a better service.

A good company to work for

We aim to be "a good company to work for" – an objective that takes us beyond the pure business life of our employees.

> Dear James
>
> Remember everyone has a life beyond the business

Most people who work for us will one day face a crisis. Usually the problem is to do with money. Credit cards, broken marriages, gambling, drugs and drink all cause financial problems. It is better for us to help than to stand back and risk problems being solved by taking money from our till.

Financial help

We actively encourage anyone with a financial problem to write to us for help. We don't always lend money, not all the letters we receive are truthful. But often we are able to provide just the help required at someone's time of need.

When you think of it, we are in the best possible position to decide whether it is the right thing to lend someone money. We know the people and can insist that loans are repaid. We usually have 60 personal loans (£80,000) in place at any one time. We have only had five bad debts totalling £2,400 in five years. Our assistance has stopped many people being tempted to solve their problem by pinching money from our business.

We want our employees to be successful. Many measure success by their ability to take holidays, buy cars and move to the house of their dreams. Our employees sometimes don't find it as easy to borrow money. Obtaining a mortgage is difficult when you receive a modest basic and a high bonus. The job of shoe repairer and key cutter is not given the social status it deserves. We like to help employees achieve their ambitions. Loans and a mortgage assistance scheme are ways in which the company helps employees to enjoy the deserved rewards of working hard for the business.

We are flexible in the way we pay people. If someone wants to be paid monthly rather than weekly we do it. If they want part of their pay put into a savings scheme, then that is what happens. If we solve employees' financial problems, they respond by doing a much better job.

Attitudes to our pension scheme are changing. In the late eighties, personal pension plans and the bad publicity surrounding the Maxwell affair reduced the number of employees who wanted to join. The mood is now different as more employees appreciate the importance of saving.

An increase to our pension fund members is an extra cost to the company, but it is worth it. It is our duty to look after the long-term interests of our employees. Employees in turn are more loyal to a company that looks after their financial future.

Membership of a company pension scheme should not be compulsory, but to counter their indifference to pensions, I write to everyone as they qualify (by age or length of service) and if they don't join, I write again every five years to point out what they are missing. After all, we have to look them in the eye when they are presented with their retirement gift.

Personal helpline

We take an interest in personal problems but the company should not interfere in people's home life. Divorce, drink problems, and bereavement remain a private matter, unless they are brought to work. But be aware of people's problems, they can explain current performance.

We actively encourage staff to seek confidential help on personal problems. They can contact anyone they feel comfortable talking to; often this is not their immediate boss. The most important step any troubled person can take is to ask for advice. We aim to make that task easy. Most problems are solved through talking. Over the years we have gained the experience to help. If we don't have the answer we can suggest someone who has.

We also offer an alternative source of help. The company subscribes to an independent helpline which provides confidential advice on a wide range of subjects from cancer to coming out. At £5 per employee per year the service is excellent value. Several times a year an employee will contact me directly – it helps that they know who I am through my regular shop visits and I am flattered they think I can help. I am not qualified to deal with most of the questions but I can find someone who can – problems last year included housing, children on drugs, threats from next door neighbours and inevitably several problems connected with debt. These personal helplines are not just simply helping the people we employ, they also help the company. Contented people do a much better job.

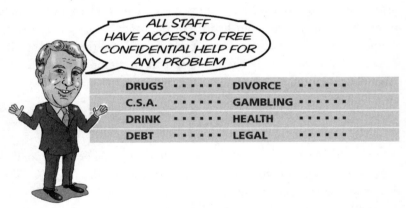

I encourage a social calendar. We have football tournaments, golf matches, visits to the seaside, discos, marathon walks, picnics, paint ball games and go karting. Where appropriate company finance is made available, but all the events are organised by staff themselves so they are never seen as being a company "do."

Our people work in small teams of two or three in shops miles apart, they benefit from meeting people from different shops. The social calendar helps these meetings to take place.

Charitable donations

We give about £25,000 per year to charitable schemes proposed by people who work for us. A regular feature in our weekly newsletter "Captain Cash" makes £500 available every month to a cause supported by someone from our branches.

We have funded a girls football team, a musicians' tour of Norway, medical treatment for a young boy in Peterhead, sponsorship for a branch manager's grandmother who undertook a charity walk for cancer research and 25 other projects during the past two years. Often we are helping our own staff in their community – the money goes to fund their son's football team, their daughter's school concert tour or their cousin's appeal to fund a special wheelchair. But just as often, we are supporting charities in which our staff play an active part.

Kelvin Reddicliffe in Newport is an accomplished musician who gives concerts in South Wales – mostly for charity. His group wanted to make a charity record but hadn't got the funds to pay the recording studio. We helped get the project off the ground and the record (which Kelvin sells in our shop) has made several thousand pounds for his favourite charity.

NSPCC

The interest our people show in charitable giving was demonstrated in 1999 when I decided the company would support the NSPCC "Full Stop Campaign" against child abuse.

It all began with a letter from the Duke. "The Duke of Westminster invites Mr & Mrs John Timpson for Dinner at Eaton Hall on 25th October 1998." It was a memorable evening eating off silver plates surrounded by two Rembrandts, a Stubbs and a Durer. There was no chance it was a free meal but I was prepared to pay. The Duke was launching the NSPCC Appeal to cut out child abuse. As foster carers it was a cause that we were keen to support.

At first I thought this could be an excuse to enter my last London Marathon. I ran five Marathons in the early eighties but such an effort at my age and weight would certainly raise a good deal of money. On reflection, during the dinner I realised this was a very selfish idea. My sons James and Edward were running in the Marathon already, there was no need for me to join them. By the time I got home that night, I had decided that all our company fund raising in 1999 would be devoted to the campaign. I went to sleep with my mind full of zany ideas to make money for the NSPCC.

We had supported individual charities in the past, not just cheques in response to begging letters but by putting collecting boxes in our branches. These campaigns have been reasonably successful raising between £5,000 and £10,000 for the chosen charity. This time we did something very different and it produced a spectacular result for the NSPCC.

With our personal commitment to children, Alex and I had the incentive to put a lot of effort into the scheme. But we had to transmit

our enthusiasm throughout the business.

We made a video to get everybody on our side. In a ten minute film with the help of an official from the NSPCC and our son James, we described the problem of child abuse and showed how we at Timpson could do something practical to help. The campaign and the video were launched at an area managers' conference – you could have heard a pin drop. The message was so strong that they immediately organised a collection amongst themselves.

The following week a copy of the video arrived at the homes of all 900 Timpson employees. It wasn't just a question of persuading them to raise money, statistics show that child abuse occurs in at least one in every four families. Our strong message could be going right home to where abuse occurs. It worked, I got the support I was looking for.

The film had a profound effect on Alan Key, manager of our Stafford branch. "After I had seen your video," he told me later, "I sat down with the family and we decided we must do something." And do something he did. Three weeks later Alan (aged 55) had the whole of his thick head of hair shaved off and raised over £300 in sponsorship.

We found an easy way to persuade customers to put money in the collecting box. "No gratuities," said a poster. "If you think you have had good service, give some money to the NSPCC!" Normally, we don't charge for very small jobs, a few stitches or a few holes in a belt come with our compliments. We have changed that slightly. In response to the question "How much will that be?" the reply became: "There is no charge, please give to the NSPCC !" As a further incentive, I promised to double the first £25,000 put in our collecting boxes. To give branch staff an incentive, we launched a competition based on customer care. Each shop was rated by a mystery shopper looking for good customer care. We also counted the amount of money raised for the NSPCC. The better the service, the bigger the funds they raised. I was astounded by all the extra things that staff did – a shoe repair marathon, raffles, a sponsored shoe shine, quiz nights, a parachute jump. Bob Northover was the star of them all when he raised over £2,500 by having his chest waxed in the middle of Taunton High Street.

Then I had to do my bit. I invented a new sort of marathon. I set out to see how many of our shops I could visit within five trading days. Monday 4th August to Friday 8th August I travelled the country. I was only allowed to visit shops during the normal trading hours and I had to talk to every member of staff and take a picture of them. During five exhausting days I went to 128 branches and raised £8,000.

We started our campaign with a target of £25,000 and within eight months reached £120,000. Even better, our branch staff voted to support the NSPCC during the following year.

Lots of winners

Every week, spare part of your time to praise people who have done well. Don't take people's hard work for granted. Special achievement should always be recognised.

Several years ago I started writing hand-written notes to shops with a particularly good performance. My writing isn't all that legible and people claim they cannot read my letters, but I soon found the notes being pinned up in staff rooms round the country. That recognition which had only cost a small amount of my time  and a piece of notepaper had been much appreciated.

I am accused of running too many competitions but the winners never complain. Prize winners get real recognition for their skills. Every year there are Timpson champions for shoe repairs, key cutting, engraving, customer service and, more recently, watch repairs.

On January 5th 2000, I held a special Millennium Lunch in the Marquee at my home that had already seen our family Millennium Eve Party and a fund raising children's party to support the NSPCC.

The Millennium Lunch was another way I could say "Well Done." During Autumn 1999 I asked for nominations from our employees for 16 different categories of excellence – Best Key Cutter, Best Manager, Best Apprentice,, Best Customer Service and so on. A short-list of three for each category were invited with their partner to the lunch – everyone received a trophy – and the winners were presented with their award by the Duke of Westminster, who as Patron of the NSPCC appeal in the North West, also received our cheque for £120,000.

Not only do winners enjoy their success but the competition helps to promote their business. A trophy displayed in the window promotes the skill of the branch to their customers. If a local paper runs an article with a picture of the staff, sales rise by at least ten per cent. I like shops that display framed press cuttings.

We find lots of reasons to present prizes. The news letter nominates our shop of the week. Each regional manager chooses his shop of the month and the company magazine publishes the top 20 managers of the year. At each area dinner prizes are given for the best trainee, the best assistant manager and the area star of the year. A press release is issued for every winner, many branches get their picture in the local paper.

We encourage our staff to enter external national competitions. If we win it sends out the right signals about our business.

If a customer sends in a complimentary letter, don't take the pride yourself. Give the credit to the person who looked after the customer. Frame the customer's letter and send it to the branch so they can show it to the rest of their customers.

Long service

Recognise long service. My grandfather started Timpson Long Service Awards when he himself completed 50 years with the Company. Since then we have an Annual Long Service Presentation for employees who have just completed 25 and 45 years' service.

The inaugural event in 1950 was an enormous affair. A presentation was made to 400 employees who had reached the 25 year landmark. They were squeezed into the largest banqueting room in the Midland Hotel, Manchester.

While we still had the shoe shops and over 3,500 employees, a large dinner was held every year to make our Long Service presentations. Now we have less than 1,000 employees and hold a much more intimate lunch at our house. We sit round our dining table. It is a very special occasion for the recipients and their partners.

The presentations mark 25 and 45 years, but we don't forget all the other landmarks. I send a letter and a cheque to everyone who reaches five, ten, 15, 20 and 30 years with the company.

A telephone call is a good way to praise a job well done. Pick up the phone and ring the shop: "I have just seen your figures for last week and thought I would give you a ring to say well done." People do not expect that from the chairman. It can have a dramatic effect.

We have one catch-all category of praise which I call the Chairman's Award. It's there for something beyond the call of duty. Winners of the Chairman's Award receive a cheque. The cheque is sent with a letter in my own handwriting detailing why the Award has been made. Anything out of the ordinary can lead to a Chairman's Award. A trainee worked three hours late on a Friday night to complete an engraving order for someone's wedding the following day because a jeweller had let them down. He got £75. One of the girls in our finance office received a Chairman's Award for spotting a fraud going on in one of the branches. She saved the company £1000, and in the process gained a Chairman's Award for £50. A branch manager worked over a weekend to win a key cutting contract worth £3000. He received £100. Whenever I send a Chairman's Award, I not only write a longhand letter but I also write the envelope. It is sent to the employee's home address. We don't put the letter through the franking machine, we use a first class stamp.

Pride in performance

Every shop has a notice board for staff to display their successes. Customers can see their achievements and staff can brag about them.

Let customers see the complimentary letters, the skill diplomas and the pictures of prize winners receiving their cup. The notice board demonstrates an individual branch character within our multiple shop chain. It shows that we take a pride in our performance.

CHAPTER 24

Listen to the experts

Dear James

Keep your eyes
and ears open
for free advice

Each week I spend an average of one-and-a-half days visiting our shops. At the end of every day I have learnt something new about the business.

In-store inspiration

Your mind is more open when you are not at the office. You are face-to-face with the problems that really matter and watching our customers being served. The best ideas come from our own staff.

Ten years ago, John Higgs, our manager in Cheadle, taught me how to display finished shoe repairs on the rack above the repair machinery. John displayed a long line of quality leather repairs with superbly finished and polished soles facing the customer. The adoption of John's technique throughout the country has transformed our shoe repair business. We have become the specialists in men's quality shoe repairing. In Leeds I spotted a display produced by our manager, Gillian Briggs, to promote the pet tag business. She produced a large pet tag and put it on a cuddly toy dog displayed in front of the counter. Her pet tag sales were three times the company average. Whenever we have cuddly toys we see a much bigger turnover of pet tags. Dennis Bramble in Tunbridge Wells taught me how to provide a proper service to shoe shops. For years we helped local shoe retailers with their complaints problems. Small stitching jobs can prevent retailers having to give customers a new pair of shoes. But every time they used our service, a member of staff had to bring the job to our shop and to collect it later. Dennis made the whole system simple. He provided each of his local shoe shops with a stock of vouchers that could be presented to their customers who brought the shoes round to us. We did the repair and charged the price back to the retailer. As a result Dennis had half the hassle and double the business. The idea was quickly copied around the country.

Suggestions

Make it easy for anyone in the business to let us have their ideas. The easiest way is the suggestion scheme. Companies launch new suggestion schemes with a fanfare of trumpets and a lot of enthusiasm. After six months the suggestions slow down to a trickle. Within a year the scheme has ceased to serve any purpose. Our suggestion scheme has been going for four years and we get as many suggestions now as we did when it started. There are four reasons why it works:

1. We publish any reasonable idea for everyone else to see.
2. Every published idea gets a cash award (generally between £15 and £50).
3. Major ideas that really work get a much more substantial award (up to £500).
4. Whenever possible we put the suggestions into practice.

Glenn Edwards from West Bromwich suggested a cleaning service to add to our watch repair business. This brought in a lot of extra business and it got Glenn the job of managing our Watch Repair Excellence Centre based in Wolverhampton.

One of my favourite suggestions was the idea of having a stock of old watches in each shop to lend to customers while their own watch is being repaired. It's the simple suggestions that make a permanent improvement, like the sticker we now put on the base of every annual trophy we engrave to encourage next year's winner to use our service.

The suggestion scheme has provided a fund of small technical tips to make the job easier. For years our engraving work was set up by a combination of experience and guesswork until John Tucker from Merthyr Tydfil invented the box system. A simple way of calculating how to lay out each engraving job. Paul Dooley invented a way to promote our water pressure testing service for watches. Whilst he was working at Derby, he put a cylindrical water tank into the display which highlighted the service and doubled our business. Steve Reilly from Warrington dreamed up a simple idea for insoles. The insoles are designed for a range of sizes small, medium and large. Steve produced a template so our staff could cut the insoles down to the exact size.

Listen to the niggles

Don't just listen to ideas, also pay attention to complaints and criticism. Everyone who works for us has a pad which is headed "Personal Note to John Timpson." It gives everybody direct access to the chairman's office. Some of the personal notes raise very minor matters but even if they are frivolous, reply to everybody who has gone to the trouble of writing to you.

These personal notes have drawn my attention to several major problems – a major quality problem with a new stick-a-sole, a problem

with our carrier. Personal notes cut across the management structure. Sometimes staff will tell me things that their area manager doesn't want revealed. Some companies won't allow anyone to go over the head of their boss, but we do. I actively encourage it. I prefer open remarks to anonymous notes. Some notes I receive are critical of the individual's line manager. We always take these criticisms seriously. Anonymous notes often don't amount to anything, but if someone puts their name to criticism, it usually shows there is a problem.

We often have meetings that cut across the management structure. Line managers have a habit of telling you what they think you would like to hear. To balance the management view, we listen to grass roots opinion, holding meetings that include people from all levels. If we are discussing the future of engraving, I want to talk to people who know most about the subject, not just their area managers. Occasionally meet a cross-section of staff with no specific agenda. It helps create a strategy developed by everybody, rather than a tablet of stone sent down from the boardroom.

Attitude

Each year we carry out an attitude survey through a questionnaire which is filled in anonymously. This gives another opportunity for employees to speak up and for management to listen. The survey measures how the business has changed from year to year – have we got better at communicating, are we still a good company to work for and have we improved pay? The comparison with last year gives an overall picture, but the real benefit comes from individual comments made at the end of the survey. This provides yet another opportunity for everyone to get a problem off their chest and help the business.

If a shop rings me I pick up the phone immediately. Never let your secretary say you are in a meeting. If every employee feels they can pick up the phone and speak to the boss, it shows you care about people and value what they have to say.

Conscience

We have introduced a conscience line. It is a confidential telephone line which people can ring up anonymously when things are going wrong. Everyone has a responsibility for collective standards. If a member of staff (perhaps on their day off), comes across a branch which is closed when it should be open, they cannot walk by without doing something. They must tell someone, the shop manager, the area manager or someone else on the area. As a last resort they can ring our conscience line.

Dishonesty

The conscience line allows people to blow the whistle on dishonest colleagues.

We have a major security issue. With over 300 shops spread round the country, each employing an average of less than three people handling cash every day, there is great temptation to take money from the till. Our shop staff know a lot more about what's going on than we do. They get to know which of their colleagues are on the fiddle; I know because they tell us about it. The best way we can control the security of cash in our branches is with the help from staff that work there. The majority of our staff are just as keen as we are to stop thieves taking money from the business. It is our job to make it easy for them to inform on the offenders. The conscience line provides them with a quick and confidential way to blow the whistle.

Problem solving

If you make an acquisition, start by talking to the staff who have just joined us. They will list all the problems more accurately than a management consultant and without the political bias of middle management.

Contact with the shop floor provides a constant insight into our core business. When I visit shops everyone assumes that I want to hear good news, but if everyone tells me that my ideas are wonderful, and that the company is marvellous, there is no way that we can improve. I want to know what's wrong, then I can make things better. Always listen to the people who know most, the people who serve the customers. They are the experts.

No shortage of good people

I had a shock recently. I rang up one of our area managers to arrange a day visiting his branches; he said he couldn't meet me, he was so short of staff on his area he was tied up managing a shop.

> Dear James
>
> Invest in people with personality

Short of talent

He blamed the labour market. "I have advertised for three weeks and only had one reply, and he didn't turn up." Shortage of staff can be a state of mind; some area managers have little problem finding the right people. Lack of staff can put a company on the slippery slope.

1. Customers get a poorer service.
2. There is no time for training.
3. We continue to employ poor quality staff for fear we can't find a replacement.
4. We start to manage by crisis and stop aiming at being the best at what you do.

If keeping to the wages budget makes you short of staff, then change the wages budget.

New recruits

Our business has changed enormously. Ten years ago we were mainly shoe repairers doing a bit of key cutting. We are now a multi-service business. The business will be as good as the people we employ over the next five years. We need to attract employees who are keen to develop a much wider range of skills than the traditional shoe repairer.

We work in a small industry. There are only 3,000 shoe repair shops in the UK and probably no more than 7,000 qualified shoe repairers.

Shoe repairers fall into three camps: the dishonest cowboy; the upstanding craftsman cobbler; and the modern manager who is good with customers. The cowboy will turn customers away and pinch the money. The craftsman finds it difficult to adapt to change. The modern manager is good with customers and can create success.

We now recruit outside the trade. If we just interviewed qualified shoe repairers, only 7,000 people in the country would match our criteria. We mustn't turn our back on the other 23 million people!

Poaching staff from a competitor has traditionally been the way to fill vacancies in our trade. As a result, shoe repairers constantly look at the same employment pool to fill vacancies. The same unloyal staff go from company to company producing a temporary improvement in sales and a permanent increase in wage levels.

Finding talent

Unless we introduce a new breed of people into our industry, the trade deserves to die. The future of our business is not just in shoe repairs but also key cutting, engraving and watch repairs. Success will depend on the quality of our branch management and the standard of service we give to our customers. The recruitment and training of the new people is a vital task. We are in the people business. The success of our shops depends on the quality of people who serve our customers. Spend money on the best job advertisements to find the best people. Plenty of people turn up for interviews if the job seems attractive. The recruitment campaign must sell the idea of a career with our company. When we used a boring advert for trainee shoe repairers, hardly anyone made it to an interview. When we produced an advertisement that stood out from the page and advertised training in watch repairs and engraving, five times as many turned up.

We don't only advertise when we have a vacancy. We hunt for new employees all the time. We like to have a waiting list of potential recruits. Our shops always have a window poster advertising jobs and leaflets to hand out to prospective employees. Applicants receive a detailed welcome pack before the interview. We send a video together with their application form. We want them to know what our shops are like before they consider working for us.

Friends of existing staff often become a success. We pay an incentive to encourage staff to introduce their friends. Under our "Recruit a Friend" scheme, an employee that finds us a new member of staff, will receive £150 after three months and a further £250 if they are still with us in a year's time.

Mr Men

We have devised a method to help area managers pick the right people. All of them started their career as trainee shoe repairers. They were brought up in a business that only employed fully trained shoe repairers or 16 year old trainees. Between 1980 and 1990, we seldom employed a man over 40 and rarely employed a woman of any age!

Good people-spotting is one of our most important jobs. There are lots of sophisticated ways to measure aptitude. We could use recruitment consultants and psychometric testing; I prefer first impressions, common sense and intuition.

We have a clear idea of our ideal personality. It's important to communicate the character of that ideal person to everybody who makes an appointment. To help, I developed the Mr Men method of people-spotting. Our Mr Men chart describes both the people we want and the people we want to avoid. It's a simple guide which brings a marked improvement in the quality of our recruits. We get people with a positive attitude and avoid time-wasters.

Problem people waste management time. Eighty per cent of an area manager's week and most of his thinking time is taken up by poor performing people.

Interviewing is an art not a science. Our Mr Men make that point

clear. The technique is simple. Tick off the Mr Men who most closely fit the interviewee. The chart helps you make an intuitive decision.

First impressions are usually correct but it is worth having a second opinion. Ensure two people interview each candidate. Don't just rely on the interview. Ask each promising candidate to work for a day in one of our branches. Pay them the daily rate (it is well worth the money for us to find out about them and for the candidate to find out about us). The permanent staff will provide a revealing thumbnail sketch of your candidate. We have another safety net. All new employees are put on a month's trial. At the end of the month, the area manager arranges a detailed discussion. The new recruits have to decide whether they still like working for our business. We have to decide whether it is worth putting our efforts into their training.

Promote from within

Every new job is advertised internally. We prefer to promote from within. Outside appointments disrupt the pecking order and undermine morale. We only look outside if the talent does not exist within the company.

A new recruit at interview puts forward the good points of their character. The problems only emerge when they start to work for us. It is tempting to think a superstar can transform the business - they seldom do. Don't recruit high fliers from outside the company, go for the person you know. We know our current employees and can judge whether they are suitable for promotion. There is plenty of talent in the business. The difficulty is spotting it. At least one in 12 of our branch staff have the potential to become middle, or even senior, managers. Spotting future talent is one of our most important tasks. We rely on the area managers to identify young people with potential, but talent spotting can't be totally delegated.

We don't open a new shop unless three directors have seen it. It is just as important for directors to know the stars of the future.

Don't totally rely on the judgement of your team. Managers usually underestimate the potential of their own staff. They find it difficult to believe their subordinates are good enough to rise to a level of responsibility higher than their own. There is no need to rely on intuition. Facts help you pick the future stars. Look at their qualifications. We repair shoes, cut keys, engrave, and repair watches, we need people who are good at doing these things. We measure the skill of each employee. That measurement tells us about skills but it also says a lot about character.

We measure our employees every week. Most branches only employ one or two people so the shop sales figures produced on a Monday directly measure individual success.

Talent spotting

Far too little notice is made of figures when assessing people. Don't be overly influenced by a good talker or someone who looks smart. Look at the figures. I like anybody who increases the turnover.

Avoid promoting people beyond their capability. Set people a temporary new challenge before making a permanent appointment.

There are lots of projects in the business which will need someone for six or twelve months. Special assignments provide an ideal opportunity to see how young managers develop their skills. It doesn't have to be a new project. You can swap jobs between two people and see how they react to the challenge. Temporary appointments give people the

THERE IS PLENTY OF TALENT INSIDE OUR BUSINESS

opportunity to demonstrate their ability. Don't promote too quickly. Someone in a job which is beyond their capability will harm the business and make their own life a misery.

You will invest millions of pounds in the improvement of our shops, you will spend months agonising over the important decisions, but the biggest influence on our future will be the quality of people who work for us. There is no shortage of good people, it is your job to find them.

Writing a training manual

We can't be "the quality service people" without spending a lot of money on training.

Our business has been training people for years. When I started 38 years ago, at least 20 people a week came to Manchester for a training course. They stayed in a company-owned hostel.

> Dear James
>
> You have to define the business in detail

In those days training was cheap and easy to do. The average wage of a sales assistant was £6/10s a week. With at least four people working in the shoe repair shop and over 15 in most shoe shops, it was simple to release trainees from their day-to-day job.

For many, the trip to Manchester was their first time away from home. Our hostel saw many young people let off the leash. Each week brought a new drama. In its last five years, the hostel recorded two arrests for drunk and disorderly behaviour, five pregnancies, one outbreak of food poisoning and two marriages. The building is now used as an old people's home.

Government funding

Training in the seventies was dominated by government training schemes. They created a second class citizen on the High Street. Only young people qualified for funding. The 16, 17 and 18 year olds became known as WEPs (Work Experience People), or YOPs (Youth Opportunity People).

Although too much of the emphasis was on administration (you had to tick lots of boxes to get the grant), the two-year training provided a lot of good recruits. When the schemes ended, the shoe repair trade entered recession, wage levels rose and staffing levels fell, and training took a back seat. We couldn't afford to release staff for outside courses, and relied on shop floor training to do the job. If we were short of skills, we recruited trained staff from within the industry.

We aimed to bring any shoe repairers up to the industry standard. We wanted our shops to turn out "a good commercial job." In 1996 "a good commercial job" was not good enough for me. To be the best, we had to be different from anyone else. To be the quality service people we needed to set a new standard.

The solution was provided by a series of garden books, written by Dr D G Hessayon. They are the ultimate fool's guide for the non-gardener. I used the illustrated concept of those gardening books as my role model for the Timpson shoe repair manuals.

I produced a rough outline in sketch form over a very wet Easter holiday in 1996. The family looked over my shoulder and described it as my "Challenge Anneka" project, suggesting that I had started a task I was unlikely to finish.

It took nine months to produce a shoe repair manual. Then we moved on to key cutting, engraving and customer care. In two years we completed the full set. During that time I developed a technique.

I started by attending a training course. You don't have to be an expert to write the manual but you do need an expert who can tell you what to say. I attended training courses for shoe repairs, key cutting and engraving, taking detailed notes. Using the notes taken during the course, I produced a list of headings and put them in a proper order. I then wrote detailed notes under each heading, checking back with the experts to make sure my facts were right. I then turned the written draft into pictures. That brought the manual to life.

All our manuals use pictures to tell their story. The words are purely there to explain what the pictures say. The fewer the words, the easier the manual is to understand. Each subject needs its own style of presentation. Work with someone who really understands what you want to say. Pick a graphic artist with considerable patience. You could

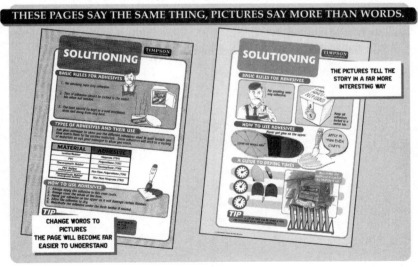

How the Timpson training manual was developed

have ten drafts before arriving at the finished result. These technical manuals were so successful we now use the illustrated techniques to teach day-to-day management. This task proved more difficult but even more rewarding.

We took 12 months producing the management manual – the detail was written by Helene Sheppherd, an area manager who had given up work to start a family. I produced a list of headings and Helene tirelessly scoured every nook and cranny of shop life to produce a manual that covers everything from how to clean the lavatory to how to lock up the shop. It covered things we had never taught before – how to discuss body odour and how to recognise the signs of stress.

The staff gave a warm welcome to this management guide. You know it is right when they say: "Every company should have this," and "Why didn't you produce it years ago?"

Even when the manual is complete, you don't have a training scheme but you have set a standard for the business. The document clearly lays out how to be the best at what we do, in a form that people can easily understand.

You have still got to organise the training programme.

How training works

When I started as a shop assistant, I learned to sell shoes in the old fashioned way, taught by Bill Branston, my manager at Railway Street, Altrincham, in 1960. There were no training courses and we were not awarded diplomas. The incentive to learn came from a bonus payment by results called "spiffs." I could earn extra money by selling expensive shoes or styles destined for the sale.

Dear James

Make everyone responsible for their own training

If things went well I earned at least 2d from every sale – Crockatt & Jones shoes at 89/lld produced the maximum spiff of 2/6d (12.5p today). Significant amounts when your basic wage was £5.7/6d.

By the late sixties things changed and suddenly there was a lot of emphasis on "in shop" training. Up and down the High Street, notices announced that the shop was closed for shop training. It must have been frustrating for customers. Many shops didn't really train while the shop was closed. They used it as an opportunity to turn up late or chat about the night before. Customers come first. Training should never be a reason for closing a shop when customers think it should be open.

Government training schemes

The enthusiasm for training was a response to Government grants. The Work Experience and Youth Opportunity programmes put money into the pockets of anyone who followed the guidelines.

Government training schemes have a political motive, helping young unemployed while reducing the unemployment figures.

In 1992, I joined a committee formed to develop National Vocational Qualifications (NVQ) for shoe repairing – it was still discussing the subject when I resigned two years later. It was my view that the only way to verify a candidate was through a practical test. The civil servants agreed but the cost of monitoring was prohibitive and, as a result, the NVQ relies on written testing and the observation of local management who tick boxes to confirm a candidate can complete specific tasks.

As a gesture of goodwill, the NVQ was overseen by the Timpson training department. It was better than nothing and helped several young people to develop their skills. There is no NVQ for key cutting or engraving – and we get along very well without them!

Companies can see training as a way of earning government grants rather than the way to improve their business. There is no need for the Government to persuade us about the need for training, we know our business and have a training scheme that aims to help us be the best at what we do. We won't change just to obtain a Government grant. We don't want to finish with a lot of administration and no real training.

Our business depends on training for success. Where else in the High Street do you find a shop where so many skills are on offer – probably by the same person?

I have no practical skills myself so I live in constant admiration of extraordinary people who can repair shoes, cut keys, engrave tankards and repair watches – all while you wait and watch. At the same time, they give amazingly good service to our customers and can complete our tedious paperwork.

Who organises training?

Our training is based on the Timpson manuals. They are the guide to being the best at all the things we do.

The manuals themselves do not train, we rely on individual employees to take that responsibility. They all have access to manuals which cover everything in the business. Everyone has an incentive to train themselves. If they pass their skill assessment, they get extra bonuses every week.

The training department is not responsible for training. They devise the skill tests, write the manuals, create off-site training courses and help area managers to organise training in the field. The training department gives everybody access to training but they never force anybody to attend. The area manager is responsible through a special area development manager (ADM) for assessing the skill levels of everybody in his area. Everyone has the right to training and anyone can ask their area manager for help with their training needs. But the area manager and ADM do not do the training themselves.

Everyone responsible for training

We assume that individuals will help themselves to get better. The skill element of our bonus scheme helps training to really happen. For every skill diploma, a percentage is added to weekly bonus payments. It is an incentive that rewards those people who develop the skills we need. As a result, our employees are keen to train themselves.

The manuals contain "help yourself" practice packs so training can be carried out in the branch. Tuition is still based on the old fashioned "on the job" system during our normal, trading day.

EVERYONE IS RESPONSIBLE FOR THEIR OWN TRAINING

The apprentice scheme

The cornerstone of our training is the Apprentice Scheme. We pick new employees on the basis of personality and provide them with training to turn them into experts at all the things we do.

Our Apprentice Scheme gives every recruit a basic knowledge of shoe repairing, key cutting, engraving and watch repairs. At the same time we preach excellent customer care. Apprentice qualifications are gained through proper skill testing – not just a system of ticking boxes. We never award qualifications simply because the trainee has turned up to a course or been employed so many months.

Timpson qualifications are only awarded if the candidate does the

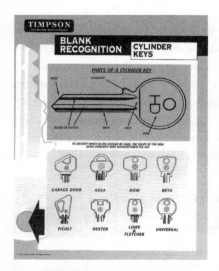

some pages from the Timpson Apprentice Manual

job well enough. Monitoring skill levels is a key responsibility of our area managers. They are our guardians of company standards, only awarding skill certificates when they are truly deserved.

Off the job

Nearly all training takes place in the shop. We have seven regional training centres but they are only used for specialist courses that can't be covered in a branch. Training away from the shop is expensive. You incur travelling expenses and pay for relief staff cover while the trainee is away from the shop.

But at times off the job training is the only alternative – when teaching specialist new skills (watch repair training and our locksmith academy are recent examples). Training centres can be the best place to teach the non-technical parts of our business – customer care and branch management.

Recently, we developed an off-site training method that covered the whole of the business at a much lower cost. We hired five motor homes for four weeks. Five expert trainees turned the vehicle into their home for a month – it was their bed for the night and the training centre every day. The novelty paid off – we called the motor homes our talking bus – as the training course was aimed to improve the conversation between shop staff and customers – a lot of people are still talking about it

The training team

Anyone in the branches can become a tutor to guide trainees through our manuals. Skilled people are well-equipped to pass on their experience to a new generation. We have a training package that trains the future trainers.

We keep emphasising the purpose of training. We are training to produce skilled people, people who are good at doing the job and good at serving customers. The skill assessment by area managers ensures that we get the right end result. The trainer's job is to help each individual to improve standards.

We provide an incentive to anybody who achieves training status. If they qualify as a tutor, they get extra pay whenever they are in charge of a new trainee. Training is no easy job, tutors deserve to be rewarded, they play a major role in the future prosperity of our business.

Pride in the job

We want to develop a culture that respects and rewards skill. We depend on providing the best quality and service. That can only be achieved by training good people.

A training scheme will only work well if the desire for training comes from the individual who needs to acquire new skills.

Our training department spends its time responding to requests for training rather than insisting that training is carried out. In that way, the training has a real purpose. We are helping people to acquire crafts so they can make their maximum contribution to the development of the company.

Being
the best

Aim to be the best

For years I ran second rate businesses – living in the shadow of other retailers who were better than me.

Footwear retailing was dominated by the British Shoe Corporation with over 20 per cent of the market. It had the best sites and the best buying team. But size does not always go hand in hand with excellence and two small competitors provided the best in quality and service: Russell & Bromley and John Farmer.

Even at Swears & Wells I spent my time envying the opposition. We were probably the best retailers of leather and fur clothing, but sales were declining and most of the opposition had already gone out of business. I was in competition with the rest of the rag trade so I walked the High Street looking jealously at Richard Shops, Top Shop, Wallis and Dorothy Perkins who were all far better at retailing than me.

Only one can be the best

At last after 38 years, I can claim to work for a business that is the best at what it does. When we took over the 110 Automagic shops we became the biggest key cutters, shoe repairers and engravers in the UK. Being the biggest has given us the incentive to aim to be the best. We might repair more shoes than anyone else in the UK but unless we maintain higher standards of quality and service, we won't remain the market leader.

After the fall in demand for shoe repairs in the sixties, the business had to diversify and found success by introducing key cutting and engraving. I feared that a multi-service retailer would be labelled a jack-of-all-trades and be a master of none. With this danger in mind, I declared a strict rule that we would only provide services where we could be the best in the UK. When we introduced a watch repairing service, I applied that principle and avoided the half-hearted approach. We set out to produce a more comprehensive and quicker service than any one else on the high street. We looked at the competition, the jewellers and the small number of high street watch repairers. Even when we looked at the best, we decided we could do better. This set the standards for training, equipment and the range of watch repair jobs we now offer.

GIVE EVERYONE A CLEAR GOAL

Recognise the best

When I was a fashion shoe buyer, I spent two weeks every year in Italy. I was the envy of my friends. The trip took me to Rome, Florence, Bologna, Milan, Verona, Padua and Venice, but I didn't spend much time in the Vatican on the Ponte Vecchio or in St Mark's Square – I was looking at shoe shops. The Italians were the best fashion creators in the world and their shoe shop windows provided our main source of ideas. Every year as I jostled with Americans and Germans, Frenchmen and Australians to take pictures of Italian shoe shop windows, I was just a follower of fashion paying the supreme compliment to the best designers in the world.

LIMIT YOURSELF TO AREAS WHERE YOU CAN BE THE BEST

I would have been flattered to have foreign competitors taking pictures of us. I said that if ever I saw a cameraman outside one of our shops, I would give him the shoes being photographed. Two years ago a photographer was spotted outside our shop near Victoria Station in London. There have been several more foreign photographers since, copying our shop design. Imitation is a true form of flattery and proof of our claim to be the best at what we do in the UK.

Only one shop can be the best on the high street, everybody else is left to copy what they do. If you provide the best service, you will be less obsessed with competition than your competitors. You can command a proper price and produce profits that can be used to invest in even higher standards.

The first prize

Second rate businesses have to rely on cut prices to get sales and cutting costs to achieve profit. Low prices are not a viable marketing strategy for a service business. People will pay for a job well done but cut prices give the impression that you are cutting corners. The only cost cutting that really improves profit is the saving of expenses you should never have occurred in the first place. Cutting costs can cut down your quality and service.

Being the best is a goal for everybody in the business to aim for. It gives pride in the job. Everyone likes to be associated with a business known for quality, especially if they make a personal contribution to the level of excellence. Encourage everybody to play their part, not just by maintaining high standards, but by suggesting ideas that can make the business even better.

Success depends on the quality of our people. Future success will depend on our ability to attract good recruits. With a national reputation for being the best, the best people will want to work for us.

BARGAIN SHOE REPAIRS

KEYCUTTING SALE

CHEAP WATCH REPAIRS

30% OFF SHOE REPAIRS

ENGRAVING BARGAINS

CUT PRICE ISN'T CREDIBLE IN THE SERVICE BUSINESS

Define the best

Define what the best is. We did this first with our keycutting business. Using the phrase "Every Key Every Time," we set the aim of cutting every key for every customer making sure that it worked every time. That set the agenda for key cutting and turned it into a £15m a year business. Similar objectives have been set for all of our "best at" business. For shoe repairs, we won't turn away any job that can be done, and the finished job should make the shoe look like new. The criteria for engraving is the Royal Warrant test – the finished job should be fit for the Queen.

BEING THE BEST GIVES STAFF
PRIDE IN THEIR JOB

There is an irritating phrase "retail is detail." In the first instance retail is not about detail. It is about getting the big picture right, getting your thinking straight. But being the best at what you do does lead to the detail. On every shop visit you will find room for improvement. Being the best is a principle that you can apply to everything. Not just shoe repairs and key cutting, but also the displays, our delivery service and even the administration.

As chairman you must passionately want to be the best – but you can't achieve it on your own. Being the best must be ingrained into the culture – persuade everyone to agree with your high standards – it will give them pride in the job and the desire to find ways to make things even better.

Fear of failure

So far this chapter might appear arrogant. I believe we should be pretty pleased with the transformation we have achieved over the last ten years, but we won't continue to be the best if we are complacent. I visit our branches each week, because I am constantly on the look-out for ways in which we can do better. Being the best is a constant striving for excellence. We must always be searching for improvements that can help the company progress.

Several times I have seen setbacks I never expected. First, when we ceased to be a family business, then when United Drapery Stores became a bid target, and later when I had to sell our shoe shops. More recently, I have observed the disintegration of Sears and the previously impregnable British Shoe Corporation and, even more improbably, the dramatic downturn at Marks & Spencer – not surprising, therefore, that I have an acute fear of failure.

I suffer from vertigo – seriously. When I took my children on Blackpool Pier, I could not go near the railings. The thought of a parachute or bungee jump is a nightmare. Just as strong is my fear of failure. I know that no business has ever achieved complete success – you really are only as good as last week. My paranoia about complacency was the only reservation I had about writing this book.

So, to make myself quite clear, let me put the message in capital letters. THERE IS ALWAYS ROOM FOR IMPROVEMENT.

CHAPTER 29

How to be the best

Everyone in the business has a contribution to make but, for a company to be the best, the chief executive must passionately believe in high standards. To be the best, a chief executive must know what to aim for. Have your idea of what is the best and avoid complacency.

> Dear James
>
> Being the best takes more effort than you imagine

Keep looking for shops that are better than yours. Check competitors on a regular basis. Every well-run shop on the high street is trying new ideas. If you want to be the best, you have to stay ahead of the game. Look abroad as well as at home. Foreign travel gives an opportunity to clear your desk and clear your mind. You are more likely to recognise good retailing in Boston than in Bishop Auckland.

Tell everybody

When you have settled on your objective, write it down. Be absolutely clear what you mean by "the best." Then tell everyone about it.

We now use training manuals to define objectives. The manuals are primarily designed as training guidelines but these pictorial text books also lay down standards for the business. They provide a precise definition of what we mean by "the best." Being the best does not just mean cutting keys that work every time. It also includes housekeeping, customer care and handling complaints.

Training manuals are not the only means of communication. Manuals have a habit of sitting on a shelf, gathering dust. You must keep "the best at" message in front of the business. Keep telling everybody through the newsletter, through your shop visits and videos. Don't assume that just because you have a clear idea of the concept it is understood by everyone else. If you don't communicate, no-one will know what they are aiming for.

Provide the tools to do the job

After buying Automagic, we spent nearly £2m on new machinery. Their shoe repair plant was difficult to operate and the key cutting machines so inaccurate that we were cutting keys that didn't work. It was not surprising that the Automagic sales had fallen so dramatically. They were using defective machinery, cheap leather, poor quality heels and inaccurate key blanks. To make matters worse, they were short of stock. They simply hadn't got enough materials to do the job.

If you want to be the best, invest in the tools to do a proper job. Only cut corners to save money if you can produce exactly the same quality result. Don't make false economies. Cheaper materials often produce a second-rate product.

Don't expand at the expense of your existing business. New shops are exciting but the highest priority is to keep your existing branches up to scratch. For 30 years, Russell & Bromley were one of the most consistently successful shoe retailers. They seldom opened more than one new shop each year. They kept investing in their existing shops, spending money on staff and customer service. Russell & Bromley expected to be judged by their poorest shop, not their best. This drove them to make sure that every branch could claim to be the best shoe shop in town. They had more staff than other shoe shops. Training took place three times a week and it showed.

Whenever I become expansion-minded, Alex brings me back to earth. "Start running the present shops properly before you think of buying any more." Our business is not about being the biggest, it's about being the best.

Excellence centres

I'm glad I'm not in the computer business. I could never keep pace with technical development that requires a business to reinvent itself every five years. It's much better being in a quiet backwater such as key cutting where nothing changes too quickly. But even traditional crafts have to keep up to date. To maintain a technological lead over our competitors, we have developed a Centre of Excellence for each of our services. These centres provide both a helpline to branches and the ability to develop new techniques. Like most good new developments, they happened by chance.

FOR YOUR ENQUIRIES YOU CAN PHONE THE KEY DEPARTMENT:-
MON-FRI. 9.00 - 5.00PM   SAT. 10.00AM - 4PM
0161-946 6213
KEY HOTLINE
ALWAYS HAVE ADVICE AT THE END
OF THE TELEPHONE

When computers started to be used for engraving in 1989, we had to have a go. The first computer was put in a room above our shop in Tonbridge to provide a house sign service by post throughout the UK. The experiment was beset by problems. We promised a ten-day service and sometimes failed to deliver within three weeks. The small team couldn't cope with the modest level of orders but, rather than asking for help, covered up the problem. Despite a buoyant demand, our shop staff soon became disllusioned with the service and house sign sales quickly faded away.

Most experiments start with a series of disasters. Determination is required to overcome the teething problems. Unhappy with the service from Tonbridge, we set up another computer engraving centre in St Helens. This was much more successful. Originally providing a service for the north of England and Scotland, its reputation grew. Orders started coming from the south. After three years, we opened a small industrial site outside St Helens, closed down Tonbridge, and established an Excellence Centre which now has a turnover of £1m a year.

Computers also invaded our key business and prompted another Centre of Excellence. The computer provides a postal service, cutting the keys by code number. The Key Excellence Centre also has a helpline. Branch staff have their key queries answered by a small team of experts at the end of the phone while customers wait in the shop. The helpline was an immediate success. The number of calls rose from an intital 50 a week and now seldom fall below 1,000. The Key Excellence Centre helped branches to deliver our promise of cutting every key every time. We became the best key cutter in the country.

The acquisition of Automagic brought another Excellence Centre, for shoe repairs. Automagic had a repair contract with Timberland. We set up a specialist factory and added other brands – Cats, RM Williams, Henry Lloyd. We also provide a service for top grade shoes and have been amazed at the demand for the £65 ultimate shoe repair. We call it the best shoe repair in the world.

Watch repairs required another Excellence Centre. Based in Wolverhampton, it already has a turnover of £500,000 a year and handles watches to the value of at least £5m.

I found it difficult to come to terms with a large investment in people who are not in direct touch with our customers. But I can now see "in-house" experts play a vital part, helping us be the best at what we do.

Our technical development is the responsibility of in-house experts. There are plenty of people in our branches who are so enthusiastic they turn their skills into their hobby. We don't have to import expertise.Our shoe repair technical manager, John Higgs, had been with the business for 40 years before he took up his current appointment. For the last 30 years he had been the branch manager of our local shop in Cheadle, Cheshire where he wrote text books on shoe repairs, built his own specialist shoe repair machinery and developed a specialist shoe repair service for professional sportsmen.

Ian Oakes, our key cutting technical manager, spent 20 years in our branches before setting up our Key Excellence Centre. Ian was fascinated by keys and became a walking encyclopaedia about them; his knowledge is now available at the end of a telephone for everybody in the business.

High Standards

Customers only give you one chance. The company's reputation is on the line every time we make a sale and our claim to be the best is judged every time a customer walks into our shops. Who better to tell us whether we are the best than customers themselves? We receive thousands of customer comment cards each year, but sales figures are the ultimate measure of success. Every sale matters. We must offer the best service for the customer who comes into Elgin at 9.30, Exeter at 10.30, Edinburgh at 11.30 or Ellesmere Port at 12.30. But with 315 shops, it would be foolish to assume that we are always perfect.

Don't assume that things are always right and don't accept low standards. If you want to be the best, you must continually check what is going on. We spend at least £200,000 a year checking up on our shops. To be the best we need skilled staff. Our training programme leads to stringent skill tests before awarding a diploma. We retest candidates on a regular basis. Customers are not interested in diplomas. They want to know whether our staff can do a good job today.

We employ mystery shoppers. Every shop can expect a mystery visit at least four times a year. They give an objective opinion of our service.

shout about it

Keep telling everybody that you are the best. This isn't arrogance, it's just good business. Shout about our high standards in the company newsletter and through our shop displays. This tells customers what to expect and lets staff know what to achieve. When we put up a poster declaring we amaze our customers with the quality of our service, the standard of service immediately improved and thousands of customers sent in postcards to say that they had been amazed.

When we put up a poster depicting a perfect shoe repair job, with arrows showing customers the quality points, the standard of our workmanship took a turn for the better! If we put up a poster saying we are good, customers think it must be true and, the staff take quality much more seriously.

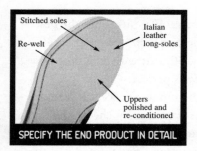

Stitched soles

Re-welt

Italian leather long-soles

Uppers polished and re-conditioned

SPECIFY THE END PRODUCT IN DETAIL

You can't expect your staff to improve standards so that the company can claim excellence without praising the people who have brought about the improvement. Run loads of competitions based on sales, quality, shop presentation and customer comments. Make special awards through the newsletter and send personal letters to high achievers. It takes effort to improve standards – don't take that dedication for granted.

Giving out justified praise is never a waste of time. People who have worked hard to improve their standards this year, will still be receptive in 12 months' time and when you ask them to do better still.

Always doing better

Keep trying to do it better. Always be on the lookout for improvements, better materials, better machinery, better technology, and better ways to serve customers.

New ideas are critical to keeping your reputation of being the best. Everyone will expect you to come up with new ideas. If you stop innovating, they will think you have lost interest.

Every day I visit shops, I fill several pages of my note pad. The notes cover problems and ideas. Sometimes I receive a sharp shock of reality. Some branches fall well short of our standards but that, in a way, is good news – it shows we've still got plenty of room for improvement.Each year seems to yield twice as many ideas as the year before. The problem isn't getting hold of new ideas to develop the business; that's simple – you just go to our shops and listen. The difficult part is getting the ideas carried out in practice. Every year we look for improvements. It's a process of annual soul searching to find better ways to cut keys, repair shoes and watches and provide an engraving service.

Every Autumn we have a key cutting campaign. We choose the early Autumn because that is the peak for key cutting. The second week of September is ten per cent better than any other week, because of children going back to school.

There is always something new in our annual key promotion. A new layout for the keyboard, a new key catalogue, a new range of blanks or a new training scheme. We have a keycutting competition based on sales and mystery shopper visits. This two month concentration on keys lifts the overall standard.

But you can't concentrate on every service for 12 months of the year. Each service has to take its turn in the spotlight.

If you leave things alone, the business will steadily get worse. Maintaining a "best at" business is like the circus act of spinning plates on sticks. Every so often each service needs a tweak to get it going again and as your back is turned, something else goes off the boil. I have been spinning the plates for 25 years and I still haven't found a way to keep them spinning on their own.

THEY DON'T KEEP SPINNING ON THEIR OWN

The ultimate helpline

Dear James

The office
influences
every shop

When a multiple retailer gets into trouble, it's never the fault of the staff that work in the branches. The problem is at head office.

Bad examples

Well before the decline of Sears hit the headlines, we knew their shoe shops were in trouble. Their sales assistants told us they didn't have the stock that customers wanted. Charles Clore's British Shoe was really created by Harry Levison, a shoe shop expert with exceptional flair. When he retired in 1977, British Shoe had well over 20 per cent of the UK shoe market. Over the next 20 years the company stagnated and finally fell under the leadership of six successive chief executives, none of whom could match Harry Levison's flair. Statistics took over and the business relied on systems for success. Control was at a head office which was out of touch with its customers.

I saw the same thing at Sketchley. In the early nineties Sketchley acquired SupaSnap the photoprocessing business and it never recovered. The SupaSnap management team got all the top jobs. They put photoprocessing into the Sketchley units but did nothing to develop dry cleaning. During a day's visit with two Sketchley executives, I went to Hitchen where a combined Sketchley and SupaSnap branch was totally dominated by photoprocessing. Nearly all the window and most of the selling space displayed films and photo albums. The shop looked like a photoprocessor that did a bit of dry cleaning, but the turnover told a different story. Photoprocessing and the photo albums added together provided only 20 per cent of total turnover. The Sketchley shop staff knew things were wrong but head office didn't listen.

At Automagic the senior management ignored the branch staff's plea to develop their key business. Most commentators agree that Marks & Spencer has suffered from having a head office out of touch with the shop floor.

Once head office thinks it knows better than the rest of the business it can produce some pretty bizarre policies. I heard of a multiple where the new management team were so convinced their vision for change was the route to success that they deliberately ignored their existing staff, especially anyone with experience. They wouldn't promote anybody who had been with the company for more than 12 months.

He's in a meeting

I have a theory that a company's performance is in inverse proportion to the time its executives spend in meetings. Ring up a company in trouble, and you often find them in a meeting. I wouldn't have made a good civil servant. I don't like meetings.

I went through my committee stage in the seventies, representing the business in a variety of outside committees.

My diary was full. I attended meetings of the British Standards Institute (BSI), the Multiple Shoe Retailers' Association (MSRA), The Footwear Distributors Federation (FDF) and the National Economic Development Organisation (NEDO).

In 1987 I started a five year stint of involvement in shoe repair committees. The National Association of Shoe Repair Factories (NASRF), and the British Shoe Repair Council (BSRC) and the Shoe Repair National Vocational Qualifications (NVQ).

In all these organisations I noticed that several committee members never spoke. They would arrive with the papers carefully arranged but meeting after meeting never made a contribution.

Most meetings took place in London. I played a game on the train. After breakfast, the important looking executives got out their files to prepare for their meetings. It was impossible not to eavesdrop. A walk to the buffet car gave you a peep at the pages to discover the destination of your fellow passengers as they headed for trade associations, union meetings and government-sponsored committees. I enjoyed mornings when the train was late. Today smart executives announce their lateness in a pompous voice down their mobiles but in the seventies they had to sweat it out: would they make the meeting on time? When the train arrived at Euston, there was a stampede for the taxi rank. Eventually, hot, late and flustered the delegates would arrive at their meeting. Half of them probably never said a word before hailing another taxi to go home.

You can't get through life without attending some meetings. Board meetings are essential but avoid Standing Committees. Committees that meet on a regular basis often become totally unproductive. Ad hoc meetings to discuss a specific subject work best. Don't forget that everyone tied up in a meeting is prevented from getting on with their job.

Helpful advice

A good head office is the ultimate helpline. Too many employees see their headquarters as a source of strife, putting obstacles in the way. I want our office to be the company advice bureau with help always at hand.

We use faxes and e-mail but life in Timpson still revolves around the telephone. Telephone calls help the office get to know the shops and sometimes they get to know them very well. Within the past ten years, we have had two long distance romances over the Timpson telephone. Two blind date encounters that resulted in marriage. Modern telephone systems look after the subscriber at the expense of the caller. It is getting more difficult to speak to the person you want or indeed talk to anybody at all. Too many telephone calls consist of pressing buttons and listening to messages. Our office is there to provide help, so we must look after the incoming caller. We don't have background music because we don't leave people on hold. I banned the voice mail because callers want their query dealt with straight away. We still have a switchboard operator who answers the telephone with a cheery voice and says who they are: "Good morning, this is Timpson House, Mrs Moor speaking."

It helps to know who you are talking to. I encourage everybody who works in our office to spend at least a day a year in our shops, that way they have a better understanding of the business and they meet some of the people they talk to on the phone. To bring all their calls to life we are now producing a complete picture gallery of our shop staff so the head office team can see who they are talking to. To ensure every call gets an answer, we have a notepad on every desk. It doesn't matter whether the request comes by telephone, post, fax or e-mail, the pad has to be completed. It describes the nature of the request and what is being done about it.

The note is then sent to the branch, so they know what has been done and can comment on the service they have received.

We had a scoring system when we started the scheme. Comments about head office were rated on a five point scale from very good to very poor. Every "very good" put money into a bonus pot shared by everybody in the office. This request scheme helped to improve the relationship between our offices and the branches. But the scheme was unpopular – I was accused of creating too much paper work and an indignant office team felt they didn't need such gimmicks to be reminded their job was to serve the shops. But I haven't given up. We need to provide constant reminders of upside-down-management – I will soon try another gimmick.

Despite these problems, our helpline is making a big difference. The office is making an extra effort to be helpful. Special orders for pink laces or extra long shoe horns used to be sent in packs of six or 12; now shops can order them one at a time. We don't insist that branches stick to our delivery schedule, if they need a special delivery, they get one. We are developing a culture where requests are greeted with "Yes, it isn't a problem," rather than "No, you can't do it."

Communication and compliments

Whatever you do, people in head office will say: "No one tells us anything." Put more than 25 people together in the same building and they will start a false rumour.

Don't be offended. If your colleagues in the office want more information, give it to them and even if they don't, give the information anyway. They are a special case. The office has an effect on every shop in the business.

It's more awkward to heap praise on people you meet every day but if someone does well, make sure you show your appreciation. "Well done" letters and special Chairman's Awards should be sent to office staff every month. Ask supervisors to tell you what is going on so you can praise individuals personally. To make sure we don't forget to recognise excellence, we now have a parking space reserved for our employee of the month.

Dreaded administration

Much as I dislike administration, it can't be avoided. The office can't purely be a helpline, some departments are essential to keep the business ticking – particularly finance, computer and property.

We have to work to a system, but ensure it fits in with the shops rather than making the shops fit in with the system.

Shoe repairers and key cutters usually find administration boring. At last, we have found the answer. A training manual – our "Managers' Guide" – contains everything you need to know to run a shop, with the tips told in pictures. Writing it really made us think. It helped us to simplify our administrative system. We cut out a lot of unnecessary work and made the essential items simpler to understand. But our people still find administration a bore and the biggest bugbear is paperwork.

Hopefully when everyone has a laptop the paper will disappear, but in the meantime, we have computers that churn out more information that anyone could posssibly read. Information that is meant to help us run the business better just gets in the way. I have sent all our managers a new waste paper basket. Everyone has my authority to put figures or memos straight into the bin.

Office politics

In a 100 per cent-owned private company you are relatively free of office politics, but they do exist. Nothing could be as bad as the memo protocol in force when I started in business. Memos had to be sent on the correct colour of paper: directors used blue; senior executives pink; junior executives green and everybody else had to use plain white. The protocol determined who got copies. People at the bottom of the organisation were told nothing and as you progressed your post bag increased. If your subordinate received a memo you had it as well. The chief executive never had enough time to read all of his post. All the recipients had to be listed by seniority. If the executives were in the wrong order, the memo was withdrawn and retyped.

A similar protocol applied to meetings and who should be consulted on decisions. Personal success was much more important than company profit and success was measured in terms of status. Status determined the make of your car, the size of your office, and where you ate your lunch. It also determined what information you were allowed to see and the meetings you could attend. We are relatively free of office

217

politics. It doesn't have a place in our upside-down management system but it will never disappear.

Dream solution

If head office is a helpline, life becomes a lot easier. Executives spend their lives solving problems rather than telling people what to do. The office stays in touch with the business and shop staff appreciate their contribution. Upside-down management should turn the office into the ultimate helpline and focus on the most important part of the business – serving customers.

spreading the word

The case for communication

Dear James

Tell everyone about it !

When I was a shop assistant at the age of 17, I was still living at home with my mother and father. One night, after they had gone to bed, I found a copy of the board meeting minutes which father had left lying around. I couldn't resist reading them. I was amazed to find out that the business was opening ten new shops, and developing computer systems (this was in 1960). There was a major investment in the development of shoe repairs. Our new head office was due to have a visit from Prince Philip. As a mere shop assistant I did not have a clue what was going on in the business and I was the chairman's son!

Why the secrecy?

Thirty-five years ago information remained the property of management and employees were kept in the dark. Although we now live in a more enlightened age, most companies are either reluctant or frightened to tell their staff what is happening. We are in the middle of the information revolution and most facts in the world are available through the Internet but managers still like to keep company information close to their chest.

It is hard to understand the reasons for secrecy. Some times silence makes common sense, particularly when the information is personal or confidential. Many businesses are paranoid about information falling into the hands of their competitors. In my experience there is little need to worry – company news, plans and ideas are of little interest to anybody outside the company. Most competitors don't understand the information, don't believe it, are not interested and don't know how to use the facts for their own advantage.

For 20 years, Automagic watched us develop key cutting. They went into receivership, still convinced that our emphasis on key cutting would do irreparable harm to our shoe repair trade.

Despite our well publicised increase in profits and market share, some competitors claim that we falsified the figures. We publish the turnovers of our best branches every week but seldom find anyone opening in opposition.

Executives worry about staff knowing too much – bad results could affect morale and good results lead to excessive wage demands. It doesn't happen like that. Being open about the bad times gives staff the opportunity to come up with solutions. Good results create loyalty.

Company secrecy adds to the feeling of status amongst middle and senior executives. Managers feel that keeping knowledge to themselves increases their power and influence throughout the organisation.

Make everything common knowledge

I am not suggesting that you run the business as a democracy. It is your job to make the key decisions. But it is certainly not a dictatorship. You can't run a successful business without the support of employees. Tell everyone everything you possibly can and involve them in the decision making process.

We don't want a workforce that just follows orders, our management style is to delegate. Don't underestimate the people in the business, most are lively and intelligent. They want to be fully involved in developing a successful enterprise. Give them all the information they need to play a full part.

During a shop visit two years ago I asked a shop manager: "How are we doing?" He replied, quite simply, "I understand what the business is trying to do and, what's more, I agree with it. It is good to be told what is going on and it makes me feel important." The more we communicate, the better chance we have of success.

Don't just tell your employees. Include their wives, husbands, partners, mothers and fathers. They all have an interest in the company and are keen to know what is going on. Tell your suppliers. Contrary to popular belief, they will not put up prices if you are doing well. They are more likely to offer attractive quantity discounts. When we needed extended credit shortly after purchasing Automagic, I got 100 per cent support from our suppliers. They trusted me because I had been consistently open with information about our progress.

Make the facts common knowledge. Report on turnover every week, not just company totals but give shops access to the figures for every other shop. It shows how they are doing and stimulates competition. Provide a regular up-date on profits, reporting company results on a quarterly basis. Every six months tell each branch the detailed profit figures of the shop where they work. A regular supply of information stops rumours. Ignorance stimulates the prophets of doom. Whenever you try to hide the facts, the workforce fear the worst.

Publish your plans

Don't just stop at the facts, broadcast your plans and your ideas. Let everybody know why we are heading down our chosen path. Tell them the thinking behind each decision. Test your ideas at an early stage; people's reaction will tell you whether you are on the right track. Harness the views and suggestions that exist within the business. Involving the workforce in the decision making process helps manage change.

Our biggest challenge has been to turn cobblers into quality service people. Everybody needed to understand why cobblers should cut keys. A continual debate about how to deal with a declining market encouraged lifetime shoe repairers to willingly take on the new tasks of key cutting, engraving and more recently watch repairs. They approved of the new direction because they felt part of the decision.

Be prepared for disappointments. Some of your freedom of information will be misinterpreted. In 1997 there was a newspaper article and a television programme which contrasted my business role with the fact we are foster parents. Most welcomed the publicity it brought to

TELL ALL YOUR STAFF EVERYTHING ABOUT THE BUSINESS

Detailed sales every week

Investment Plans

Profit every six months

Share your thinking

Test your new ideas on the staff

Broadcast the company strategy

223

MEANS OF COMMUNICATION

Weekly news letter

Quarterly magazine

Occasional letter

Video

Road show

Area manager conference

Area dinner

Suppliers lunches

Public relations

the business and saw our fostering as an indication that we cared for people. But this was not a universal view. One customer wrote to me from Preston suggesting that instead of spending money on looking after other people's children, I should reduce the price of our shoe repairs. Following the television programme which included reference to our Caribbean holidays, one employee wrote to say I should not spend so much money on holidays but increase wages instead.

Don't be put off by the minority, being open and honest does much more good than harm. One word of warning, always make sure your senior executives are the first people to know anything. The status associated with Company knowledge is still very strong and going over the heads of your management will undermine their authority.

Channels of communication

Once you are convinced that communication is a powerful management tool, there are plenty of ways to use it. The quarterly company newsletter is a classic way of distributing information. Don't delegate its production to a PR company; you will finish with a bland publication produced by someone clearly out of touch with the day-to-day business. Our quarterly newsletter concentrates on policy issues and analysis, news stories are published on a weekly basis.

Our weekly newsletter has become the main information bulletin for the business. Most of it is written by the staff themselves. It is a weekly collection of news from all parts of the business. It is the item (after their salary cheque) that staff most look forward to receiving through the post.

I don't like head office circulars. If something is worth saying, it should be said in the weekly newsletter. I have one exception – memos sent by myself! But these are seldom, if ever typed. I write them out freehand so they will be noticed.

Videos work well. People read pictures, not words and a video follows this principle. We often send the video to everybody, addressed to their home. In this way we communicate not only with employees but their families as well.

Company dinners give another chance to talk directly to wives, husbands and partners. It is a golden opportunity to demonstrate that we are a good company to work for.

Over the past few years I have held a suppliers' lunch, which has helped to develop our relationship with the rest of our industry.

Good PR does not just speak through the media to customers but is also noticed by our employees. People believe what they read in the newspapers and company news broadcast in the press has much more influence than an internal memo.

The best way to get any message across is through meeting people face to face. I do that regularly on my weekly shop visits. Five times over the past 11 years I have used the road show, a nation-wide tour that covers up to 20 venues over a period of three weeks. It is a way of getting a major message across, particularly if the company is going through a time of change. But be warned, it is expensive (tot up all the travelling expenses involved) it takes a lot of your time and it should not be repeated too often otherwise the road show gets a bad name.

My favourite opportunity to talk about strategy is the area managers' conference. With four meetings a year, it provides the opportunity to develop strategy in public, ensuring that senior management get the message first.

There are plenty of channels of communication open to you – plenty of ways to tell everyone in the business everything you possibly can. But communication in itself is not enough. You need to be communicating clear ideas that get the right company message across.

Once you have taken communication seriously, you will find it takes an awful lot of your time. But it will force you to think and will help you to get to know the business better. In developing your communication you will also draw up a clear plan for the business.

Writing a speech

Most of us are not natural speakers. The select few who can command an audience are singled out at an early age. They were the stars of the debating society and took the lead in the school play. But the ability to make a speech is a vital management tool. Fortunately you can teach yourself speaking skills, and most of the learning is through experience.

Dear James

It takes a long time to write a good short speech

Speechmakers must know what they are going to say and know what they are talking about.

Writing the script

Think carefully about the content of every speech. Sometimes your words will be predetermined. At a long service lunch, your job is to talk about the people receiving presentations, make them feel good and proud to be present. At a company dinner you should convince the staff and their partners that they are involved in the best business in the country. You talk to bankers or venture capitalists to persuade them to invest in you and your business.

With general management meetings, you have the freedom to choose your topic but you must have a main theme. Restrict yourself to one main message. Before writing a speech be absolutely clear what ideas you want to get across. Talk to colleagues and find out what they think you should say. Make a list of the possible contenders for your speech. Messages that are important to the business such as:

1. Why we should be the best at what we do and how we can achieve it.
2. Being the best company to work for.

3. Raising our standards of retailing.
4. The importance of diversification and learning new skills.

Having chosen your theme, begin to write. Allow plenty of time. Your talk may only last 15 minutes but it should take over four hours to prepare.

Write down everything that comes into your head about your chosen topic. Produce a long list in random order. If the importance of watch repairs is your chosen subject, the list could be as follows:

1. Is the training easy?
2. What is the competition for watch repairs?
3. How big is the market?
4. What will the shops look like?
5. How much extra profit can we make?
6. Short history of the business
7 What experience have we got so far?
8. How mature are our current services?
9. What is in it for our shop staff?
10.What is the investment?

Reorganise your topics into a sensible order and give special attention to how you begin and how the speech will end. Having decided the order, talk it through to yourself and then try the list of contents on a colleague. Through this process the detailed words of your speech will start to emerge.

Visual aids?

You not only decide what to say but how to say it. Choose a speech-making method that suits the occasion and suits yourself.

If you want to make things easy write the whole speech in longhand and read it out word for word. That is the best technique for your debut, but it is not a method you should always use. Shorthand notes produce a more spontaneous speaking style, particularly when you fully understand your topic. Your notes should be sparse enough to allow

List everything that comes to mind

NOTE Stick to the theme

Theme: Being the best at what we do:-

Training	Repairs
Service Talk	Training Manuals
Check Machinery	Mystery Shoppers
New Materials	Guarantee
Starting Levels	Opening Hours
Packaging	Warehouse Services
Speed of Services	Compliments

REMINDER
WHAT IS THE MESSAGE YOU WANT TO GET ACROSS ?

Organise into Headings

Introduction
Customer Service
Manuals
Mystery Shopper
Complaints

Branch Appearance
Display Guidelines
Housekeeping
Refits

Training
Skill Test
Training Courses
Apprenticeship Manuals

Materials & Machinery
Maintenance
New Technology
New Materials

HQ Service
Warehouse
Phone Calls
Paperwork

Maintaining Results
Mystery Shopper
Complaints
Sales Figures
Conclusion

Check with someone else

Write your detailed notes

PRACTICE!
PRACTICE!
PRACTICE!

Introduction
Why we are the best....
Pride
Price
It works
We can do it!

What Matters ?
Quality
Service
Appearance
Reliability

IF NERVOUS WRITE VERBATIM NOTES!

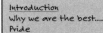

Choose the best delivery...

WARNING Don't be ambitious

STRAIGHT TALKING WITH
NO VISUAL AID

OVERHEAD PROJECTOR

VIDEO

USE ONLY ON RARE EVENTS

AUDIO TAPES

FLIPCHART

SLIDES

SLIDES WORK BEST!!!

free expression but sufficient to ensure you stick to the subject. Never distribute notes before you start speaking, or you will lose the audience before you start.

Avoid the overhead projector. This visual aid has been so badly used by presenters over the years, that you can hear a collective yawn throughout the audience as soon as the wretched machine is switched on. It is excusable to use an overhead to show visuals (line drawings or pictures), but certainly not to display words. There is nothing worse than seeing someone projecting a list onto the screen (which is a copy of the notes for their speech), and then go through the items one by one. The biggest bore of all is when the presenter takes a piece of paper to cover up the text, so that the speech is revealed, tedious item by tedious item.

I prefer old fashioned flip charts, they at least give the impression that you have gone to some trouble to prepare your presentation.

You can use video but be careful, often this can be a cop-out. You should do the talking, not delegate the job to a film. Make sure that visual aids are there to supplement your presentation. They should not be allowed to take over the show.

The slide show

My favourite is the slide projector. Thirty years ago while visiting a computer exhibition, I saw a big black box which turned into a self-contained projector and screen, I didn't learn anything about computers but I bought the box and have been using it ever since. It has given slide presentations to countless employees, pensioners, consumer groups, Government departments and prospective investors. The black box played a leading part in obtaining funds for our management buyout and was still used when we bought Automagic 14 years later.

To produce a slide show, start as you would for any talk by choosing the main theme and listing the detailed content. The trick is to turn your shorthand notes into pictures. The pictures become your prompt for the talk. When I started using slides, I took a lot of pictures. Pictures of fascias, displays, competitors and people, all illustrating the points I wanted to make. Now I have a large picture library but each new talk

231

still requires a few new slides.

Slide shows need lots of rehearsal. You must be sure what every slide means! Go through the slides several times, talking out loud until you know what the next slide is going to be before it comes up on the screen. Your slides now provide all the notes you need and even if you lose your way, the next slide will bring you back to the script.

Don't leave anything to chance. Lots can go wrong. Hotels promise equipment they have not got. Take your own extension lead and spare projector bulb. Drop the carousel and all the slides fall out jumbled up on the floor, (insulating tape round the carousel will prevent this problem). Never be satisfied until you have tested the slides at the venue to make sure everything works.

Rehearsals pay off

Fully prepare for every speech. The more you rehearse, the better the speech will be. Turn up to the venue early. Don't be worried about being nervous and don't use alcohol to overcome tension. A few nerves can enhance your performance, drink certainly does not.

Before the speech concentrate on your opening words and how you will finish. Get off to a good start and things will almost certainly go well but you must know how you are going to end!

Take your time, many speeches fall down because they are rushed. But don't be tedious and boring, react to your audience, you will soon sense whether everyone is listening. As you gain experience at speaking, you will learn how to change your pace and even the content in reaction to the different types of audience. Remember you are there to sell yourself as well as selling the message. It is a communication exercise and communicating is two way. You are talking to people not to the wall – or your notes – so you must make eye contact.

Once the ordeal is over, have a private inquest. Decide what went well and what went wrong. Which visual aids work and which ones don't? The next time you speak you will have learned from the experience. But never get complacent, however experienced you become, it still takes four hours to produce a good 15-minute speech.

CHAPTER 33

The company magazine

Timpson has published a company magazine three times a year since 1954. I have read through every one of them.

They are a good guide to the history of the business, they tell you what the company was doing and what it planned to do. The pieces about people give a good indication of the company culture of the day.

> Dear James
>
> Keep everyone up to date with your thinking

What's it for?

Remember what the company magazine is for. It is the board's bulletin to the business. It is a fairly serious publication covering plans and performance with analysis of the company strategy. Plenty of space should be given to employee achievements.

Don't just cover what is going on. Say why you are doing it. You are talking to employees, pensioners, suppliers, possible investors, visitors to head office and your employees' families. After they have read your magazine, everyone should know more about the business, its current performance and future plans.

The topics are serious but the style must not be boring. People read pictures not words and a magazine with lots of writing and few pictures won't be read. Your style should be somewhere between the *Daily Mail* and the *Sun* rather than *The Times* or *Guardian*.

Editor in chief

Never allow your magazine to be produced by a PR company or by the personnel department! You must write it yourself. You are the journalist, the sub-editor, the editor, the feature writer and, in some cases, the photographer. The magazine should reflect the culture of the business and it is you, as chief executive, who sets the tone. There really is no option. You have to write the magazine yourself.

Don't be overawed by the task. If you follow the simple guidelines in this chapter, you will produce the first draft of a magazine in four hours and during that time you will also have thought a lot about the future of the business.

Start by listing topics you want to communicate. This will cover major events since the last magazine and the new things which are about to be launched. You need a financial report on turnover and profits. There should be some analysis or news about each of the major parts of the business. Give plenty of space to news about your workforce. People are much more likely to read a publication that mentions their name.

When you have listed your topics, decide on which page each item should appear (our magazine had eight pages). Decide on your front-page headline. Keep the serious and financial news to the front and use the last three pages for news about people.

Script writing

Take two pages of A4 paper and fold them both in two. Put them together and you have eight pages of A5. Use your notes to draw up the shape of your magazine, writing a headline for each item and indicate where you want to put the pictures.

Check several times to make sure you are happy that each page is interesting (there should be plenty of pictures), and that the headlines will attract the reader. Check the content really does get the important messages across.

You are now ready to write the words . Using a dictaphone, produce an article for each of your headlines. When I first started the magazine I made the mistake of asking other people to contribute articles. I waited ages for my colleagues to come back with the required words. I find it so much easier to do the work myself.

To make articles more interesting, I pepper them with personal

THE METHOD

❶ List the items for your Newsletter

New Warehouse System 6

Watch Repairs 1

Profit Review 1

New Shops 2

Car Key Stocktaking 3

Training Interview 1

Locksmith Services 8

Computer 2

Shoe Repairs by Post 3

Scottish Dinner 4

Top 20 Manager 8

London Marathon 6

Greyhound 6

New Badge Range 7

Shoe Repairs in Canada 7

❷ Decide which page the items should be on

❸ FOLD TWO FOOLSCAP PIECES OF PAPER

❹ DRAFT OUT HEADLINES AND FEATURES

❺ DICTATE THE COPY

❻

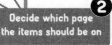

CHECK DRAFT MAGAZINE

quotes – (e.g. "This is a major step forward for the company," commented managing director, Kit Green, or, "Our refit is already getting some highly favourable comments from our customers," said Peter Smith, manager in Huddersfield). The quotes, of course, are pure products of my imagination as I speak into the dictaphone – but I do check with the people concerned before I publish their words!

The in-depth interview is a good way to get an important message across. You still use a dictaphone but for this exercise, you are both the interviewer and the interviewee. I have even, from time to time, taped an interview with myself.

Often I have written the magazine when I am on holiday, dictating the detail as I walk along a beach or sit huddled in a cottage sheltering from the Scottish mist. Anyone near me on the beach in Majorca 18 months ago would have heard me dictating this part of an interview.

TSR News: "Well, John, what are your most important achievements over the past 12 months?" John Timpson: "I am sure the speed in which the Automagic business has become part of Timpson has been our greatest success." *TSR News:* "What has helped most in that Automagic success?" John Timpson: "It's the co-operation we had from Automagic people who have quickly changed to the Timpson way of thinking." *TSR News:* "How many of the Automagic branches have you seen now?" John Timpson: "All of them once, and most of them two or three times." And so it goes on.

Editorial balance

Think carefully about the section of the magazine devoted to people. The stars and high achievers must be mentioned but the magazine should have a human touch. Features on hobbies, charity work, and employees who have made the newspaper headlines will add life and make the point that the business is full of characters who lead interesting lives.

As well as dictating the copy, you need to choose the pictures. Some will be of shops, keys and shoe repairs, but most of the pictures must be of people. Avoid having too many pictures of the chairman and the managing director. Your readers want to see pictures of the people who really do the work!

When your dictated notes have been typed, check them in detail and cut them down to size. Dictation makes you verbose. Your magazine doesn't need many words, you tell the stories through your headlines and pictures.

It is now time to pass your draft to the publisher. Inject a sense of urgency. You want your notes printed as soon as possible, otherwise they will sound stale. Insist on a draft at every stage of its publication and check the draft carefully. There will always be mistakes.

Think about how your magazine is distributed. Don't send it in the normal weekly mail. If you want it to be read, send it to each employee at their home. It might cost extra postage, but it ensures that all your hard work will be worthwhile.

The weekly newsletter

Dear James

Don't let anyone cut the newsletter to save paper !

Our weekly newsletter was created by chance and in two years has become the most important communication tool in the business.

How it started

Early in 1996 as part of a road show to introduce Automagic staff to our business style, I gave everyone a notepad "Personal Note to John Timpson." This gave everyone direct access to the chairman's office.

The personal notepad worked. Every Monday morning I received between ten and 20 notes from all over the country. The messages contained problems and any criticisms. The system helped to highlight important areas but for me Monday morning with nothing but a new collection of problems. I decided I needed some good news.

To cheer myself up I sent everyone a "Good News" pad. In contrast to the personal note, this pad was for the exclusive use of people with a cheerful message. The "Good News" pad was an immediate hit. The first week I received forty notes, mostly from shops reporting excellent turnovers. Two branches reported their competitor had closed down and one manager told me that his wife had just had a baby. I put all the good news in a letter to every shop, giving a prize of £20 to the best news of the week. Our weekly newsletter was born.

News gathering

For the next four months, my secretary, Barbara and myself spent every Monday morning converting the "Good News" notes into our newsletter. One week, Barbara said I had written too much, it couldn't fit on one sheet of paper and wanted to know which "Good News" to cut out. I left the good news in and added another sheet of paper.

Most businesses have a wealth of statistics on computer but don't know much about what really goes on. My little notepads provided information that no computer could reveal and most of it was good news. I decided to send out more notepads.

I called the week before Easter our "Amaze Me Week," offering £2,000 in prizes for news that amazed me most about branch success. Everyone received a notepad: "To John Timpson, this will amaze you, I claim my prize!" This produced a bumper postbag and, amazingly, an extremely good week's trading.

Later in the year, I used another notepad, for an unusual job competition. Entries were reported in the weekly newsletter and as the unusual jobs were published, I received even more bizarre entries. People had repaired shoes for clowns, made pet tags for elephants, cut keys for handcuffs and engraved a vibrator.

Four years after the newsletter was launched, we still get 50 to 100 good news notes a week, and our newsletter has extended to average 16 pages.

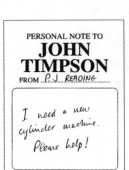

Spreading the news

We have added many extra features. Every issue gives detailed figures of company sales, and lists the top 20 branches for all our main categories – shoe repairs – key cutting – engraving – watch repairs and merchandise. I give my personal comments on trade the previous week.

We advertise every job vacancy through the newsletter and mention personal landmarks, marriages and births as well as long service.

We include lots of pictures. We are building up a photo library of every member of staff, so if they get a mention, we can show what they look like. I normally write a report on the branches I visit, illustrated by the pictures I take of the staff as I go round. We include local press cuttings that feature our shops.

A section is given to head office. Executives are not encouraged to send out memos; they are expected to use the newsletter.

Other features come and go. We have had caption competitions, pictures of employees' pets, and staff with unusual hobbies. We publish complimentary letters and mention celebrity customers, particularly those who have been persuaded to sign one of our leather soles for display in the shops. We continue to report the unusual jobs and even quote the "customers from hell". There is a regular contributor of cartoons and for a time we had a racing tipster.

In the early stages, we introduced "Captain Cash." Each month we made £300 available for a charity nominated by our staff. As a result, we are now sponsoring several local sports teams and support many charity appeals which are near to the hearts of our employees.

Popular press

Ninety per cent of our weekly newsletter is written by the branch staff, through their regular "Good News" notes. We publish every bit of genuine good news and ensure that the news we receive on a Monday is sent out in our newsletter the following day. There is always a chance of winning a prize. Every week cash prizes are given for the best news, the most interesting news and to the branch of the week.

The newsletter has gained such status that we are now starting to produce special supplements to announce major company initiatives.

The newsletter has been a dramatic success. Not only is it read by most staff, but they take it home to their families. I am now being asked to produce more copies – one for every member of staff to take back home to show to their wives, husbands, mothers and fathers.

Our weekly newsletter had been so successful that the company magazine had ceased publication – the weekly news became so instant and comprehensive I could not see a role for the magazine.

I forgot that the magazine went to our pensioners and our suppliers. We didn't need a magazine inside the business any more but we still needed to talk to the outside world.

We think we have found the answer – a two-monthly collation of our weekly newsletter – it seems to work not only for pensioners and suppliers but also in a new and important direction. We are now using the bimonthly news as a customer newsletter – for waiting customers. They seem more interested than I expected. Our newsletter has made a major contribution to the company culture, thanks to the cheap little "Good News" pad.

CONTENT OF THE NEWSLETTER

ALWAYS SHOW THE FIGURES

SHOP OF THE WEEK

NEW SHOPS

STATE OF THE TRADE

FUTURE OF THE BUSINESS

MESSAGE OF THANKS

NEW APPOINTMENTS

ADVERTISE EVERY VACANCY

PERSONAL LANDMARKS

NO LIMIT TO THE NUMBER OF PAGES

NO H.Q. CIRCULARS, EVERYTHING MUST GO IN THE NEWSLETTER

CONTENT OF THE NEWSLETTER

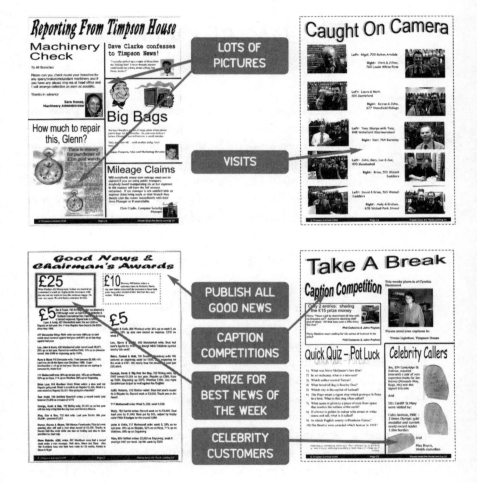

LOTS OF PICTURES

VISITS

PUBLISH ALL GOOD NEWS

CAPTION COMPETITIONS

PRIZE FOR BEST NEWS OF THE WEEK

CELEBRITY CUSTOMERS

The special message

Dear James

Make a special
effort if you
have a special
message

A few times every year a special message needs to stand out and be noticed. You cannot send lots of special messages – otherwise they wouldn't be special. But there will be major events, a major change to the management team or the purchase of another business when the story must be told in a different way. Use a variety of innovative ways to make your message special. Here are a few ideas that have worked for me.

The personal touch

The easiest way is to write a circular, but you must make sure it doesn't get buried with the rest of the company postbag.

I send the letter in my own handwriting. Sometimes I put a picture or cartoon (often of myself), at the top to emphasise it is different. My handwriting is difficult to read, even my secretary, Barbara has difficulty at times. So when I send out a circular, I write as legibly as possible, so everyone gets the message. They also understand that it was written personally and not created by a spin doctor. I use a fountain pen and I get through a lot of ink. The "Well Done" notes I write to members of staff after a good week, or letters sent following a bereavement or birth, are written with the same fountain pen. Even if the body of a letter is typewritten, I will still add a postscript in my own hand! It is important to get the personal message across.

Our system is designed to save postage costs. Branch mail is only sent out from the office on a Tuesday and a Friday, if you produce something on any other day, it waits for the next posting day. Post your letter separately from the other mail – to make it really personal avoid the franking machine and use a stamp. If the special message is properly received, then it is well worth the cost. Send the letters to each employee at their home. A first class mail shot to all 800 staff, costs little more than £200. It is the cheapest way to ensure everybody gets the message.

Hitting the headlines

I use the weekly newsletter, either by writing the front page or by the addition of a supplement.

The most effective way is to hijack the front page, by creating a bold tabloid headline. This was how we announced the acquisition of Automagic. Recent headlines have covered watch repair, dishonesty, and a record week.

If you have advance warning, such as the launch of jewellery repairs, or a new range of shoe repair materials, publish a magazine supplement to the newsletter. This is a four-page A5 edition of the company magazine concentrating on the one issue. This provided an excellent launch pad for our new training scheme in 1998. In 1999 a supplement described the background behind our move into watch repairs.

Our biggest communication challenge followed the acquisition of Automagic. We entered the final round of bidding on a Thursday morning, almost certain that our main competitor, Mr Minit, would defeat us.

After a nail biting 28 hours, we unexpectedly won the battle. At 2.30pm on a Friday afternoon, we signed an agreement which made us owners of 110 Automagic shops at 9.00 am the following Monday.

Fortunately, the office team were more optimistic than me. They assumed we would do the deal and put together a complete communication pack that not only told our new employees about the acquisition, but also introduced enough paperwork to ensure takings immediately went into the Timpson bank account.

This was a message that had to be delivered personally. Over the weekend, all our area managers, plus a number of volunteers, came to Wythenshawe to collect the information packs. One hundred out of the 115 shops received the information from a member of Timpson management by 3pm on Monday. The remaining shops were informed by 11.00 am the following day. On Wednesday I set out on the road myself, visiting all 110 shops over the next four weeks.

Serious issues

Our weekly newsletter is now the most important opinion former in the business. The front page has carried headlines that have made a real difference.

When we launched our fund raising support for the NSPCC the newsletter carried a picture of a child with the headline "Please Help!" A company-wide survey into drugs was introduced with a front-page article: "The Question of Drugs?"

One of our biggest issues is dishonesty. We work in an industry with a history, (almost a tradition) of petty crime. We use test shoppers and covert cameras to catch the culprits, but I don't just want to deter criminals I want to eliminate dishonesty from our culture.

My answer is to appeal to peer pressure. I hope that my crusade against employee theft will have the same success as the drink driving campaign. In February 1999 I was particularly upset – we had caught 16 people pinching money in the previous two months. My knee-jerk reaction was to write a hard-hitting front-page article for the newsletter. It was the headline that caught everyone's eye: "Betrayed." That one word did more than anything before or since to spread the vital message.

Timpson – the movie

We have put several messages onto video, with great success. We have found a video producer who will work closely with us and produce a quality product at a sensible price.

We don't want an expensive film studio with the emphasis on their artistic flair and little attention to the message we need to get across. Nor do we want a home movie. Amateur videos are just not good enough. Produce a video in the same way as a speech or produce the company magazine. Only think of making a video if I have got something very important to say. Before meeting the video producer, have a clear idea of the main message and list all the points you want to make.

Work with the producer. Tell him everything to do with the project, not just the detailed notes, but also how that project fits into the total company strategy.

It is nerve-wracking watching the finished video product for the first time. We have had our disasters. Once we took a chance casting our own staff as the actors in a role-play situation. Most of them couldn't act and the whole video had to be done again. Don't be put off. We have always, in the end, had an extremely good result.

Our customer care video was preceded by a long discussion on why customer care matters, not just to our customers but also to our staff. Because of this discussion, the film not only concentrated on customer care, but also sold the idea that giving amazing service makes the job more interesting, creates loyal customers and increases individual bonus payments.

At an early stage we decide on the format of the film: do we use actors or real people? Am I going to be interviewed at my desk or just voice over? Am I going to be involved at all? You don't have to spend a fortune to get the best results. We tend to make our films for about £4,000, just enough to provide a quality result.

When the producer comes back with his detailed proposals, I have always accepted his method of making the film, that's where he is an expert – but I look through the script in detail, not only to ensure the message is correct but to see that they are using our terminology.

Very often I take part in the video with a filmed interview. Once they have set up the lighting, the camera equipment and the autocue, the filming itself can take less than an hour. One of the great attractions of the video film is that it doesn't take much time.

The first videos we produced were just used at meetings, at road shows or by area managers when they called a shop. Once I discovered it only cost £1.50 to produce a duplicate, we had a change of plan. We now send videos to everybody in the business. They are personally addressed to everybody at their home. At first I was concerned that this would be seen as an invasion of personal privacy. That doesn't seem to be a problem, but make sure you get the packaging right. The first videos we issued were sent in plain brown envelopes. Four people complained that their wives suspected that they were ordering unsavoury films through mail order. We now put a clear message on the outside to indicate what film is inside!

If a job's worth doing

Writing the headlines for a newsletter or discussing the script of a video might not seem vital jobs for a chief executive, but one of my most important roles is to communicate.

Our management style is based on persuasion and delegation – everyone in the business needs to know what is going on. The important messages must come across clearly – it is up to the chief executive to write the headlines.

Area managers' conference

Our area managers have the most important role in the business. They look after the people who look after our customers. They ensure standards are maintained in every branch and turn head office ideas into action. But area managers have an isolated role. They need regular meetings to keep up-to-date with company facts, understand our plans, give their views on our ideas and, perhaps most of all, to meet their colleagues from other areas.

Dear James

Area Managers are your best link with the shops

You need four area manager meetings a year. They are more important than board meetings and should be planned well ahead, with the dates kept firmly in everyone's diary.

Setting the agenda

The meetings usually start in the middle of the morning and last until lunchtime the following day. I open the meeting with an up-date on our business plans. There will always be a closed session when the area managers meet together to discuss where they have problems with company policy or head office management. Their views are reported back confidentially to myself and Kit Green, our managing director.

The most important part of an area manager meeting is the evening at the bar when they can compare notes with their colleagues. Don't interfere with the process. The last thing they want is head office management getting in the way by organising a formal dinner.

The purpose is to help them to do a better job. Tell them the things they want to hear, it is not the right time to issue orders. Help them understand how the company is thinking and talk through the its ideas. Don't just talk about your priorities but explain why you have chosen them. Try and get an outside speaker to widen their experience. We have had guests from Vision Express, our PR consultant, Max Spielman and the NSPCC. The conference should have a main theme. Weeks before the meeting, decide the message you want to get across. Ask yourself two questions: What will most help area managers to improve profits? How can I make their job easier? The answers give you the content of the conference. The theme should strengthen a main plank of company policy. It is easy for area managers to get buried in the detail and lose sight of the main principles. One conference, based on "being the best at what we do," gained the support of area managers in our drive to become fully qualified watch repairers (not just people who put in watch straps and batteries), and it highlighted the critical role of our training programme. We explained we wanted to "be the best" so that we could become a market leader that did not rely on low prices, and they welcomed the idea. For two days they told us how we could do better rather than giving reasons why it couldn't be done.

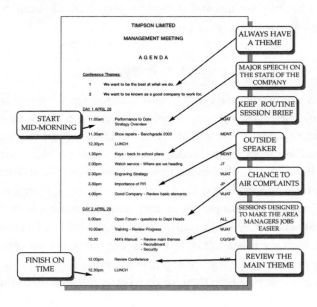

Make it fun

You want your area managers to look forward to their conference. A history of well planned past conferences will make a big difference. A reputation for running conferences that are interesting, relevant and help make an area manager's job easier brings an audience full of enthusiastic anticipation.

The social side is as important. Don't be mean. Choose a comfortable hotel with a leisure centre. Ask the area managers which hotel they prefer. Once a year we organise a special event linked to the conference – a half-day activity designed to take everyone's mind off work. Paint balling, go-kart racing and clay pigeon shooting have all been excellent curtain raisers to a successful conference.

Good speakers

Never allow the conference to be a soapbox for head office executives. Anyone who contributes to the conference must sell their ideas. For years I have been preaching that head office provides a service to the branches. That style of management must be reflected throughout the conference. Every speaker should persuade, explain and never issue orders. Everybody should be willing to listen to area managers' comments.

No session should last longer than 40 minutes and everyone must keep to the timetable and stick to their script. The conference should have been carefully planned and fully rehearsed.

Don't use poor speakers, however good they might be at their job, if they cannot make a decent presentation, find someone who can. This gives your executives the incentive to acquire good presentation skills. You must be present throughout the conference, listening to every word. Be prepared to interfere if things go wrong. The biggest problem is timekeeping. Some speakers don't know when to sit down!

The longer they speak, the more they stray from the point. It is your job to keep discussion on the chosen theme. As chairman, you must ensure that the area managers have a chance to say their piece. You

251

already know what head office has to say. The new ideas from the conference will be raised by area managers.

If you seriously want a good conference, train your senior executives how to make a presentation. Make sure they know the importance of visual aids and fully understand that their 40-minute talk may take at least six hours of preparation.

Opening remarks

Allow several hours to prepare your own opening address. Start by giving as many facts as possible about current company performance and then talk about business policy.

Over the past ten years, I must have given 40 different talks to area managers about our company plans. The content of my speech does not vary much from one meeting to the next. The consistency of the message is important. People don't want to work for a business that does "U" turns, they don't like being marched up the hill one minute and back again the next. It is reassuring for a team to see ideas work in practice and company policy gradually unfold to create success.

For ten years I have been talking about the decline of shoe repairs and how we need to react. I have made the case for improving our key cutting and engraving skills. When I introduced this theme, our key cutting was worth £2m a year and engraving as little as £250,000, today we have a £15m key cutting business and engraving exceeds £4m. The shoe repair market has declined by 70 per cent during those ten years but our business has prospered.

There are other messages that I gave year after year. I urged everyone to create an excellence gap, to ensure our service was always better than any competitor. That, I said, gave us the chance to charge a better price and be the company most likely to survive in a difficult market. I also made a consistent plea for good customer care and for years have been encouraging the area managers to develop the quality of the people who run their branches, using the turnover figures as their main indicator of success.

I have been using these messages for ten years and they are still as important now as they were when first introduced.

The conference provides a golden opportunity. It makes you develop the company strategy and provides the perfect means of communicating it. Four times a year when you write your opening address, you will have to spend a full day thinking carefully about strategy.

Your main roles as chief executive are to develop the company strategy and communicate it. The conference is the forum that brings these roles together.

CHAPTER 37

The road show

Dear James

Three weeks of face to face contact needs detailed preparation

There are times when it is best to meet everyone face-to-face. The way to make this possible is through the "road show."

Why go on tour?

It is essential at times of major change. After we sold the shoe shops in 1987, I talked to everybody to explain why the deal had been done and announced our plans for the shoe repair chain.

When we bought Automagic in 1995, we had to convince them that a change of ownership meant a change for the better. The road show provided the best way to demonstrate the Timpson culture.

We have used it to introduce other parts of our strategy. It worked well when we introduced the phrase "Amazing Customers" as the objective of customer care. It has also given us the opportunity for some straight talking about theft.

They should not be entered into lightly. It is like taking a sledgehammer to crack a nut. Four weeks planning, three weeks travelling and when it is all over, all you have done is to communicate one company message.

It is tempting to think that you do as much good by sending out a carefully crafted newsletter or an effective company video. But, if the road show is well organised, you will meet most people in the company within the space of three weeks and will end with a much clearer sense of how the atmosphere feels.

Before you commit yourself, make sure you understand what is involved. To cover the country you must visit at least 15 venues in three weeks. Most meetings take place out of the normal shop hours and that means lots of evenings away from home, living out of a suitcase. You will find it almost impossible to do your day-to-day work.

I strongly advise against a road show every year. Once every three years is enough and only then if your message is so important that it is worth giving up three weeks of your time to deliver.

The content

Before you even consider booking a conference room, think carefully about the content of your road show. It is not just a question of whether it is worth you spending three weeks talking to branch staff; even more important is whether the branch staff should stop serving customers to come and listen to you!

The choice of hotel or conference room is important, (don't forget you will be staying in some of the hotels you choose for your road show). Make sure it is easy to find, with adequate parking. Choose a hotel that is good enough to have proper conference facilities. I have suffered at the hands of cheap hotels who do not have the promised equipment. Make sure your venue lives up to the standard of your presentation.

Don't attempt a one-man show. Kit Green and I have always done them between us. We developed a standard format which seems to work well. The presentation lasts between 90 minutes and two hours. For some reason we seem to go on longer with each successive performance. The programme is split into five sections of about 20 to 25 minutes each. My introduction produces up-to-date facts about the business, profit, turnover and recent trends. That is followed by an update on our business strategy and an outline of the themes we will develop. Before introducing our main theme, Kit will talk about another subject dear to our heart – such as good housekeeping, dishonesty in branches and quality control.

We then use a video to introduce our main theme. Immediately after the film, Kit repeats the main points using slides from the video.

I conclude the session by talking about our future plans, allowing time for questions. To end I hand out a take-home pack which summarises the two-hour session.

The audience

Road shows are not just for shop managers. We invite everybody. Most take place in the evening, to avoid taking staff out of the branches during trading hours. Everyone receives an official invitation and the area manager arranges transport. You can still expect some people to turn up late. Don't wait too long, always start the session ten minutes after the advertised time, even if you start with a number of absentees.

People who turn up early can be just as much trouble, particularly if they find the bar. Drink beforehand causes problems. Within 15 minutes the first one disappears to the lavatory and that literally starts a steady stream. Then some of your audience starts to get drowsy and some even go to sleep, however lively your performance. But even this is preferable to those who stay awake and get noisy, laughing at the wrong bits of the video and asking questions just to be awkward. Area managers must not only get everyone there on time but keep them out of the bar.

Slide presentations are easily the most effective. They let you vary your talk according to the audience. It is tedious giving exactly the same presentation 15 times and the ability to inject something different each time keeps it fresh. The use of slides holds an audience's interest longer than a straightforward speech.

The take-home pack is important. It ensures that you send your audience away carrying your message with them. The pack should repeat the slide presentation and the video. Area managers can use the pack on future shop visits. It also gives a flavour of the presentation to those 20 per cent of staff who, for various reasons, cannot attend.

When you have completed the 2,750 miles and you think the road show is over, you still have one more task. You must give the presentation again, this time to the staff at head office.

The road show involves a major personal commitment, but can deliver a powerful message. Every few years it gives you a unique way of coming face-to-face with the majority of the employees. It helps shape the future of the business.

The company dinner

Many people view company dinners with trepidation but to me they are the most enjoyable business occasions of the year.

Dear James

Invite everyone to your company dinner

They have changed a lot over the years. The first ones I went to in the early sixties were formal, even stodgy. Everyone was smart and on their best behaviour. The speeches were dry and we always ate chicken.

Relaxed atmosphere

Things today are much more relaxed, we try and make sure that everybody has a good time. The objective is to say thank you. In doing so, we hope to persuade them Timpson is a good company to work for. The best way to say thank you is to make the evening as enjoyable as possible.

Some years ago we gave area managers total responsibility for local expenditure, and at the same time gave them a bonus linked to area profit. The first thing they cut out was the company dinner. It is an expensive occasion. We invite 150 people at a cost of about £6,000. After four years without one I realised how much we missed them. We now insist that every area has a dinner every 18 months. We don't just invite the managers, we invite everybody who works for us. We also send an invitation to any pensioners who live in the area.

The area manager is in charge of transport (they usually hire some minibuses), it is their job to get everybody to the dinner safely and on time. We organise the rest. It is a formal dinner but because of my earlier experiences, I insist we never have chicken. We generally finish up with lamb or beef with a vegetarian alternative. We start with drinks at the bar and end with a disco. We choose a hotel which is a bit better than expected and more expensive than most people thought we could afford.

Despite the efforts of the area managers at least one mini-bus load of partygoers arrives late. But most arrive early, some very early. The attraction is the free bar. Until recently, drinks were only free before the meal so there was every incentive to turn up very early and down as many drinks as possible before dinner. The free bar was particularly important at Scottish dinners. Some would order a pint of beer accompanied by three large scotches. After one sip, the whiskies were poured into the beer. If repeated three times, they are well set up for the dinner! Some did so well on the free bar, they never made the dinner at all. Once, in Perth, I sat next to someone whose head slowly sank and fell into his soup. This exhibition of excessive drinking made us change the rules. We now have a free bar all night. Surprisingly, the new format has sobered up our dinners.

Although the invitations clearly state jacket and tie, not everybody dresses so formally. That is fine by me, as long as everyone feels comfortable. Most of the girlfriends who come certainly dress up for dinner, and they are ready for the disco.

The format

Everyone is invited at 7pm for dinner at 7.30pm. By the time I arrive, generally at 7.10pm, the bar will be packed. Before the meal, the head office people (usually a small team of six), meet as many invited guests as possible.

When dinner is served, there is a final frantic rush to the bar to obtain beers to drink during the meal. I am beginning to think that jugs of beer on each table would be more welcome than wine.

During the meal I have two main tasks. First, keep the conversation going on my table (we sit in tables of eight or ten), but also keep a close watch on the waiters and waitresses. In some dining rooms the team act with military precision, but others are less organised and staff seem to go missing and the meal can go on for ages.

Once the pudding has been served, I go round to talk to every table. This is my best opportunity to have a word with everybody individually.

As soon as coffee has been served, we give a ten-minute warning that speeches are about to start. Unless we give some sort of indication, we have half a dozen people in the lavatory when Kit Green stands up to say his words of welcome.

The speeches

Kit only speaks for about two minutes, welcoming everybody to the dinner, especially the wives, husbands and partners, and explaining that the dinner is our small way of saying thank you for all the hard work that everyone has put in since the last dinner was held.

My speech takes considerably longer. Over the years I have changed the format and I now give a slide show. But the content has not really changed for ten years. My job is to speak to everybody, not just the employees but also their guests, to tell them something about the company, our performance, and our future plans, but particularly to heap praise on everybody who has been successful in the area.

The highlight comes at the end when I present the prizes. First, I award three mystery prizes with the winners drawn out of a hat. The rest are awarded on merit, to the young employee of the year, the most improved branch, some special prizes and the climax of the evening is the manager of the year, chosen from three nominations which have been announced on the menu. The winner who gets a cheque for £200 is listed inside an envelope which I open at the end of my speech.

The area manager gives a short vote of thanks to the company and then the tables are cleared for the disco. The great advantage of the disco is the noise. I cannot hear anyone speaking and I might just as well go home. I have generally gone by 10.30 pm leaving the area manager and our other senior executives to ensure that everything is kept in reasonable order until the minibuses leave somewhere around midnight.

suppliers' lunch

Seven years ago I adapted the company dinner idea into a suppliers' lunch. This has now become a regular event in the shoe repair trade calendar. It takes place in early December.

We invite all our main suppliers, not just the leather merchants and the makers of key blanks, but also the suppliers of paper bags, public relations, property people, our insurance brokers, lawyers, bankers and the accountants. In addition, I also invite some middle managers. I send a personal invitation well in advance and hardly ever receive a refusal. We have a prompt start at an excellent restaurant, the food is much more important than the wine. People nowadays drink very little in the middle of the day.

My speech takes the form of an annual report, showing the figures, analysing trade and disclosing our future plans.

My guests are always surprised how readily we open up our books and how honest we are about our plans. Many of our suppliers' fortunes are closely linked to our success and they have every right to be given as much information as possible about our progress. My speech finishes in the same way as a company dinner, by making some presentations. Mystery prizes are followed by awards for the best delivery performance of the year, the best innovator, the best new supplier. I also make some special awards to our own staff, for this is the only occasion on which I can publicly praise members of our senior management team.

We finish with the three nominated suppliers waiting anxiously to see who is named in the envelope as our supplier of the year.

I receive lots of letters of thanks after our lunch. You would expect polite suppliers to write letters like that, but the real evidence of success, is the speed in which suppliers accept our invitation in each successive year to hear me make another 30 minute speech about the business.

In favour of Public Relations

Good PR is often the best way of communicating to your staff. We don't advertise. We have never proved that advertising works, but we spend at least £50,000 a year on PR.

> Dear James
>
> You can't delegate PR

The point of PR

One of the things that appeals to me is the idea of getting something for nothing – persuading the media to write about the business without having to pay for advertising. But PR does cost money and it is necessary to justify the expense.

We have no shareholders, so there is no point in seeing our name on the City pages. We are, however, interested in getting our message across both to customers and our staff. They are the target audience of our PR campaigns.

There are two messages. First, we want to be the best known company in our industry. We want our name to be the one that is associated with shoe repairs, key cutting, engraving and more recently watch repairs.

Secondly, we want our name to have a number of positive attributes. We want to be known as the experts with our shops recognised for amazing service.

To the property developers we want to appear a modern successful business with an excellent covenant. To our employees we want to be a good company to work with a rosy future.

Creating a story

Don't let a PR consultant try and change the way you run the business. Their job is to communicate what you do, not change the way you do it. Don't be tempted to get all the staff to wear Union Jack hats or increase the level of discount to students, just because your consultant thinks it will create a good PR opportunity.

Beware of the advertorials where PR is advertising in disguise. It is not the job of PR to propose paid-for advertising or a series of cut price promotions. Special half price offers in the *Daily Mail*, or 25 per cent off for all newly married couples, are marketing ideas and should not be confused with PR.

You will think up most of the good ideas yourself. Do not delegate responsibility for PR. Outside consultants don't know the business well enough to identify things of interest to the media. Don't let an outsider change the business purely to make it more media friendly. As soon as you stop taking a close control of PR, it will become a lot more expensive and a lot less effective.

PR can be great fun. Have the courage to be eccentric. It makes life interesting and can bring a lot of unexpected publicity. Two recent fun promotions have been particularly successful.

In 1996 we introduced our own version of the "Footsie Index" in the City of London. We distributed 20 per cent off "Well Shod City Vouchers" within the Square Mile and used a points system to measure which firms used our service most. The winner of the "Footsie Index" was the firm that brought in the most shoe repairs, in addition, the more shoe repairs we received, the more we donated to Centrepoint, the City charity for the homeless. The scheme captured the imagination of the diary writers. Every quality newspaper carried the story. We had only just acquired our eight City branches and the publicity helped to establish our name in the minds of the commuters.

During the 1997 General Election, a range of blue, red, yellow and white plastic key tops were given to every key cutting customer. Throughout the campaign we published regular results of our key poll showing the percentage of customers who took key tops in red

263

(Labour), blue (Tory), yellow (Liberal), or white (other). We concentrated on the key marginal seats. Our polling method did not correctly forecast the result but it brought a considerable amount of local publicity.

Although PR can be fun, don't get too carried away. You will have some failures, some schemes which seem good to you, just don't appeal to journalists. Don't spend too much time on this type of PR. Even if you come up with a successful idea, don't be tempted to repeat it.

A collection of interesting facts about our business works well with the regional press. A survey of the names used on our house signs got nationwide coverage and attracted in-depth analysis as to why some people stick with the traditional "Bungalow" or "Rose Cottage" whilst others reveal their character by calling their house "Bedlam" or "Wits End."

Unusual jobs also proved popular. Although the articles concentrated on the bizarre, like repairing a leather pouffe and cutting keys for a chastity belt, they showed Timpson as an expert business where a wide variety of useful jobs can be done.

Communicate your culture

Promote the company culture by announcing relevant initiatives. My first, and probably still my most successful PR campaign, was based on the launch of our Code of Practice, published in 1975 with the support of the Office of Fair Trading.

That Code of Practice had all the elements of a PR success. It was innovative, it was about customer care and, most important, it had Government backing. The resultant publicity gave Timpson a reputation for good service and established good customer care firmly in the minds of most Timpson employees.

We try to position the company as the consumers' champion. A current campaign about car keys follows this trend. We are publicising the problems that result from the sophisticated electronics now put into car security systems. We applaud the higher security but at the same time the poor customer finds it enormously difficult to get duplicate keys made. We have produced a consumer guide to the new car keys, showing we are on the consumers' side.

Be the media star

The person who runs the business is always in the best position to get the company message across. If the chief executive is seen to be on the side of the consumer, everyone will assume the whole business cares about customers.

Most companies have the attention of the City press at least twice a year, when they publish their results. The City desk is not interested in private companies but they are interested in people.

With our surname (Timpson) being the same name as the business, we are potentially the best PR asset the company has got. You have to accept a certain loss of privacy and allow your personality to be the lead of every press release.

The name is particularly useful on radio and television. The broadcast media are reluctant to provide free publicity by mentioning company names but they can't avoid your name even though it is the same as the company. If there is a radio or television interview, don't delegate. Do it yourself.

If possible, go to the studio. It is never as easy to do an interview down the telephone. Even a local studio, with a special telephone line is not always as good as it should be. Twice, at Radio Manchester, I have tried to give a telephone interview while listening to my own words in the headphones being played back seconds later. It is always better to see the interviewer face-to-face.

It is not always plain sailing when you go to the studio. In the early days of commercial radio, I went to the BRMB station in Birmingham.

It was a little office stuck in the suburbs. There was no receptionist, you just picked up a telephone when you arrived. I was told to go upstairs and walk straight into the studio, where I met the presenter. As soon as the presenter saw me, he walked out and left me watching the records go round. No-one had spoken to me and within a minute of arriving, I was in charge of the studio. I could have been anyone walking straight off the street.

If you know your subject, most interviews will go well. Smile, sound friendly and only answer questions that are relevant to getting your point across. The more practice you get at interviews, the better you are likely to be, but every so often you have an absolute disaster. Don't worry about it, interviewing is like riding a bicycle, once you have got experience you don't lose it, if you fall down, have another go as soon as you possibly can.

If you are the front man you have to accept an invasion of privacy. When the press started to show interest in our life as foster parents, we had to decide how much of our personal life we were willing to reveal. We decided that any publicity would be good for the business and would encourage more people to volunteer as foster parents. We have not regretted the decision. Most of the publicity has been complimentary and anyway, you cannot run a business and remain incognito.

Is it time consuming?

Involvement with the media is not particularly time consuming. You might think the business is intriguing but the media soon gets tired of your news stories. Interviews arise infrequently but at short notice. When the chance comes to be on national radio or television, drop everything and do it.

I was amazed in Autumn 1999 when BBC Radio 5 ran an hour-and-a-half phone-in programme about Marks and Spencer and the company declined to send a spokesperson. They should have put their own side of the story.

Personal appearances don't take much time but PR management does. You have day-to-day responsibility for corporate communication and that includes PR. It is worth spending time to get the right message across.

PR will take a good slice of your thinking time but it helps you develop the corporate strategy and is one of the most enjoyable parts of running a business.

Plug your local stars

There is nothing to beat getting a good picture of a branch manager in his local paper. Good local publicity brings an immediate improvement in turnover. When Stan Knagg, our manager in Kirkby, became the shoe repairer of the year and appeared on North West television, his sales increased by 50 per cent.

Local publicity is the main objective of our PR programme. We run regular competitions to find the best shoe repairer, best key cutter, best engraver and now the most expert at watch repairs. We pepper local newspapers with press releases and at least 40 per cent get a mention with half the articles carrying a picture of our shop. Sometimes we get a major piece on the front page. You can't do much better than that.

We look out for stories that will appeal to the local papers. Long service presentations, special hobbies and the awards given at our company dinners, all provide material for local press releases.

We encourage local branch staff to seek their own publicity. It ensures that if any press approach them, they welcome them with open arms. But publicity achieved by the initiative of local staff is a bonus. It is our job at head office to organise the press releases. All we ask of the staff is to smile at the camera.

Does PR pay?

It is difficult to measure the benefit of PR. Our £50,000 a year compares favourably with the cost of the airtime and column inches we achieve. It is impossible to link any turnover benefit directly to PR, although there is evidence that sales increase at a local level.

PR does a great job for internal communications. When we

launched the Code of Practice in 1975, we immediately improved our customer care. The publicity about our fostering in 1997 encouraged employees to see us as a good company to work for. On the evidence, PR gives good value for money and beats advertising at getting our message across, but always keep an open mind on advertising.

The success of PR isn't determined by how much money you spend, it depends on the effort you personally put into the project. With your commitment and a certain amount of luck, PR will get your message across.

Confession

I have a confession. This book started as a PR exercise. It was the brain-child of Michael McAvoy who has advised me on corporate communication for 23 years. I was trying to find a way to improve our standing on the high street. I have always felt that our type of shop is underestimated. We are tarred with a cobbler's image of being amateur, dirty and old fashioned. His idea was to publish a book to emphasise that we are modern, well managed and a good company to work for. He expected me to find a ghost writer, never thinking I would write every word myself.

Now it is written, I don't care whether it is a PR success. Forcing me to sit down and pass on the tips of 35 years is, in itself, a worthwhile exercise. If this book improves our image at the same time, let's treat that as a bonus.

what business books don't tell you

Be approachable

You can't run the business by being aloof. Status symbols and personal lavatories get in the way of good communication.

An incident that occurred 30 years ago still sticks in my mind. We had a large head office and warehouse employing about 400 people. There was a big car park well away from the office and (closer to the front door), parking bays numbered 1 to 35, the lower the number the nearer your car to reception. The number of the parking bay was as precise a measure of progress through the business as a golf handicap. One day, a branch manager was called in to see the personnel department. He was unaware of the parking system and selected bay two because it was empty. Twenty minutes later, Geoffrey Noakes, the deputy chairman, arrived and found that his bay occupied. He parked his Rolls Royce directly behind the car blocking his way and he stayed in the office until 6.30 pm. The poor shop manager, who had made a special journey on his day off, had to stay all day waiting for his car to be released. You don't win over the workforce by pulling rank.

When we moved to our present offices (just for the shoe repair business) in 1987, I had no parking bays. Seven years later we painted white lines to fit all the cars in the car park. Everybody comes on a first come first served basis; it is just as likely to be my car parked by the rubbish skip. The only designated space, just by the front door, is for the employee of the month.

Walk the office

The way you go about your work at the office really matters. I don't go

there for a series of meetings, I go to meet people. It is just as important to find out what's on everyone else's agenda as it is to push the ideas
that you think important.

Most days I wonder where the time goes. I can get to 5.30 or 6 pm
and wonder what I have achieved. I never stop for lunch, having a sandwich in my office, so I must be busy all the time. What on earth have
I been doing? Mostly, it has been talking to people.

I hate the internal telephone. Our offices cover 10,000 feet on two
floors, it takes no more than 40 seconds to walk from one office to
another. I have never made an internal phone call. The telephone is a
rude interruption. Its insistant ring makes the caller more important
than anyone else in the room. If you ring someone else's office, you may
be interrupting a conversation. My aversion to internal telephone calls
gets me walking round the office. Sometimes I barge in on other people's
conversations, but instead of using the telephone, I do it personally. I
find out what people talk about when they don't think I am going to
be there ! By constantly walking round the office and warehouse, and
leaving my own door open, I talk to a lot more people than I would sitting in an ivory tower. I give a frosty reception to anyone who rings me
on the internal phone but I welcome any outside calls from shop staff.

At the end of the phone

It takes a lot of courage to ring the chairman. A call from a member of
the shop staff, is more important than anything else I might be doing.
Sometimes, they ring to report a fantastic week, but usually they are
looking for help.

When I visit shops I never promise anything. I will do what I can
to help, I can't promise because it will be some else's job to sort things
out. I tell them to contact me again if we haven't solved their problem
in a week.

Often the problem is personal- a financial difficulty or a family
problem. I am delighted they feel they can ring me for help.

We tell everyone that if they have a problem they should talk to the
person they feel most comfortable with. Lots of problems can be solved

just by talking, but you have got to choose someone you trust. Their immediate boss may not be the right person at that time.

Direct calls from shop staff help me. They tell me what really is going on. Sometimes they tell me where other staff are being dishonest. We always investigate. These calls are a genuine response to our campaign to cut out dishonesty. Writing a memo to say you will listen and leaving your office door open will not in themselves get people talking. It's a great advantage to have the reputation of being someone who listens. To be a good listener you must be willing to start the conversation.

Who do you know?

If you take an interest in people's lives, they are more likely to show an interest in your business. You will find we have employees with fascinating hobbies – from a female boxer to a ferret breeder, elite athletes, channel swimmers and Olympic weight lifters and the whole kaleidoscope of family life. Tragic stories of premature death and tear-jerking tales of a widower bringing up his four children.

When the business discovered that Alex and I are foster carers, I formed a special relationship with a significant number of employees who have been fostered or adopted themselves.

A lot of our friends are customers and they mention my name when they call at their local shop. I don't understand why, but they are amazed the staff know who I am and have met me. I suppose most people think that you run a business sitting behind a desk.

Travelling back from London, I struck up a conversation with the person opposite. He was a merchant banker working in the City and was one of our customers at Bank Tube. We talked about business from Euston to Crewe. The thing that impressed him was that I knew our manager's name was Martin Wynter. I also knew Martin was on holiday in the West Indies for the next fortnight.

Listen to criticism

You have got to learn to take criticism. Your job is to listen. School masters taught me the benefit of a calm reaction. With five children of our own, and ten times as many foster children, we have made countless visits to the headmaster's study. They have an excellent response to angry parents. They listen, they thank the parent for coming and are absolutely non-committal as to what they are going to do.

If you are criticised, listen and think. If you haven't got the ready answer, don't give one. Don't get ruffled, who knows you might actually be wrong.

Part of the family

To be approachable you have to give of yourself. You can't keep your private life totally away from a family business.

Talk about your holidays and your children, the employees are interested in your lifestyle, who you are and what you do. If I spend a day going round shops with an area manager, the branch staff don't want to know what I said about the business, they want full details about my car (a Lexus, because it looks anonymous and is less vulnerable to vandalism in the multi-story car parks).

A lot of employees visit our home in Cheshire. We hold our Long Service Lunches at home, when we present awards to people who have been with the Company for 25 and 45 years. Every third year, we have an office barbeque. We close down the whole of our office in Wythenshawe, and ship two bus loads of people to spend most of Friday in our garden. Before the business expanded, we held area managers' meetings at our house. Ten area managers fitted comfortably around our dining room table. We now hire meeting rooms at hotels. The area managers now only come to our garden for a paintballing competition. In a family business, it helps for the employees to feel part of the family.

Know the business

There are loads of books to read about gardening, golf, motoring, computing and any other pastime you can think of, but there is no book that tells you about key cutting.

To do your job properly, you need to know everything about the industry. You can't read about it, you have got to find out for yourself.

Out of the office

It is a good excuse for getting out of the office.

When I was a fashion shoe buyer, finding out about the business meant trips abroad. Two separate weeks in Italy, two visits to Paris and two more to Germany. Every other year I went to the United States. I was in search of nice shoes, and also found nice weather and restaurants. Fact finding tours for footwear repairs are less glamorous. Foreign trips are infrequent. Our shops are ahead of the rest of the world, so there is little to learn from our foreign counterparts.

With no trade magazine to spread the news, our suppliers have become the source of gossip, they are also an important source of advice. As the market leader, our prosperity has a profound effect on our suppliers. They are very keen to help us do well. Visit suppliers and make them feel part of our own business. They will be surprised but flattered that you consider their advice so important. You will receive some useful ideas to develop the business.

Link scheme

We now recognise the importance of suppliers through our Annual Suppliers' Lunch. When I was involved in retailing, the relationship I had with footwear manufacturers and agents, was so vital that I introduced what we called a "Link Scheme."

The Link Scheme was a series of measures designed to improve communication. We had an annual Open Day, which included a tour of the warehouse, personal interviews with any member of the Timpson management, and an open forum on suppliers' problems. The Link Scheme provided suppliers with sales information and gave the chance for their staff to work in our shops to get high street experience.

To encourage suppliers to visit branches, we issued a shop contact card, which guaranteed that our branch staff would welcome the supplier and answer questions. We encouraged suppliers to visit our shops because we know that's the best way to get to know our business.

Branch visits

Visiting branches is an essential part of our job. With the introduction of mobile phones, there is now no excuse for sticking behind a desk. Visit some branches every week. It is amazing how quickly you get out of touch.

I run a feature in our weekly newsletter reporting back on shop visits including pictures of the staff I have seen. This tells everyone that I am visiting shops and also pricks my conscience. It makes me go out every week.

I don't normally warn the staff I am coming, so (at least for the first shop of the day), my visit will be a complete surprise. News soon spreads that I am around. One morning I went to Huddersfield and moved quickly on to Bradford, where the phone rang. I answered it and a voice said: "The area manager has asked me to call to let you know that John Timpson is about."

People expect me to carry out a meticulous inspection and point out anything out of line. I don't. Just talk to everybody. Praise anything good and find out as much as you can about the people who work for you. I haven't gone to the shops to tell them what to do, I am there to find out about the business. I want them to tell me what I should be doing.

Staff are much more likely to come up with their impressions and their ideas if you put them at their ease. Don't just talk about the business. Talk about their hobbies, their home, their families and whether they are going on holiday. When they find you are interested in them, they will be much keener to give you their views on the business.

I don't have a routine for shop visits, but I always look at the figures. I cannot understand anybody visiting a branch without wanting to know the exact sales for last week, even for yesterday.

Talking shop

The prime reason for shop visits is to meet the staff, for them to know you and for you to get to know the business. But there is a spin-off. You get lots of new ideas.

Always carry a notepad and a camera. You think you will remember that bright idea but it will be forgotten by the end of the day unless you make a note.

Keep a careful watch on your competitors. I try to pick a route from the car park to our shop that takes me past the opposition. I try to peek at rival shops unnoticed, but we are a small trade and often I get recognised and, if the competitor wants to have a chat, I feel duty

THE MOST IMPORTANT TOOLS OF YOUR JOB

CAMERA

NOTE PAD

bound to stay. A friendly chat with your competitor's staff can tell you just as much as visiting your own shop.

We keep a list of all the shoe repairers and keycutters in the UK. If a new competitor appears, our staff soon tell us about it, particularly when it affects turnover. They are not so quick to tell us when the competitor closes. More than once I have sent a letter congratulating a shop on excellent figures before I have discovered the real reason for the improvement!

Don't always go out on your own, as it's an opportunity to get to know middle management, not just area managers, but head office executives as well. A full day one-to-one conversation in a car can teach you a lot.

I try to go to every shop every year and usually fail, but I only miss about five shops in any 12 month period. We design the shops to look exactly the same, so why visit them at all? The shops might look the same, but the staff are all different and it's the people that really make the business, that's why you have to go and talk to them all. By regular visits, I keep a picture of each branch in my mind. I can tell you which side the key board is, whether the branch is trading to potential and where they have changed the local car parks. I see all the shops after a refit and check out any new competitors.

I take the shop visiting task very seriously. I receive a detailed list of every shop's turnover every week and every week after a quick glance, I throw the information into the wastepaper basket, but I keep the figures for the last week of December. I use that December list as my record of shop visits, as each shop is seen I cross it off the list. By July or August, I will have been to about 200 shops, only another 100 to go! That's when I go to the garage and buy another road map. On the map I circle every shop I haven't visited, this helps my journey planning from then until December in my quest to visit every branch.

Statistics

I don't learn much about the business from our computer. It isn't there to give you new ideas, but it is useful to check out your theories.

For 25 years my mood has been reflected by the weekly sales figures. A big increase on last year put a spring in my step but being down was real worry. Our constant contact with the shops gives a feel for the level of business every day, but judgement comes on a Monday morning when the computer reveals a precise total for the previous week.

I used the weekly sales figures as a trigger to send complimentary letters to people who had done well, but in our business turnover can fluctuate wildly – a big trophy order or a contract for key cutting can suddenly produce a record week.

I now base my congratulatory letters on a monthly print out, but even those figures are not the perfect basis for praise. A well done letter means so much more when you know the person you are writing to.

Gossip

I like to keep up with the business gossip. Since the introduction of our weekly newsletter, I can now read about events in Timpson which are just as colourful as Coronation Street. The informal tone of our news letter, tells us a lot about what's going on. The lists of unusual jobs and star performances, celebrity customers and impossible complaints all bring the weekly sales figures to life. The newsletter reflects the mood of the business, it is a thermometer to measure morale.

I want to know as much about people as I am told about figures, especially the special events in their lives. When I hear of births, marriages, or a tragic bereavement, I write a letter, always hand-written including a hand-written envelope.

I have met most of our people, several I know particularly well, but it's not possible to know all 900, so I cheat. We have our "known as" list, which shows the manager of every branch and the name by which they prefer to be called. It's amazing how many people don't want to be called by the name their parents chose. Write every personal note by hand and use proper ink, including the Christmas cards. We send out about 1,200 Christmas cards a year to pensioners and staff. It is well worth signing each one individually. Make sure the Christmas cards don't go through the franking machine.

You cannot know enough about your own business. A chief executive spends most of his time gathering information, not from figures but by walking about. Everyone looks to the chief executive to make the right decisions. A close knowledge of the company gives him the best chance to get things right.

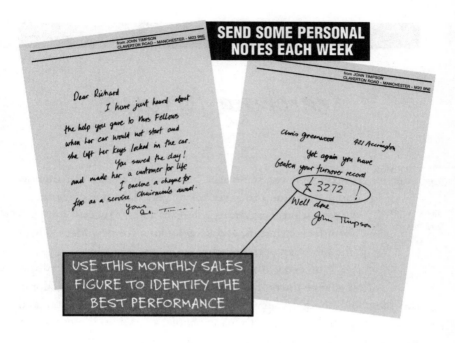

SEND SOME PERSONAL NOTES EACH WEEK

from JOHN TIMPSON
CLAVERTON ROAD - MANCHESTER - M23 9NE

Dear Richard
I have just heard about
the help you gave to this Fellows
when her car would not start and
she left her keys locked in the car.
You saved the day!
and made her a customer for life
I enclose a cheque for
fifty as a service Chairman's award.
yours
J. Timpson

from JOHN TIMPSON
CLAVERTON ROAD - MANCHESTER - M23 9NE

Chris greenwood   421 Accrington
Yet again you have
beaten your turnover record

£ 3272 !

Well done
John Timpson.

USE THIS MONTHLY SALES FIGURE TO IDENTIFY THE BEST PERFORMANCE

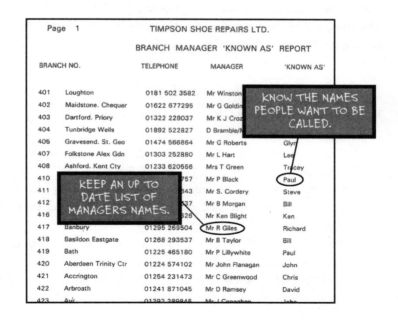

Page 1	TIMPSON SHOE REPAIRS LTD.		
	BRANCH MANAGER 'KNOWN AS' REPORT		
BRANCH NO.	TELEPHONE	MANAGER	'KNOWN AS'
401 Loughton	0181 502 3582	Mr Winston	
402 Maidstone. Chequer	01622 677295	Mr G Goldin	
403 Dartford. Priory	01322 228037	Mr K J Croz	
404 Tunbridge Wells	01892 522827	D Bramble/N	
405 Gravesend. St. Geo	01474 566864	Mr G Roberts	Glyn
407 Folkstone Alex Gdn	01303 252880	Mr L Hart	Lee
408 Ashford. Kent Cty	01233 620556	Mrs T Green	Tracey
410	757	Mr P Black	Paul
411	543	Mr S. Cordery	Steve
412	37	Mr B Morgan	Bill
416	326	Mr Ken Blight	Ken
417 Banbury	01295 269504	Mr R Giles	Richard
418 Basildon Eastgate	01268 293537	Mr B Taylor	Bill
419 Bath	01225 465180	Mr P Lillywhite	Paul
420 Aberdeen Trinity Ctr	01224 574102	Mr John Flanagan	John
421 Accrington	01254 231473	Mr C Greenwood	Chris
422 Arbroath	01241 871045	Mr D Ramsey	David
423 Ayr	01292 288845	Mr J Conaghan	John

KNOW THE NAMES PEOPLE WANT TO BE CALLED.

KEEP AN UP TO DATE LIST OF MANAGERS NAMES.

KNOW THE NAMES OF MANAGERS NAMES.

279

searching for ideas

> **Dear James**
>
> It's your job to look out for new ideas!

No company can stand still. However successful you are now doing the same thing year after year does not constitute a successful business strategy. Regard today's success as a platform for expansion, and keep looking for new ideas. That's the job of an entrepreneur.

Not every one will welcome new ideas. Most people find change uncomfortable, it's much easier to carry on doing the same old thing. A new concept threatens the status quo and inevitably entails hard work. To many people, a new idea is tantamount to criticism. The very suggestion that things can be done better implies that the current team are not doing a decent job. I take a different view. The challenge of running a business is managing change and the fun is developing the ideas that make change happen.

List of problems

Always have a list of problems to solve. Here are five problems I have at the moment:

1. We are short of good staff in London. How do we recruit the right calibre?
2. Our mystery shopping tells us that only 35 per cent of staff have a conversation with their customer. How do we get them talking?
3. Most people in the engraving business do well with trophies. We don't, so what are we doing wrong?
4. Our type of business is given a low priority by property developers. How can we improve our image?

5. Area managers are reluctant to adopt our upside-down management – how do I get them to delegate more authority?

Some people would respond by giving the reasons why the problem can't be solved. An entrepreneur never looks for excuses, but looks for for the ideas that solve the problem.

On the look out

Always believe there is a better way of doing things and constantly look out for ideas that make it happen.

Just because you know the problem, don't expect the answer to pop up straight away. Always be on the look out for a good idea. Good ideas can appear in the most unexpected places. Whether you are at work or at home, reading a book or on holiday, you will be surrounded by good ideas just waiting to be discovered.

In 1995 we were desperately searching for a new shop design. We wanted to upgrade the traditional cobblers' image to become a modern good quality multi-service business. It was important to change the fascia to give the right initial impression. Six months work and £9,000 in design fees failed to provide a solution. One day, I was visiting our shop in Bath when I suddenly realised that I was surrounded by good fascia designs used by other retailers in a quality high street. I photographed every fascia I liked, we stuck the resulting pictures on a board and selected our current fascia design. It was perfect for the job.

Sometimes you don't know you have even got a problem until you see the idea that is going to solve it. Keep an open mind and always be on the look out for someone who is doing something better than you are.

281

Ideas file

If you find yourself saying "that's a good idea !" write it down immediately and, if possible, take a photograph. I keep a file full of good ideas, the ones I have seen but never used. The file has photographs, newspaper clippings, leaflets, sketches and scribbled notes. You seldom get an idea when you need it and if you are not careful, by the time it's useful, you will have forgotten all about it. As well as the file I keep a list which is updated every few weeks. Some ideas are transferred from one list to another for years before they get used.

Six years ago, I had the idea of developing our own special brand of shoe polish, I wanted to call it Cobblers Cream, a special secret formula developed by the people who know most about looking after shoes. Nothing happened for five years, until in 1998, inspired by the success of "Moneysworth and Best" in Canada, we started developing our own branded shoe care products, including Cobblers Cream.

Most good ideas don't need to wait that long. The longer you wait, the less likely you are to give the idea a try. If you sit too long thinking about your latest brainwave, you will come up with your own reasons why it wasn't such a good idea. It is much better to be impetuous and go for good ideas as soon as you discover them. You will make mistakes and some people will think you are a fool, but the ideas which really work will be remembered long after your failures have been forgotten. The best ideas will be remembered because they make a lasting difference. Here are some of my ideas that have stood the test of time.

Shoe classification system

Shoe complaints have always been a headache to footwear retailers. In 1975, when I took the side of the consumer and introduced a generous complaints policy, I put the Company at the mercy of the professional complainer. Although I advertised a money back promise, the wording clearly stated that the customer had to have good reason for complaint and I gave authority to the shop staff to decide whether the complaint was justified.

I told the staff "to put themselves in the customers' shoes." If they felt the complaint justified, they should give customer a replacement pair or the money back.

Our complaints department received more and more unjustified complaints. When I saw that we had given a full refund on a pair of slippers that were covered in mud, I knew I had to do something.

My classification system came to the rescue. I got the idea from the legal concept in the Sale of Goods Act of "fitness for purpose."

I classified footwear according to end use. Using six categories, from indoor wear to heavy duty, I gave customers an idea of the fair wear they should expect and provided our staff with a basis to judge whether a complaint was justified.

Most people thought I was mad. We sold five million pairs of shoes a year and I wanted to put a classification card into every shoe box. We had to send the cards to every supplier, not just in Great Britain but also in Portugal, Italy, Hong Kong and Taiwan I was guided by my youth and ignorance. I ignored the extra administration, the aggravation and cost and six months later, we had a classification card for every shoe we sold. It worked. Our reputation for customer service went up and the number of complaints went down. After three years, the costly classification cards were replaced with more economical stickers. The scheme gained even more credibility after five years when we started subjecting every sample to detailed tests at the Industry Research Association. We left it to the scientists to decide the fair wear category. Ten years after it was introduced, the classification system still applied to all Timpson footwear and it was being actively discussed by the British Standards Institute as a possible European standard. When I sold the shoe shops, the classification system rapidly disappeared from Timpson Shoes, thus saving me the embarrassment of being the originator of a Euro-specification for footwear.

Closing down sales

I learned how to run a closing down sale by accident. The accident was a fire in our shoe shop at Wilmslow. From that incident, I saw that a sale works much better if you close the shop for a few days before it starts. I got the idea from a fire sale, but it also works for floods, bomb damages and closing down sales. Or any sales at all. The longer you close the shop, the better you will do when you start the sale. Cover the window with posters apologising that the shop is closed and announcing the start date and exact time of the sale. To make it even better, advertise while the shop is shut. Even if you don't advertise, I guarantee a queue.

The biggest difficulty of my closing down sale idea is convincing other people that it works. My most dramatic success was the Timpson July sale in 1975. We closed on Wednesday and Thursday, started the sale on Friday, and had a record ever week. Every shop beat last year's figures except Northampton. He had ignored the instructions, never closed his shop and started the sale two days early.

The only other company that uses this type of sale is Next. In their early days all their shops closed for two or three days preceding half yearly sales, but as the company got bigger and more institutionalised, such frivolous tactics were thrown out. But they still block the window with enormous sales posters.

I now run a shoe repair business where the closing down tactic is fairly useless. Even so, I still use it. It even clears off surplus stock of key rings, tankards and shoe polish.

Big keyboard

The big keyboard (which I describe elsewhere in the book), is an example of how a simple idea can completely transform a business.

Dramatically increasing the size of the keyboard display inside our shops has taken our key cutting sales from £2m to £14m per year. It was the trigger that turned us from a struggling shoe repair business to a flourishing multi-service retailer.

Terra nova news letter

In September 1995, I was appointed the Chairman of the Governors of Terra Nova School, a prep school in Cheshire which had already taught four of my children and was in the process of educating a fifth. It was time for me to put something back into the school that had done so much for our family.

I knew I was taking on a difficult task. I had been a Governor for the previous six years and seen a gradual fall in the number of pupils. Immediately prior to my appointment, the school had parted company with its headmaster. The Common Room reported that morale was low (due to pressure of work, and lack of resources), and the gossip at the dinner parties was not good. Some were even whispering that Terra Nova would be closing down.

For two years things got steadily worse. I was consoled by other business men who had joined me on the board of governors, who pointed out that in any turnaround things get worse before they getbetter. While the numbers and morale declined further, we appointed our new headmaster who received a warm welcome from the parents and he, in turn, appointed some excellent new members of staff to form his senior team. The school was starting to get considerably better but the chat about Terra Nova around the Cheshire dinner table was still downbeat. We had to do something about our image. We hired a PR consultant who caused us to spend £40,000 and made little difference. In my spare time from Terra Nova, I was still running the business. I had just introduced our "Good News" notes and started to print the first editions of the *Timpson Weekly News*. It seemed sensible to copy my own idea. I distributed the notes to Terra Nova staff, children and their parents and I used the good news that came back to start a Terra Nova newsletter. It seemed to do the trick, at last all the excellent things that had been happening at the school with our new Common Room team were being spread round the district. Pupil numbers at Terra Nova flourished and there was a rumour going round the Cheshire set that there could be a waiting list.

Necker Island

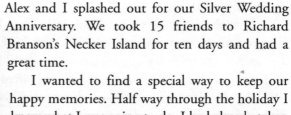

Alex and I splashed out for our Silver Wedding Anniversary. We took 15 friends to Richard Branson's Necker Island for ten days and had a great time.

I wanted to find a special way to keep our happy memories. Half way through the holiday I knew what I was going to do. I had already taken lots of pictures, some of the Caribbean but mostly of people. When I got home I wanted to tell the story of our ten days in words and pictures.

Hello! magazine provided the way to get my message across. I spent a month reliving the holiday and writing my account in the *Hello!* style. I sent a spoof copy of the magazine to everybody who joined us on the best holiday ever.

Dear James

I already know that one of the better ideas was to write this book. During eight months preparing the transcript, I had an excellent chance to think what is most important in the business, sifting through the successes and failures of the last 25 years.

The business will continue to thrive as long as we believe it can be improved. The constant search for ideas will be at the centre of any future success.

CHAPTER 43

Making ideas work

Prepare yourself for the most frustrating part of the chief executive's job. Finding ideas is tough enough but the really difficult part is putting ideas into practice.

Dear James

Make your ideas attractive to everybody !

The quick and easy way is to issue an instruction, but the unilateral approach seldom succeeds. If your idea hasn't got the support of the rest of your team, it is probably doomed to failure.

Unhelpful advice

People will be keen to point out the pitfalls of a new initiative. Their well-meant advice is really designed to stand in the way of progress.

"We have tried it all before."

"We will have a go but you won't be pleased with the result."

"I'm just being the devil's advocate."

"Have you thought of the side effects?"

"Once we have decided, there will be no turning back."

"You could be undermining the staff."

"We are opening the floodgates."

These phrases come from well-intentioned employees who don't share your vision. You must use your powers of persuasion to secure their commitment. That is never easy.

The man who tells you why your idea won't work (Mr "Ah But"), is not nearly as dangerous as the one who agrees with you all the time (Mr "Gunna"). Mr Gunna gives you confidence that you have got good ideas, but he has absolutely no intention of carrying them out, his style is to agree with the boss and do nothing.

Make life easy

Win the support of your colleagues. Their help will increase the chances that your idea will be a success. It is so much better to push on an open door.

Before setting off on the horrendous task of persuading everyone to back your project, make sure it's worth the effort. Be absolutely certain that it really is a good idea. Only back ideas that are very important and have an excellent chance of working. Don't waste time on a pet project unless it will have a major impact on company progress. If your only support comes from people in the business who always back you on principle, assume the idea won't work. You have to make the idea attractive to everybody. Counter the major objections. Look through everybody else's eyes and pose the question "What's in it for them?" People will embrace ideas that are to their own personal advantage. You are much more likely to get the backing of branch staff if the proposal gives them the chance of a bigger bonus. Most people like ideas that make their job easier. Take every objection seriously. If you don't investigate all the pitfalls you won't get wholehearted support.

Be a salesman

It's your job to sell new ideas throughout the organisation and that takes time. Ideally you want everybody to adopt the new thinking as if it was their own, this will happen if you involve others in in the development of the new scheme.

We communicate our strategy through quarterly management meetings. Whenever a new theme is introduced, I explain why we think it will improve the business. I also cover the known objections, giving my reasons why they don't create a stumbling block. I outline the plan and ask for a debate. Three months later, I repeat the process, having taken on board all the comments made at the last meeting. By this stage the scheme is not just an embryo but a well developed plan. I still want their comments, so we have another debate. At the third meeting, six months after the project had its first airing, I am ready to announce firm plans which are still subject to final comment. By this stage, everyone is familiar with the scheme and some claim it was their idea in the first place!

Do a test

If possible test every new idea before you are committed. Carry out the test with the people and in the place where you expect it to be most successful.

Some people suggest tests should be carried out under difficult circumstances "if it works there it will work anywhere." I totally disagree. Give ideas the best chance of success because if it doesn't work there it won't work anywhere else. Don't let anyone else tell you how successful the test has been, go and find out for yourself. Statistics don't always give a proper reading of a new idea and they certainly don't tell you the reason why a scheme has not worked.

We once introduced a new key cutting machine to cut keys for Ford cars. Three out of the ten test branches reported no sales at all. I could have thought there was no business in Ford car keys. But I visited the shops and found a different story. Two branches didn't have any trained staff and in the third hadn't

TEST THE IDEA IN A SMALL WAY

TEST ZONE

GO WHERE IT IS LIKELY TO SUCCEED

VISIT THE TEST PERSONALLY

even received the machine

Test an idea with people who will spread good news if it's a success. Your employees are ten times better than you at putting the message across. Always be ready to change your mind. It doesn't matter how committed you are and how much work you have put into its development if you get the hint it is not going to work, drop it.

In the end, all the good ideas are enthusiastically adopted. If you fail to sell your plan, it probably wasn't such a good idea after all. But if you are successful, leave the implementation to everybody else. Your job is to go out looking for some more good ideas.

Respect your team and delegate

I can't do the most important jobs in the business. I can't cut a key and I can't repair shoes.

Dear James

Let them get on with it !

My first 25 years were concentrated on shoe retailing, I always got a buzz out of serving customers and thoroughly enjoyed working as a sales assistant, particularly on the busy Saturdays before Christmas. I should have grown up to be an expert handyman. My father was able to tackle any job around the house and for a hobby made radio sets and televisions from a kit of parts. He sent me to a school, Oundle, that specialised in engineering, each term we spent a week in the workshops. When it came to the practical skills, I was bottom of the class. When I got married, Alex soon stopped my attempts at DIY, the only room I ever decorated had to be redone by the local expert.

I regret not being able to serve customers when I visit a shop, but my lack of expertise emphasises the importance of delegation. Our business is full of people doing jobs that are beyond my capability.

Some star performers

In 1996, we set the target of refitting 250 shops in just over three years. Rod Umpleby who already looked after all the maintenance, the displays and the opening of new shops, took on this daunting task.

We expect all refits to be completed within a week. It's much easier to organise a big job than lots of small ones, but Rod only added one more member to his staff. Every one of our shops is different, no refit is the same. Half way through the programme I made matters worse by introducing watch repairs. All the refits that had taken place had to be altered, and all the refits yet to be done were made more complicated. Six months after the refit programme started, Rod failed a medical and had a heart bypass operation. He was away for ten weeks and I thought we would really miss him. But the programme continued. Thanks to his careful planning we hardly needed to change anything before he recovered and returned to work. Rod knows how to delegate.

Modern technology makes me feel inadequate when I walk round the office, I am one of the few people who doesn't have a personal computer. Even the telephones have got more complicated. I find it impossible to transfer calls from one office to another, but our switchboard operator can deal with ten lines and do two other jobs at the same time.

Our area managers have a daunting task, they have the responsibility to ensure all branches are fully staffed with skilled people throughout every trading week. Their team is constantly changing, although our staff turnover is lower than other people in the industry, it is still high and they have to find suitable replacements. They are also having the problems of holidays and illness.

I spend about 15 days each year with different area managers. As we travel round in the car, they receive a constant stream of problems: "Can I change my day off?" "George rang in and will be sick for three days." "Gillian will be starting her maternity leave next Thursday and my replacement has taken another job."

I was once in Scotland with an area manager to carry out a detailed inspection. We followed a list which took us into every nook and cranny of the shop. We checked the window displays, the fire extinguisher and the lavatories. No stone was left unturned. , I was about to check the float in the cash box. "There's no point," said the manager. "What do you mean?" I asked. "There's nothing there," said the manager. "What do you mean?" I asked. The area manager looked flustered "It's all at home," the manager said. Within 20 minutes the area manager had checked all the cash, suspended the member of staff, organised for a replacement from the shop down the road, informed head office and before sending the manager home, ensured that he signed a form so that we could reclaim our losses from his accrued holiday pay. To help the area manager complete this task, he asked me to go for a walk and keep out of his way ! I returned 20 minutes later to help him run the shop while we waited for the replacement.

I see humbling examples of excellence every time I visit a busy shop. In places like Milton Keynes, Reading and Hammersmith where we have over 2,000 customers a week, there is a constant hive of activity. I just stand back in admiration and watch them serve the customers.

What makes a good manager?

Good branch staff excel at five things: shoe repairing, key cutting, engraving, watch repairs and most of all, looking after our customers.

The sales in our bigger branches are fairly equally split between the four main services so it is quite possible within 15 minutes for the same person to repair a shoe, cut a key, engrave a tankard and repair a watch. To do that and be really pleasant to customers at the same time, takes considerable skill, a pleasant personality and a lot of patience.

I am asked what makes a good manager and I don't know the answer. All I know is that good managers take good money.

We have a way of measuring each manager against the very best. We call it potential. Potential is the average weekly turnover that is achieved by an expert team good at all our four services and excellent with customers. It is, in other words, the turnover when everything is perfect. This theoretical figure is set by the managers themselves in consultation with their area managers. A bonus is paid each month for sales in excess of potential. It gives everyone a high target to aim for and points out the under-achievers. Where turnover falls you know there is a problem. The manager will usually give you a good reason: "All the shops round here are quiet." "Our competitor has cut his prices." "They have moved the car park." "It's the one way system." It would be easy to accept these excuses, especially as I couldn't do better myself, but a good manager can nearly always put things right.

Let yor managers manage

You have to set standards for the business and do its thinking. You have to communicate the ideas and pick the right people to develop its future. You have to find the ideas that will increase pay. In addition, you must leave time for your family with a few hours left to play golf or tennis.

You can't be a chief executive and run the business at the same time. You have appointed a team to manage the business, let them get on with it. Your job is to advise and to help and particularly to praise but don't go telling everybody what to do, they know much more than you do. There is no need to get involved in day-to-day problems. If a shop burns down, there are plenty of people to deal with the problem.

One of our main suppliers has never had a holiday for 15 years. He is so involved with the day-to-day running of the business he owns, he is fearful of what will happen if he goes away even for a week. I take nine weeks holiday a year, sometimes four weeks at a time, and I don't bother to have the figures sent while I am away. If there is something important, they will soon be in touch.

Recently I did contact the office. Alex has the same lottery number every week and the ticket ran out while we were on holiday. I sent a fax. The reply confirming the new lottery tickets had been purchased ended with a statement "Sales 14 per cent up on last year, stay away". One of the most important jobs of a chief executive is to develop a strong management team and let them get on and run the business for you.

Family business

It's a privilege being born into a family business but every privilege brings obligations. The family firm becomes part of your life from a very young age, whether you like it or not, if the company is a household name, part of the business is bound to invade your household.

Dear James

Its a privilege
- if you use it

Free choice

I first became aware of Timpson at the age of six when I ran in the junior obstacle race at our company garden party. Around the same time my father and mother took me on shop visits. Usually, we visited our shops at Preston, Fleetwood and Blackpool so that business could be combined with the Pleasure Beach.

I involved my own children at a similar age. When we went shopping on a Saturday morning, I couldn't pass one of our shops without calling in. The children particularly enjoyed the time when I was running the Swears & Wells leather and fur business. A favourite Saturday morning game was to get inside the circular rails of coats and twirl them round as fast as they could. The shop managers were always very nice to the children but sighed with relief when they left. In 1975 our three eldest children featured in our window displays. Their pictures appeared alongside quotes – "My mummy loves Timpson," and "This is my daddy's favourite shop." It worked well as part of our campaign to establish a family business reputation for customer care.

The family business becomes really important when choosing a career. I always assumed that I was going into the business. I was probably asked if I wanted to, but I can't remember. My generation didn't really have a mind of its own until the age of 21, so I probably just followed what was expected. You can't dictate to today's teenagers, in fact it is dangerous to do so, a firm parental push in one direction could well lead to a tenacious teenager doing exactly the opposite. So never assume that a son or daughter is going into the family business. There shouldn't be any pressure and certainly no blackmail, but it is always an option. I have given that option to all our children. They have had experience working in our shops and made up their own minds. Two have pursued careers elsewhere, one a teacher, the other a barrister but as they have the same name as the company, their lives are still touched by being part of a family business.

Work experience

If you decide to join, there is no job interview. Father sent me to see the personnel director (causing me to buy my first business suit). I was given a long lecture about company rules and told that my starting salary would be £5.17s.6d per week plus commission. But there was never any doubt that I was going to get the job!

But there are plenty of informal interviews. The workforce put you on trial. They take note of everything you do and everything you say. In particular, they notice what you look like, (are you smart?) they notice your timekeeping, (can you get out of bed in the morning?) and most important of all, they notice how well you get on with people. The big test is whether you are able to work alongside colleagues to the extent that they almost forget who you are.

For the first few years you are severely judged by your peers. It's the

THE ENTIRE WORKFORCE PUTS YOU ON TRIAL

people on the shop floor that will decide how far you go, not your mother, father or the board of directors. You work alongside some very hard task masters who expect you to be better than anyone else.

Don't think you are better

just because you have got the same name as the company. If a young man or woman waltzses into the family firm brandishing their silver spoon with an aloof air of superiority, they will not gain the respect they already think they deserve. You don't inherit a reputation, you gain it through hard work. If you are to lead the business, the employees have to trust you. You must gain that trust at an early age.

To be a success, the business must be a large part of your life. Your commitment must be total. If, on the other hand, you go into the family firm purely for a job, that's all you will get. Our son Oliver who, at the age of 23, still finds it difficult to get to grips with life, falls in the latter category. His first spell with the business came to an end when poor timekeeping led to three warning letters and the inevitable dismissal. No member of the family can be allowed to undermine their area manager.

The younger you are when you start, the easier it is to work at the shop floor. All our children have cut keys, repaired shoes and served customers before the age of 19. School and University holidays are ideal for work experience. When I left school, my father wanted me to have a year in accountancy. I joined an audit team in Manchester but after six weeks I couldn't face any more ticking off figures and became an assistant at our local shoe shop in Altrincham. I was hooked, I loved the business, and from then there was no doubt where I wanted my career to go.

It's a good idea to get experience elsewhere. My father was right to suggest I didn't go straight into the business. In my case the accountancy didn't work, but after I had been to University, I spent six months working at Clarks Shoes in Somerset. Most of the time was spent working on a production line making children's sandals. Not being a practical sort of chap this was a particularly difficult task. The most enjoyable part was the three days when the factory went on strike!

It was fairly easy to gain experience in another company when I was young. Clarks ran a "customers' sons scheme," (presumably it wasn't expected that daughters would go into commerce). Today it's not so easy to get a job, as our son James found when he left university. After several interviews, it was clear that other retailers were reluctant to

employ somebody with a well known High Street name. We used shock tactics and produced an advert offering James's services on a six months free trial. Six national companies received the advert, three responded and one came up with a job. Johnsons the Cleaners were attracted by the inventive approach and offered James the chance to sell textile rental hire in the north-east of England. Twelve months cold calling as a sales rep to the Geordies was an extremely good grounding.

Making a mark

It helps to come to the business with some experience having made your first mistakes elsewhere. But don't be deceived. When you get your first role you are not an experienced executive. There is still a need to get your hands dirty and work unsociable hours. A 12 month stint working as a shop assistant is the best possible training for retail management and the best way to gain the respect of colleagues.

Don't stop getting your hands dirty when you get promoted. The advantage of experiencing day-to-day business has been very well demonstrated in a television series called "Back to the Floor." Meeting customers face-to-face teaches the chief executive much more than a meeting in the board room.

Christmas is a good time to work in branches. When I was running the shoe retail shops, I always spent the last two Saturdays before Christmas as a shop assistant in Liverpool or Manchester. I am pleased that James is carrying on the tradition with his 'Christmas Challenge'. Five branches challenged him to work a day in their shop during December to show whether he could increase sales.

The biggest problem for a father or mother in a family business is to be objective about their children. The temptation is to promote too quickly and pay too little. You need someone else to tell you how the rest of the world sees your son or daughter. I rely on my non-executive directors, Patrick Farmer and Roger Lane-Smith. Patrick spends a lot of time with our son James. He knows him very well. He has determined the pace of his promotion and checks his level of pay. You should always ensure that family members get paid the proper rate for the job. No more, no less.

When your name is the same as a shop on the High Street, your family is always on show. Many people think you are rolling in money, particularly local traders.

Several years ago I wanted to have a family photo taken as a birthday present for Alex. I was getting quotes of three or four hundred pounds. I asked Alan Ackrill, a colleague in the office, to find a photographer. He succeeded in booking a session on a Saturday morning for £45 inclusive of all proofs and prints. The only snag was I had to announce myself as Mr Ackrill and discipline the children not to say who they were. It all worked well. The children behaved themselves and within fifteen minutes the portraits were taken. The final result was so successful, it is still hanging both at home and in my office.

Circle of friends

The family has an impact on your local shops. Our Northwich manager recently told me: "You have an awful lot of friends." People whom you have only met once suggest they are bosom pals when they are customers. When I was a shop assistant, customers said how well they knew my grandfather or my father expecting me to come up with a discount. I never revealed my identity.

Shortly after we got married, our family connections seemed to bring a wider and wider circle of friends. But later when the business was taken over and we found life more difficult, we discovered who our real friends are. After a time you detect superficial friendships.

It is not easy marrying into a family business, as Alex discovered on her first visit to a Timpson shop after our wedding. She took a pair of shoes to be repaired in Lloyd Street, Altrincham. The assistant who was filling in the ticket asked for Alex's name. "Timpson," said Alex. "You what?" said the assistant in disbelief. "Timpson," repeated Alex. "Yes, and I'm Queen Victoria," said the assistant. Alex doesn't have any problems like that anymore. She is fairly well known round the business, not only is she my greatest supporter, she is also my greatest critic, particularly when it comes to standards of housekeeping. We were in Berkshire for a wedding in 1998 and it gave us the chance to visit our unit in Asda on the outside of Reading. The cleanliness fell well below Alex's standards and she decided to do something about it. I have a picture hanging in my office of Alex hoovering the carpet in Reading as a constant reminder of the standards we have to maintain.

The family doesn't want to hear about business all the time – this becomes a problem as soon as a son or daughter gets involved. Before long you are talking shop across the dinner table. Try to keep business talk in the office, for the sake of the rest of the family.

When I was young I saw the problems that can be caused when family members don't see eye-to-eye. Fortunately, I have enjoyed total support from the family during 25 years. Too many family members can be bad for the business. There are not that many big jobs to go around, but it's essential that there is at least one member of the family to look after the shop. Once you hand the management over to someone else, it's time to think about selling the business.

Don't underestimate the value of family management. Fairly recently I listened to the strong views of a banker who could only see things in terms of black and white. Professional management on the one hand, family management on the other. All he had to do was to look for family businesses and there was a business that needed turning round. He got it totally wrong. A family business has a tremendous advantage,

people know where they stand, they know who they are working for and there are no politics getting in the way. There is a big advantage being a family member heading a family business, it's up to us to use it.

CHAPTER 46

Life must go on

Your contract of employment as chief executive doesn't specify the number of hours. You decide. You must find the right place in your life for work. Don't feel guilty about taking time off from the office, the happier you are, the better job you will do. You have to devise your daily routine and monthly calendar to keep work in its place and allow you to live a life of your own.

> Dear James
>
> The most important side of life is your family !

Sporting life

I got the sport bug at an early age, hours of my childhood were spent kicking a football or batting a tennis ball against the garage door. Lack of talent didn't dampen my enthusiasm.

I was a keen spectator. In the fifties it was acceptable to support Manchester City and Manchester United. Later ,when I had to make a choice, I expressed my individuality by opting for City. I was a junior member of Lancashire County Cricket Club. On several days each holiday, my mother packed me off with a box of cheese and tomato sandwiches and I got a bus and a train to watch the play at Old Trafford. I am one of the few people who watched every ball at Old Trafford between England and Australia in 1956 when Jim Laker claimed 19 wickets.

When I was at university I played golf nearly every day. I was very lucky, golf was not as universally popular as it is today, so I was one of six students who could play at Wollaton Park Golf Club, 400 yards from my Hall of Residence. The Golf Club charged a special university subscription of £3 per year of which the University Union paid half.

As I was playing five rounds a week during the University term, my golf cost me a penny a round.

Back home, a regular working week came as a shock after the freedom of university, but I filled the weekends with sport. During the summer it was golf in the morning and cricket in the afternoon Saturday and Sunday. In the winter I replaced cricket with hockey.

Things changed when I got married. I didn't play golf on a Sunday afternoon. When my daughter was born, I stopped Saturday morning golf. By the time we had three children, my sporting weekend almost disappeared. I started playing squash and joined the local club that had a monthly league. In theory you got four games every month, but it was difficult to fix a convenient time with everyone else in the league. Eventually, my sporting life had been reduced to a game of squash every fortnight.

When I sold the shoe shops in 1987, I changed my routine and sport came back on the agenda. I started to play games when normally I had been at the office. It felt strange at first, playing when I should be working, but I overcame the guilt by finding people who would play with me early in the morning. I started by fixing a regular weekly tennis lesson at 8.00 am. I then met up with a friend, Gordon Long, who was happy to play golf at 7.30 am. We have been playing once a month for the past ten years. I then started to be more adventurous and played sport during the working day. I had a weekly game of squash and more recently tennis with Tom Wrinch, this is usually an early start, another 7.30 am game but sometimes creeps into the afternoon.

In the last three years I have discovered Real Tennis and that takes two hours out of a working day. Weekend sport is back on the calendar, whenever possible I play golf on a Saturday morning. During the Winter I hold a fortnightly snooker evening when we consistently prove what a large gap there is between the ordinary amateur and the professional game.

Each year I play one or two golf challenge matches against Thomas Black, an ex-shoe trade colleague who is the most competitive individual in Britain. An example of his keeness was shown one day when I played against him at Hoylake. The weather was so bad no one was on the golf course but, when I arrived, Thomas was changed and ready to go. Responding to his determination I came up with a new rule – "The first person to suggest we give up loses." The rain was unrelenting. After four holes I was so wet I gave up using the umbrella. It was the most miserable game of golf I had ever played, but I was in the lead so there was no way I was going to suggest we walked in. Hoylake goes all the way out to the ninth green and you don't see the club house until you have played 13 holes. By then Thomas was three down with five holes to go and soaked to the skin, I thought there was a strong chance he might throw in the towel. He didn't give in until missing a four foot putt through hailstones on the sixteenth green to lose the match.

Fortunately, the rest of my golf is more relaxing and living near the Lancashire coast play at some of the best courses in the country including Lytham, Birkdale and Hillside.

Outside interests

I am not a committee man but have occasionally been tempted to take an interest in things outside the business. It's easy in a weak moment to be flattered: "If you want someone to do something, go to a busy man," and, before you know it, you are sat round another meeting table.

I have been fortunate that in most outside interests I have fulfilled the role of chairman, so at least I have had some say on how long the meetings are going to last.

I have been chairman of the Regional Citizens' Advice Bureau Committee, I was chairman of the Governors at our local Secondary School in Wythenshawe, Brookway High School and I spent a short period working as an Adviser for the Princes' Business Trust.

My longest involvement has been with the local preparatory school, Terra Nova, first as a governor and subsequently as chairman of the Governors. Being chairman of a prep school goes well beyond just sitting in meetings. You find you are running another business. Terra Nova has a turnover of over £1m employing 50 people. But is not as easy as running a business because you not only have responsibility to the staff you are also closely vetted by the parents. Our shoe repair customers don't ring me up out of hours. I don't get a key cutting customer giving me a call at home but some parents see nothing wrong in ringing the chairman of governors on a Friday night.

Working routine

In an attempt to get the right balance between work and leisure, I have introduced a few self imposed rules.

I try to visit every shop every year and I always visit some shops every week, except when I am on holiday.

We hold a board meeting every month (apart from August), and the dates are firmly fixed 12 months in advance. We have a meeting of area managers four times a year and hold a company dinner in each area of the country every two years. I usually try and go out with each of the area managers once a year.

Anything I have put in the diary I regard as a firm commitment and that rule applies equally to business and pleasure appointments. I avoid staying away from home as much as possible, although some overnight stays are inevitable. I can't avoid the early morning starts. Living in Cheshire with the majority of our shops based in the South, I have the permanent problem of negotiating the M6 through Birmingham. As long as I leave home before 5.30am I have every chance of missing the worst congestion.

Family fun days

For several years I took Tuesday off; it was the regular day each week when Alex and I went out together.

During the first year of this arrangement, we spent some time fighting an application to dig a sand quarry near to our house. We just failed to stop the Council approving the application but in the process we got to know our neighbours. We spent our days out pursuing places listed by the National Trust viewing gardens open to the public and following the advice of the *Good Pub Guide*. We discovered the pleasure of going racing. Once or twice a year we visit Chester and Bangor on Dee and also visited Cheltenham, Chepstow, Ascot, Windsor, York and Kelso. (Although we don't take racing very seriously, Alex would love to own a racehorse. I am happy to leave that as a yet unfulfilled ambition.) The nearest we have got is a greyhound. The business has owned two greyhounds. They were both based at Belle Vue. Greyhounds usually run every week and not only win prizes but they get appearance money. We reported on the progress of the greyhound each week. All the greyhound's winnings were awarded to our shop of the week.

Full time fostering

The regular day out together worked well for three years until it was Alex who changed her routine. The foster children took over. Alex now spends more time working with children than I spend working on the business.

Originally foster children stayed with us for six months and then were gone. Today we are not only involved with the children but are also in close contact with the parents. The plan is almost always for the foster children to return to their family home and Alex becomes closely involved in helping the mother and sometimes the father to be reunited with their child. The relationship often continues when the foster child has left our home. Inevitably Alex maintains her interest in the family and has, as a result, an ever increasing list of past foster families in which her interest goes well beyond buying presents at Christmas. Few people understand the dedication that Alex has to her fostering commitments, so a few years ago I wrote about it. (That account is included in Appendix 1)

With the regular Tuesday off erased from our calendar, we had to find another way of meeting up. The answer was holidays.

On holiday

I do some of my best work when I am holiday! I have written our company newsletter in Majorca, Barbados and St Lucia. I developed our training schemes while I was in the Isle of Lewis and the notes for this book were written when in Mustique.

The only holiday that completely excludes work is when we go skiing.

We enjoy going away with friends, have had some wonderful holidays with the children but the best holidays of all are when there is just the two of us. I spend a minimum of eight weeks a year away on holiday and at least half of those weeks are just with Alex.

Work is much more fun when you have got a holiday to look forward go. I can keep going for months in the knowledge that in January I will be sitting on Macaroni Beach in Mustique.

Holidays are our extravagance. It's the only time when we spend a substantial amount of money on ourselves and the real extravagance is Necker Island, Richard Branson's holiday home near Virgin Gorda which really is better than you ever imaged. You rent the whole island, so you have a holiday surrounded by your friends and family. Necker is our special treat, we go there once every three or four years.

In 1997, during a television programme about our time as foster parents, the interviewer asked Alex whether she ever felt guilty about going on such expensive holidays. She quickly answered "No." "Perhaps we should feel guilty," she added, "but we both work pretty hard and why shouldn't we spend some of the money on ourselves?"

No peace at home

"It's all right for you, you can get out to the office for some peace," complains Alex, who is permanently tied to her place of work. She is absolutely right. Our home Sandymere is no resting place. One of the sad things about a home that has everything is that you feel guilty that you don't use it enough. We have a beautiful garden, croquet lawn, all weather tennis court, covered swimming pool, even a small golf course, but you can't use those things all the time. Alex has her answer to that problem. She invites other people in to use the facilities, particularly the swimming pool. Cubs, Brownies, the local Hospice, and the primary school together with people with bad backs all use the swimming pool. Sandymere is full of people. Not just the family and the foster children, but the domestic staff and their children. The gardeners and often the decorators, the window cleaner and the friend that is dropping in. It is not unusual to find more than twenty people around at lunchtime.

We live in a lovely home but we have to go away to have a rest. Fortunately, we not only have our holiday but we also have a bolt hole – a small house in Uppingham – bought for convenience when we had children at the school there

Working Sundayss

Don't feel guilty about working at home on a Sunday. There are certain jobs you can't do at the office – thinking and planning ahead are two of them.

An office has its problems. It's a place where you meet other managers in the business and that is good. You can develop your strategy by chatting it through with the rest of the team. Office workers fill their diary with meetings and that's bad. Meetings are given undue priority above everything else, as they tie everyone to the office and stop the management viewing the real business out in the shops. My open door policy leads to constant interruptions and prevents the peace and quiet required for clear thinking. There are times when you need a place where the office door is firmly closed to be left on your own to think through future strategy and plan your diary. The study at home provides peaceful isolation.

Planning the diary

Diary planning is an important task that can't be delegated. It sets your routine. I am usually in the office on Monday and Tuesday and out for the rest of the week. Pleasure is just as important as business. Two hours careful diary planning can create an awful lot of leisure time during the months ahead.

New challenges

I need the challenge of tackling something new. There always has to be a project. This book has been the latest challenge. I started it in

Mustique in January 1998 and took considerable determination to finish the first draft before December.

The London Marathon set me on a series of physical challenges. I had already taken part in the trade charity 26 mile walk when I watched the first London Marathon on television. It was the spur I needed. Despite being a slow runner, within days I was hooked.

I was unable to do any better than five and a half hours on my marathon debut on a hilly course near Bolton.

The London course is flat, encouraging fast finishing times. I was able to set a personal best of four hours and 20 minutes, which I beat by ten minutes the following year. These marathons were a good way of raising money for charity by putting unashamed pressure on suppliers. I collected an average of £5,000 each time.

I entered the London Marathon for a third time but my application was rejected. I entered the Paris Marathon instead. I travelled to Paris on a package coach tour. There was a snag. The coach left the finish five hours after the start, anyone unable to run a marathon in less than four and a half hours would miss the bus. I made it with over half an hour to spare. I spent seven hours in the coach and on the ferry surrounded by sweaty people, all looking forward to a shower. Eventually we arrived at Waterloo Station. I took a taxi to the hotel where Alex was waiting in our five star bedroom. I woke her up as I stumbled through the door, expecting to hear a warm welcome but all she said was, "God, you smell, go and have a bath."

After five marathons, the next project was on a bike. To coincide with my Presidency of the Boot Trade Benevolent Fund, I decided to cycle from Clarks, in Street in Somerset, to Startrite in the middle of Norwich. It was 300 miles, took four days and I never wanted to ride a bike again. But I did get back on a bicycle, on a mountain bike trip to France. Most of the party had only just started mountain biking and I was fresh from my trip across England. It was a pleasant three day trip. Three years later, I joined the same party mountain biking in the Yorkshire Dales. Since our visit to France they had all become serious mountain bikers. I hadn't been on a bike at all. With no training I was soon left behind. It is unlikely that I will take up a major physical challenge again.

The biggest challenge

Most big projects are connected with the business but the most important difficult challenge is to achieve the right balance between your business and family life.

Disaster stories

Business can be associated with failure as well as success.

Business biographies don't often mention the disasters. Bad news is swept under the carpet and soon forgotten. But you can learn a lot from mistakes, so I have put together a collection of blunders from our past.

Inexperienced buyer

Shortly after I had been given a job in our ladies' shoe buying department in 1966 I made my first purchase. Jim Aulds was the salesman, a charming man who had imported his Irish gifts of persuasion to work for Lotus in Staffordshire. It took him ten minutes to persuade me to buy some of the most hideous shoes that have ever been put into a shop. They had big wide toes, an enormous metal buckle with uppers made of patent leather. Square toes, metal buckles and patent leather were all out of fashion. But I was keen to be an innovator. I bought 288 pairs – 144 black, 72 red and 72 white. Black sold the best – in 12 months we cleared 20 pairs. Four months after delivery to the shops, we sold our first pair of white! The real success came in January when we sold the 250 pairs that remained in ten days after I reduced the price from 59/11d to 17/6d. That was the last time I tried to be a fashion leader.

Ranger slipper

Before any chain stores started selling footwear, we had an enormous slipper business. Our biggest purchase in 1956 was a novelty children's slipper – a boy's bootie made out of felt that had a pouch on the right foot which held a toy gun. It was such an attractive item that we bought 100,000 pairs. They all arrived from the Far East during July and August well in time for Christmas.

An advertising campaign was planned, featuring the young cowboy appeal of the "Ranger Slipper." But even before the first advert appeared, success seemed certain. In the second week of September, we sold 3,800 pairs and started to investigate whether repeat quantities would arrive in time for Christmas from the Far East. When the first advertisement appeared two weeks later, sales climbed rapidly. It was clear that 100,000 was not nearly enough to satisfy the demand.

While we were busy selling our slippers there was an important murder trial going on at the Old Bailey. The trial became known as the Craig and Bentley case. During a burglary 16 year old Craig had shot a policeman. His accomplice, 18 year old Bentley, had, prior to the gun being fired, shouted to Craig: "Let him have it." They were both found guilty of murder but only Bentley (due to his age) faced the death penalty. As the trial was nearing its conclusion, a woman wrote to the *Daily Express* complaining about our slippers that provided guns for young children. The press took up her comments and the Ranger Slipper hit the headlines for all the wrong reasons. Our novelty slipper, intended as an innocent toy, was now inciting young people to become violent criminals.

During September sales had climbed to nearly 10,000 a week. In the first week of October we only sold 5,000. By the end of October sales were down to a trickle. Fortunately, we hadn't placed any repeats but we still had over 70,000 pairs to sell. We were faced with a dilemma. In view of all the adverse publicity should we withdraw the style from the shops altogether. We didn't have to decide, the decision was made for us. We started to receive complaints of the slippers falling apart in wear. By the third week of October, our complaint rate had soared to ten per cent of sales. The whole batch was declared to be faulty, taken off sale and returned to the supplier. We had a lucky escape.

Fire disaster

On my visits to Italy and France before Christmas in 1970 and 1971, I saw that the shops, did an enormous business in candles. We were developing a gift business in the shoe repair shops and so I persuaded the buyer, Charles Noakes, to add candles to his range.

Shortly before Christmas, the St John's Precinct in the centre of Liverpool was destroyed by fire. We had a shop near the market right in the centre of the precinct. The fire covered a big area, 150 shops were destroyed and it was several days before we could get access to our branch.

There is a fire risk associated with shoe repairing, sparks can fly into our dust containers and smoulder overnight. Despite our rigorous health and safety instructions, small fires have occurred in our shoe repair machinery once every three or four years. We were anxious. Could the major destruction of Liverpool's new shopping precinct be down to us?

Seven days after the fire, we were allowed back to inspect our branch. We were not the cause of the fire, but we suffered almost total damage. All our machinery had been destroyed, the customer's shoes had been burned to a cinder, the shoe polish had melted and the key blanks distorted by the heat. Searching through the charred remains the only thing the salvage team could find were the candles – totally unaffected by fire. To have candles that don't burn must be one of the biggest quality control failures ever seen.

Five year diary

We had very few complaints about the Christmas gifts we sold in our shoe repair shops.

We stocked a random selection of items all selling at under £1. Typical parts of the range were motoring kits, jewellery boxes, golf tee holders, toasters, notebooks and cuddly toys.

We catered for those people who had to buy a present for somebody, out of duty, and didn't care what it was, as long as it was cheap.

As a result, most presents from the Timpson shoe repair gift range were put in a drawer and never used.

One year we sold five year diaries. They were very successful. Out of the 1,000 purchased, 890 were gone by Christmas Eve. It wasn't until February that we discovered a problem. A lady returned a diary to one of our branches pointing out that each month only had 28 days! We only got the one diary back, the other 889 are probably still stuck in drawers.

Tote bags

One of our best sellers in the seventies was tote bags. Canvas bags mainly used for shopping that sold for about £3. The bags created a display problem. When hanging on the wall they looked like a collection of deformed bats. To improve their appearance we stuffed them with paper. The shops looked better and bag sales increased. To make life easier for our shops, we arranged for the suppliers to deliver the bags pre-stuffed ready for display. When the next delivery arrived, the suppliers had done just as they had been asked. The new stock was well stuffed and our branch staff had been saved a job. We only discovered the problem three weeks later, when a woman in her sixties returned to one of our shops with a serious complaint. She had no problem with the bag but its contents caused her severe distress. Our supplier had stuffed all the stock with shredded copies of *Playboy* and *Mayfair*.

The Chairman's shoes

In 1975, shortly after Timpson became part of the UDS Group, we were asked to open heel bars in all the UDS Department Stores. One of the units we opened was in Whiteleys, a department store in Bayswater, London.

Whiteleys was the nearest store to the home of UDS chairman, Bernard Lyons. He sent his chauffeur with a pair of high grade crocodile shoes to test our repair service.

When the chauffeur returned a few days later, he presented the repair ticket but the finished repair could not be found. We had lost the chairman's favourite shoes and they have never been seen since.

The size four problem

In 1969 we had the sort of experience buyers dream of. We bought a range of corduroy lace shoes from Holland which sold out in less than two weeks. We had a real success on our hands. In 1970 we copied the style in the Far East and I bought 80,000 pairs.

Just before I placed the order, a discussion group of shop managers pleaded for better labels at the end of each box. It was not easy working in a shop in those days. Faced with loads of boxes, you had to rely  on your knowledge of the style number to know what was inside. We decided that the answer was a clear picture on the box end label.

I knew that Far Eastern suppliers were unreliable and often didn't follow instructions unless they were given with explicit clarity. I sent a detailed example of a labels to show the size, the style number, the price and, of course, a picture of the shoe.

The end result was perfect. All 80,000 pairs were delivered with the correct label and the perfect picture and they were all marked size "4."

Spectacular failure

In 1986 we opened a shop in March in Lincolnshire. I had visited the town on two occasions with two of my senior colleagues. Escalating High Street rents meant that city centre shops were too expensive. We decided to expand the business by opening shops in small market towns and March was selected to test this type of location.

In the first full week the new shop only took £350, less than half our initial target. I went to the branch and recommended some changes to make things better. Two weeks later, sales had fallen to £250 per week. For the next two months sales never rose above £275 per week

We changed the staff. When sales settled at a consistent average of £175, we decided to cut our losses and close the shop. The whole exercise cost £30,000. The lease was acquired by another shoe repairer who appeared to have a successful business from the day he opened. He obviously knew how to trade in a market town. We abandoned our market town strategy.

Record price reduction

The worst fashion purchase ever made took place in Swears & Wells. A new and enthusiastic assistant buyer went to the Frankfurt Fur Fair, where she fell in love with a monkey skin jacket which had been dyed bright blue. At £550 each, the jackets were among the most expensive in the fair, so she only bought two of them. The two jackets were given pride of place in Oxford Street, retailing at £1,495. After three months, neither of the jackets had been sold. They were put on a rail in the back of the shop and forgotten until someone noticed a smell. Within two weeks the smell was so bad the jackets were reduced from £1495.00 to £100 for a quick sale. No one bought them. Eventually they were reduced to £10 and still no one bought them. They were thrown away with the rubbish.

Caught on camera

We use video camera to monitor customer service and cash security. One hidden camera revealed much more than we ever suspected. Twenty per cent of the takings went straight into the manager's pocket. But that was small fry compared with the other criminal activity caught on camera. Most people coming into the shop were buying and selling stolen goods and drugs. When we handed our film over to the police, they had clear evidence to incriminate not just our manager but 14 others.

Big trouble

All the disasters related above were merely timely reminders that things

go wrong, but none of them caused many sleepless nights. The real test comes with a rapid fall in sales or profits.

My worst experience was when our shoe retailing business started to decline. Increased competition affected our sales and profits fell so dramatically that we were heading for financial disaster. The sale of our shoe shops in 1987 probably saved the company from receivership. The experience was good preparation for the troubles of shoe repairing ten years later. From 1993 to 1995 our shoe repair business declined by 22 per cent. The development of key cutting and engraving was not enough to offset such a big drop and our profits fell by 65 per cent.

Most business stories paint a picture of uninterrupted progress. But life isn't like that. Every business will go through difficult patches. Bright ideas and clever deals can create success but it's the way you deal with difficult times that will determine the long-term survival and prosperity of the company.

Art of survival

British shoe manufacturers taught me how to be cheerful and inventive in the face of adversity.

When I started in the shoe trade, imports were less than 20 per cent of UK sales. They are now well over 80 per cent. In the face of low priced foreign competition, only the nimblest UK manufacturers could survive.

A master survivor was John Hirst. For years he took on the Italians, the Portugese, the Brazilians and the Taiwanese. His factory based at Waterfoot, Lancashire, made 25,000 ladies' fashion shoes a week. He had the daunting task of finding orders to fill the factory. Every six months he created a completely new range of footwear. Tooling up for new materials, new colours and new toe shapes. It was a risky business.

His Autumn 1971 range included a new toe shape found in France. It was an unknown quantity but I bought 10,000 pairs and had them delivered early in July. By the end of August, it was clear the new style was never going to sell. In five weeks we sold little over six per cent of our stock. I was facing some large mark-downs.

But John Hirst had a bigger problem. He had sold 30,000 pairs of the new toe shape to the British Shoe Corporation (BSC) and was running late with delivery. If the BSC got a hint the styles were not selling, they would cancel his order. During the first week of September, the BSC buyer was chasing delivery. He had seen the shoes in our shop window and couldn't understand why John hadn't delivered any stock to BSC. John saw his opportunity. To provide prompt delivery, John offered to send some stock direct to BSC branches in Liverpool. They arrived on a Friday. On the following day, 12 girls from the John Hirst factory went shopping in Liverpool and between them bought enough pairs of the new style to register on the BSC computer that they had a winner. BSC was happy to accept the whole delivery, even though it was three weeks late.

survival kit

No one is immune from a recession. You won't go through a decade, never mind a whole career, without hitting a solid wall of problems. When it happens, don't panic.

The natural reaction is to stick in the office and bury yourself in a meeting. Don't. If there is an answer, it will be out in the branches. Go out to the shops and look for it.

Don't look for a solution until you have found the problem.

If sales are going down, ask the branch staff. Visit lots of shops and then think about what they have said. When you come up with a theory, visit more shops to test it out and then visit alot more.

Spend as much time as you can thinking and talking and visiting shops until you know what the problem is. Then start discussing possible solutions.

When our shoe repair sales dropped so severely in 1994, I had to decide whether we had got things wrong or whether we were suffering due to a downturn in the market. I decided our shops were just as good as the year before – probably better – and the quality of our service had improved. The problem was to do with the market. I then had to decide whether this was was a permanent downturn or a temporary blip.

At least we knew all our competitors were being affected just as badly. If we had caused our own downfall, the answer would have been to reverse the decision that had caused the problem. As we were coping with market forces, the solution was more difficult to find.

We decided to do three things:

1. Continue our wholehearted commitment to shoe repairs. There was still a possibility that the market would bounce back.
2. Continue to develop our key cutting and engraving service vigorously in case the shoe repair demand continued to go down further.
3. Do all we could to become the best shoe repairers in Britain. That way we could increase our market share.

This thought process created confidence. We felt we knew what the problem was and had a solution.

When faced with a major problem it is tempting to make a rash decision. Often you make matters worse. Don't ever take action until you have visited lots of shops. Don't do anything until you know the problem and how to solve it. Often the best solution is to do absolutely nothing and wait for the problem to disappear.

CHAPTER 48

Nothing to worry about

I first suffered from stress in 1976 but in those days you didn't talk about it. If you openly admitted to the problem, you were labelled as a person who would buckle under pressure and couldn't take the strain.

Dear James

Don't keep your worries to yourself!

The stigma of stress makes the condition worse. You try to hide your affliction by working harder, just when your body is suggesting you take things easy.

When I first started to run the shoe business nothing seemed to go wrong. For six months I was an unqualified success. Suddenly, I lost confidence and the thought came into my head that pride comes before a fall. Perhaps the success story of my dreams was never going to happen and I wasn't so clever after all. Within a week lingering doubts about my ability had turned to despair. My life totally changed.

I couldn't concentrate for more than two minutes but, at the same time, I couldn't get my mind away from the business. Half the time I was nervous and twitchy and for the other half I was feeling depressed. I became forgetful too. Once I completely forgot a game of squash. Forgetting an appointment like that further undermined my confidence. I stopped planning ahead. I have kept my diaries for the last 12 years and I can tell the times when I suffered from stress, because the diary is empty. There was no desire to face up to the future. All this made me irritable and bad tempered, so it was a good thing I didn't fix up appointments, the less people I saw the better. For six weeks I hid the problem from everyone at the office and at home. Eventually Alex detected my change of mood and sent me straight to the doctor.

Popping anti-depressant pills helped a bit, but the talk with Doctor Angus Luscombe helped a lot more. He talked to me about how stress is created, that it's the body's way of saying enough is enough. Too much adrenaline and tension will, in the end produce a breaking point. He told me the condition would soon disappear. I didn't believe him, but he was right. Three weeks later I had forgotten all about stress and everything was back to normal. But before too long it reappeared.

One day I set off for London full of confidence and, for no reason at all, returned home in the depths of despair. I had nothing to worry about, so why should I be worried ? I ignored the problem, thinking it would go away, but it didn't. It didn't go away until I returned to see Angus Luscombe. I had learned a lesson: you can't beat stress on your own. You should never be too proud to ask for help.

Fortunately, stress has never really affected me when it has really mattered. Odd really, but for all the critical times, both at home and at the office, I have always been 100 per cent fit. Perhaps it is significant that it's seldom a big thing that knocks my confidence. Missing an appointment, giving a poor speech or interview, or even problems at the school where I have been Chairman of the Governors, have all been triggers for a period of stress. I still have bad days, probably always will, but at least now I know what to do.

As soon as I recognise the signs, I tell those nearest to me (wife and secretary), that I am not on top form! I know it is not going to last for ever. But when you are depressed, time seems to pass very slowly and even a week seems like an age. If I am still stressed after a week, I go and get medical help and do exactly what I am told. I have learned to be patient, and within another week the tension has gone and is completely forgotten.

Stress makes you irritable but more tolerant of others with the same problem. Many more people are affected with stress than like to admit it.I am writing frankly about how it has affected me in the hope that I might help someone else.It helps to be prepared.

I did wonder whether writing this chapter might be a stressful experience, but having got it all off my mind, I have never felt better.

CHAPTER 49

And finally

James, I did warn you that this was an odd book. But it is the best way I could devise to hand down my experience.

Dear James

Over to you!

It tells you what has worked in the past. You will have to work out the best methods for the future. Treat this book as a guideline, but don't follow everything I suggest. It isn't a text book. You will want to develop the business in your way. It won't be enough just to keep things as they are.

The business will need to change to survive, to develop and to grow. In 15 years our business has transformed from a shoe repairer to a successful service shop on the high street. My job satisfaction has come from overseeing that transformation. The business will probably change even more dramatically during the next 15 years. As you oversee the development, you will probably add many more chapters to this book. For most of the time you will find that your work will be your favourite hobby, but make sure it is you that run the business and not the business that runs you. Our financial independence gives you the freedom to pursue whatever course you and your employees think is going to be the best for the business, and the security of knowing that no-one can knock down your share price or tell you what to do through the financial press. Despite my strong belief in independence, even that part of this book should only be treated as a guideline.

If, in the fullness of time, you find the business has become a treadmill that you can't get off and you run out of ideas to make the profits grow, then look round for another member of the family to take over your role. If there is no one left in the family to run the business, then you should sell it. Just in case you are wondering, I hope to be available for work until 2013.

"My wife brought something extra into our marriage"

On the way back from taking our son Edward to nursery school, my wife Alex was stopped for speeding. The policeman, filling out his form, asked: "Do you have a job or are you a housewife?" To which Alex replied, crossly, "I have two jobs, I am a housewife and a mother."

Alex was a nursery nurse (a nanny) when I first met her. From leaving school at 16 to the time she married at the age of 21, her life was spent looking after children.

The gap from child care was short lived. Thirteen months after we were married, our first child, Victoria, was born. James arrived two years later and Edward two years after that. Thus we were set for a typical family life. I had a new stimulating job and we had moved to the house that Alex regarded as the perfect family home.

The change occurred when our youngest child Edward went to school. Perhaps it was the policeman who queried Alex's employment who started the thing off. Whatever the reason, Alex very quickly found long days with no children in the house difficult to take. She tried the charity committees, but soon discovered she was a lady that did not lunch and decided she really did need a job as well as being a housewife.

She wanted to work with children. After some discussion, Alex decided (I only offer advice), that, rather than go out to work with children, we should find a way for more children to come into our home. We started to investigate fostering.

Once Alex has an idea, she goes for it. Soon I was face-to-face with my first social worker. Morven Sowerbutts had a social worker's sort of name, and was good at her job. This initial interview was designed to find out whether we knew what fostering was about, (which I didn't) and put us off the whole idea unless we were really determined to go ahead, (which Alex, of course, was).

A more serious in-depth interview followed. Then two of our friends were asked all about us. Another social worker checked that Morven had the right impression. Eventually, the fostering panel approved us as short-term foster parents.

Nothing happened for six months. We expected a child to arrive within a week. After two months, Alex became so concerned that she went to the Social Services. They promised a child would arrive soon.

Fostering had gone from my mind when one Friday I returned from work to find two extra children. The boys aged three and four had led a pretty unstructured life. These were free-range children, not used to regular bedtimes or meal times and had never used a knife, fork or spoon. Their language impressed our children. The three year old rode a tricycle round the room shouting "f....off" at the top of his voice !

Their behaviour was certainly different , as I discovered the following morning. I took the two boys on a shopping trip to Wilmslow. In Silvios, the then crowded bakers in Grove Street, the four year old tugged fiercely on my arm and shouted pointing at some poor unfortunate woman, "John, John, that woman's got big busters." Everyone looked at me. After telling the young boy to keep quiet, I smiled at the well-endowed lady with an expression which I hope said: "Very sorry, but I am a new foster parent and this is my first day."

They soon fell into our routine. They trusted Alex immediately and they gained the affection of the rest of the family (apart from young Edward who hid in his bedroom). After three weeks they were part of the family.

On the fostering front, Alex does the work. I get the nice bits. As the weeks turned to months, more of the nice bits appeared. I told bedtime stories and took them for walks in the woods, while Alex helped them develop as people. It was amazing to see them grow up in such a short time. They came with little knowledge. They had never seen a cow or a sheep. When they looked outside our window on their first morning, they asked to play in the park (our garden). When we went to North Wales, they called the sea a big puddle.

Fostering changed our approach to dinner parties. We don't relish the social scene and I find dinner party conversation difficult. Then we started fostering. It is a subject that you cannot avoid. Someone asks you about your family and that starts it off. "How many children have you got ?" is a simple question for most people, but quite difficult for us. I reply "Well, it depends what you mean". Immediately my inquisitor thinks I have a string of ex-wives. To clear the air I say we are foster parents. Fostering then dominates the conversation. There are expressions of sympathy, disbelief and embarrassed admiration. There are ten questions people always ask. Question one: "Don't you feel awful when they leave ?"

Despite all the interviews before our approval as foster parents, we had no formal training. When the first foster children arrived, no social worker came to see us for four weeks. In those days foster parents were left to work it out for themselves. It was assumed that if you had your own children, you would be good at looking after someone else's. We thought that Alex, with her training, would have no problems. There was no talk of child abuse or behavioural difficulties.

We were approved for short-term fostering, which meant a maximum of six months. The first foster children arrived in May. We were not asked to any case conferences to plan the boys' future. Indeed, no future had been planned. They left us three weeks before Christmas and went straight to a children's home in nearby Knutsford. As soon as they had gone it was clear that Alex had become emotionally attached. She waited until the New Year but could wait no longer and went to the Children's Home, peered through the fence, and saw the two boys playing in the playground. The visit was repeated several times during the next four months until Alex heard that the boys had moved to another foster home. Alex had learned a difficult lesson. She never got so emotionally attached to any of the 60 or more children who have come since.

Another favourite dinner party question: "Which children do you remember most ?"

We have looked after several families of three and they certainly stick in the memory. They change the family routine by sheer weight of numbers. Not long ago, I arrived home from a day trip to London, unaware Social Services had rung, to find an extra three pairs of school shoes and three pairs of trainers in the kitchen that Alex had put out for me to clean.

Each group of children brings unique characteristics and that family (a girl and her two younger brothers) argued incessantly, from 5.30am until bedtime. They took all of Alex's experience. By the time she had achieved harmony amongst the foster children, the rest of us were so tired we started arguing amongst ourselves.

Our most disruptive visitors were six month old triplets. They only stayed for four weeks but we will never forget them. Alex had extra help from the Social Services during the day, I was on duty at night. Early morning and late night feeding was a joint effort. We started at 5.30am to ensure the triplets were fed before our own children went to school and I left for work. Alex relished the task and enjoyed taking the triplets out in a specially made three berth buggy to incredulous stares from Wilmslow shoppers. Triplets were even rarer then and strangers approached Alex with an odd question, "are these real live triplets?"

Another threesome were the children of an English mother and a West Indian father. They quickly fell in with our routine and became pupils at the local primary school. They stayed for five months and we all enjoyed their company. Their stay was marred by the attitude of a social worker.. We experienced discrimination, prejudice and political correctness. The team leader was convinced the children should not be with a white family. Eventually the children were taken to another foster family who were just as white as we are but lived in a smaller house.

Our privileged background is a disadvantage. Some social workers, particularly those who did not know Alex, thought our big house was unsuitable for foster care. But young children are not influenced by material things in the same way as adults. What children look for is precisely what Alex provides, the loving protection of a caring family. The prejudice was particularly marked in social workers with no children of their own and no experience of parenting. Some new social workers, seeing our house for the first time, furtively observe the large garden and indoor swimming pool. Alex tackles the problem face-to-face, inviting them to look round. "We really are quite normal, I can assure you," she tells them.

Some foster children make a dramatic arrival. Usually a social worker telephones to see whether we are available. Most calls come during the day and the children arrive within hours. There are false alarms that never result in an extra child, but on many occasions I have arrived home from work to find my family has increased in size.

We are on an emergency register. I took an emergency call one Saturday morning; we had had no foster children for some months so, without consulting Alex, I said we were happy to receive the child. An hour later, two police women came down our drive to deliver our latest foster child. Alex was already in her foster organisation mode. Bedrooms had been reallocated and by 10.30 am I was in Sainsbury's filling the trolley with baby food and nappies. Some children come in the middle of the night. Recently I returned from a business dinner at midnight and was surprised to find the bedroom light still on. Alex had spoken to the emergency services and a five week old baby was on his way. Alex got some much needed sleep, in anticipation, while I waited. The social worker arrived with the baby at 2.30am.

We have particularly fond memories of those that stay longest. Years ago we looked after a brother and sister who were a particularly attractive pair. They were welcomed to our local primary school and appeared at the outset to be normal balanced happy children. Alex, was, however, disturbed to observe the way the young girl played with her dolls. This was not a game of babies and nurses, but acts of violence which would have fitted well into a horror movie. Her brother was even more violent. On one occasion, we found him at the end of the garden having smashed every one of our garden cold frames. The distressed little boy was surrounded by 100 broken panes of glass and a hammer. We were observing the behaviour of children disturbed by the physical abuse they had experienced from their stepfather.

Alex enjoyed the new-born babies. Twice we looked after Downes Syndrome babies. The first was successfully adopted by a remarkable couple who went on to adopt another Downes baby. That is the sort of commitment that Alex and I could not even contemplate. The other Downes baby stayed with us for two months. The child was the result of a pregnancy which had caused the couple to get married but after the child arrived, the couple's relationship broke down. Some weeks after the child came, Alex met the mother and got to know her well. Over time their relationship developed and Alex saw the bond of love developing between mother and baby. That placement had a happy ending. The Downes girl returned to her family, the couple restored their marriage and then had another child. Alex kept contact for several years.

As we have got older, nights disturbed by screaming babies have been more difficult to bear. I have, however, managed to retain the ability I had when our own children were born of sleeping through any noise however loud it is. Alex is disturbed by absolutely everything. Most of the young babies we have fostered screamed an awful lot. The biggest screamer of all, had good reason for making a noise. Her mother was taking hard drugs and her baby was born addicted to heroin. She had been in hospital for ten weeks before coming to us and she yelled day and night. Gradually, things improved and when, four months later she left to live with her father, she was eating and sleeping like a normal child.

The social services system has improved considerably during our involvement. Nowadays, foster parents play a role in case conferences and their advice is sought in deciding the future of the child. Short-term fostering is no longer just for six months but often goes on much longer. Two boys stayed with us for the best part of a year and became very much part of the family. We went to their school concerts, a Nativity Play, parent/teacher meetings and their schoolfriends came to play at our home. We got to know their parents well. The children had been placed in care because both parents were addicted to drugs and were in a rehabilitation centre fifty miles away, near Sheffield. Over the months, Alex made several trips with the children to see their parents and eventually although the marriage had broken down, the children went back to live with their mother.

When the first enquiry comes from the social services, we have no idea how long the children are going to stay. Normally, we are asked to look after the children over a weekend or for a few days. Sometimes, this is exactly what happens. Usually, however, the days become weeks and often the weeks become months. One call came just before we were going on holiday. We had booked a family fortnight in a house in Portugal. The social services rang five days before we were due to depart. As it was late July, there were no other suitable foster parents available. The only alternative was to make arrangements for the two boys to join our family party. This proved more difficult than I expected. The holiday company were less than sympathetic, despite being told why these children had appeared at short notice. They talked about late bookings and proposed an exorbitant rate. I ignored them, booked two separate flights through a bucket shop and the two boys were able to join us. We expected them to stay for two or three more weeks on our return from Portugal. Six months later, they were still with us. They were half brothers. Eventually the younger one left to become the long-term foster child of his parental grandparents. The elder boy became our only long-term foster child.

The media often concentrates on the negative side of fostering. There are some tragic stories of children abused by foster parents, but most cases relate to placements many years ago. Today the vetting process is thorough and professional.

Before we became long-term foster parents, we went through the same checks we experienced when we started fostering. In depth interviews of ourselves, our children and our friends together with cross-questioning by a Guardian *Ad Litem* who looks after the interests of the child. We never resented the process. As long-term foster parents you not only look after the child, you are also responsible for his development through to adulthood. Every precaution should be made to ensure you are fit to do the job.

Over our years of our fostering, the quality of social workers has improved significantly. But there has been a progressive introduction of political correctness and we are now expected to toe the correct political line.

Our long-term foster child joined us when he was seven and stayed for ten years. Once he came into long-term care, we decided he should become a member of the family in all respects. Our short-term children have their own room, their own space and have the same range of Christmas and Birthday presents as our own children, but with our long-term foster child it went much further. He was a member of our Golf Club, and joined the local Cricket and Hockey clubs. Most significantly he went through the same education system. We moved him from the local primary school to the prep school that our children attended and he progressed from there to go to Uppingham. He proved to be remarkably adaptable to the changes in his life. It was particularly pleasing that he retained a strong relationship with his mother who he saw on a regular basis.

Research has shown that children who are moved to a different social background want to return to their roots. This has happened to us. When he reached the age of 14, he started to see more of his mother. He acquired the social graces that we taught our own children but he never discovered the will to work hard. His GCSE results were so poor that he had to leave Uppingham. He joined a local college but his laziness ensured that this latest stab at academic success was doomed to failure. He was spending more and more time with his Mother until at the age of seventeen, we had to make a firm decision and he moved back to his roots. We still keep in touch, and he contacts us if he has a problem. We sometimes wonder whether we made a difference, but he gives us the answer by still calling on us for help.

Alex managed to increase the size of her family shortly after a hysterectomy! During her convalescence, her mind turned to unfulfilled ambitions. A significant change in our life was just around the corner. We planned to move to a smaller house, to keep expenditure in line with our income. But Alex had a much more major change in mind.

Alex started talking about adoption and one of our social workers listened. Early that summer, Alex went back to the same children's home in Knutsford which received our first foster children.. I joined her on the second visit and for the first time met Roy, an undersized six year old, who was full of energy and a bag of nerves. After several visits, Roy came to live with us and shortly after his seventh birthday he was adopted and became Oliver Timpson.

Alex felt she was in need of a real challenge and in Oliver she found one. Before the adoption could go ahead, we went through that vetting process again. We were approved but no one gave us the slightest hint that we were about to be put through a supreme test of parenting. Oliver has found good behaviour difficult. Most children misbehave, they are disobedient and they tell lies. With Oliver this had become a way of life. Alex was undeterred. The same love and discipline was applied to Oliver that she had given to our own three and the foster children.

Oliver made progress but it was two steps forward and one step back. Schooling was difficult. Just when we thought we had got Oliver settled in a school, something went wrong and we moved him elsewhere. He is a talented singer. He had such a beautiful treble voice, that he joined Chester Cathedral choir. Just when that seemed to be going terribly well, he fell out with the choirmaster, (something to do with passing round sexy playing cards during Evensong). He was good at games but never became a permanent member of school teams; he failed to turn up in time for practice. This sort of behaviour becomes less acceptable as you get older. He only spent five terms at Uppingham before I suggested to the Headmaster that Oliver left before the red card was issued. During his short five term career, Oliver ran away twice, broke most of the school rules and set up an agency selling booze and cigarettes to members of the school on behalf of some of the local traders. Shortly after he left Uppingham, Oliver performed one of his most memorable and frightening exploits. We were still looking for his next school, so he was living at home, being taught by a local tutor who really earned his money. One morning Oliver, aged 14, was gone, and our small family car was missing. We informed the police and for 48 anxious hours waited for the telephone to ring. The car and Oliver reappeared two days later. He had arrived as he had gone, in the middle of the night, leaving the car abandoned half way down our drive. He crept still dirty and smelly into his bed, where we found him fast asleep the following morning. It turned out that he had driven back to Uppingham. His plan was to restart the agency selling drink and cigarettes to Uppingham pupils. Before this enterprise could get underway, however, he discovered he had come out in spots. Fearing that he was suffering from chicken pox he persuaded a man he met at a garage to fill the car up with petrol and drove back home.

We managed to find the right school for Oliver. Witherslack Hall in Cumbria specialised in children with behavioural problems (mainly statemented by local authorities). The strict discipline and reward system suited Oliver well and he thrived. But the same two steps forward one step backward still applied and shortly after he left Witherslack, he ran off again. This time I had to drive down to Baldock at 4am to recover Oliver and a schoolfriend. Oliver had planned to work in a night club owned by the friend's uncle. It was the uncle who had called me out in the middle of the night to rescue him from the boys. He was not a night club owner but the manager of a Working Men's Club.

Oliver then went to a special school in Canada, where he survived for over two years, gaining five GCSE's and the love of the Principal's daughter. In the end he was asked to leave at short notice. I was driving around the M25 at the time the call came from the Principal in Canada: "Oliver will arrive tomorrow morning. Please pick him up from Gatwick !"

The previous summer, Oliver had stopped living in our house. He was friendly with some local boys and became involved in drugs. One evening he was so abusive about Alex that we had a fight. As a result he decided not to return home. All his belongings were moved to a neighbour's house and in due course were sold by Oliver to raise money to buy drugs. It is impossible to achieve two steps forward and one step back when you are hooked on drugs but, thankfully after six months, Oliver contacted us and shortly after gave up his habit. He then asked whether he could have a job in the business.

As an employee, Oliver displayed the same bizarre colourful contrast that had been present through the rest of his life. He was excellent with customers, charming with his colleagues and lousy with time keeping. He frustrated his area manager by being the star salesman who often failed to turn up.

When Oliver was 19, encouraged by Alex, he went in search of his mother and found her. Eventually, he went to live with her. We were delighted they met up again hoping that his renewed relationship would change his behaviour- it didn't.

To gain experience, he was working in London during December 1997, when I received a call on a Saturday morning. It was our son Edward, reporting that Oliver had spent the night in a police station and was still held in custody. Nine months later, Oliver appeared in the dock at Southwark Crown Court accused of assaulting a police officer.

During a tense four day trial it transpired (thanks to Oliver's excellent barrister), that the policeman who claimed he had been assaulted was using Oliver as a way to obtain financial compensation from the police. The judge was clearly unimpressed with the policeman's claim that he suffered from post traumatic stress syndrome following a scuffle with Oliver in the police station. Oliver had been arrested in a pub where some of our shop managers were holding a Christmas party. The police were called because a fight had broken out, most of the party disappeared as quickly as possible, but Oliver stayed and was arrested for being drunk on licensed premises. Being drunk on licensed premises is not an arrestable offence, it was, therefore, established in Court that Oliver had been subjected to a wrongful arrest and was entitled to use reasonable force when he was detained against his will, which is exactly what happened at the police station. Thankfully, after three and a half hours deliberation, the jury found Oliver not guilty and brought an end to another fine mess that Oliver had got us in to. One would have thought that it would have made a dramatic change to Oliver – it didn't. He returned to taking drugs and his time keeping got even worse, so bad in fact that he received three warnings and was dismissed by his area manager.

After six months work stacking potatoes on a lorry, he asked me for his job back and returned to have another go.

All the way through his life with us, Oliver has retained the most endearing personality. It's that charm that makes the whole of his education even more frustrating. During the seventeen years since Oliver came to our family, we have experienced considerable despair, relief on many occasions, we learned an awful lot, but the greatest feeling of all is frustration.

Another dinner party question: "Why did you choose to adopt that particular child?" It just happens. These things are not planned – they are just meant to be the way they turn out.

When Oliver was 13 and showing the first signs of adolescence, we adopted another child! Henry was only a few days old when he came to us as a foster child. At a time in life when most people are thinking of grandchildren, Alex's mind turned yet again to adoption. We went through the vetting process once more. It took some time to get approval from the Adoption Panel, on account of our age. Finally, it was agreed The 18-month-old Henry became our adopted son. Since then he has done a wonderful job of tiring out Alex but keeps both of us young at heart.

Another dinner party question: "What do your own children think of it all ?" There is bad news and good news to report. Edward showed it was not all plain sailing when the first foster children arrived; he hid in his room. But later he took such an interest in fostering that (at the age of 16), he gave a talk to the whole of his school about fostering and adoption. Now a barrister, he has a special interest in family law.

Our daughter Victoria has always been concerned at the strain put on Alex. She saw her mother's tiredness and sometimes suffered from it. But Victoria's interest in children has developed into a career as a primary school teacher.

James was often the strongest objector whenever Alex took on a new challenge. But James has become superb at looking after young children, readily giving his time and gaining their confidence.

Despite the difficulties of bringing other children into our home, there is no doubt that our family, (including Oliver and more recently Henry), has gained much from the fostering experience which will certainly stand them in good stead if they become parents themselves.James has already proved this to be true.

We get a lot of help in looking after the various children in our care, not just from our own family but from friends and, in particular, people who work in and around our home. The star role has been played by Eric Done, who is a permanent member of our staff at home, together with his wife Janet. They have been through the full vetting process and are also approved foster carers.

Outsiders often assume that short-term fostering, long-term fostering and adoption are much the same. They are different, particularly the emotional bond that develops between us and the children. Short-term fostering is similar to looking after a relative's child who is staying for a long time. Long-term children enjoy a much more permanent bond without the deepest emotions that are extended to a member of your own family. An adopted child is a member of your family but the lack of responsibility for the genes makes you more objective when receiving poor school reports or dealing with the difficulties of adolescence.

Our recent short-term foster children have often been more disturbed than the children we cared for twenty years ago. We now recognise the results of child abuse and Alex has become expert at dealing with behavioural problems. We have never, however, taken on the most difficult challenge, teenagers or children with special needs. Caring for a difficult teenager takes a special kind of dedication that deserves the admiration of everybody. We got some insight into the problems of caring for handicapped children when Alex, early on in our fostering career, decided that we should join a Home from Home scheme. You took a child into your home for one weekend a month to give the parents some respite. Our first Home from Home child was a 15-year old Downes Syndrome boy. Dealing with a young adult who is still a child has its problems. Bath time and bottom wiping were particularly difficult. But we enjoyed taking our visitor for walks or on shopping expeditions. We soon got used to other people staring at us. We used to walk on the other side of the road if we saw someone with Downes Syndrome; the Home from Home experience completely changed that attitude. But we also learned that looking after handicapped people on a permanent basis is not for us.

Another popular dinner party question: "How do you get on with the social workers?" In most respects, we get on very well. The social services have generally improved, but in one way things have deteriorated. Every time the government tries to improve child care services, or legislates to prevent an abuse reoccuring, they create more paperwork. Our social workers call it "pressure of work" and "lack of resources." It now takes far too long to resolve the future plans for children in care. Sometimes the social workers take so long to make up their mind it is probably too late.

A major benefit of the recent Children's Act is the closer contact we have with the children's parents and family. That has changed our answer to another dinner party question – "Do you ever see them again?" Over the past five years, Alex has forged a permanent relationship with several of our foster children's families.

One mother of four children, who briefly came into our care, rang Alex out of the blue two years later. She had taken an overdose and wanted Alex to come and look after her children. Alex took her to hospital and contacted the social workers. That was the first of several such emergency calls. On each subsequent occasion, Alex brought the children back to our house and that was enough to avoid the suicide threat.

Alex got to know another mother well during the six months her son was fostered with us. The mother wrote to Alex a year later to say she was expecting another child and wanted her son to stay with us when she gave birth. I had forgotten about the letter when Alex woke me up at 2am. The mother was in labour and asked us to collect her son. I arrived back at 3am, not only with the boy but also his very smelly guinea pig.

Many of the mothers of children in care were themselves in the care system and had no personal example of being a parent. Many of these mothers are younger than our own children; they look on Alex as a mother figure able to help them learn to be a parent.

Recently, a mother of another short-term foster child invited Alex to be the birthing partner at the arrival of her new baby. The mother, the new baby and the foster child all stayed with us for a week after the birth and were regular visitors for the next three years. They became members of Alex's large extended family.

Alex has also looked after children who have not come through the Social Services. Sometimes these are friends' children staying while their parents go on holiday, but Alex has provided the solution to more difficult problems. Divorce and adolescence have caused children to come and stay with us, some for as long as nine months. Alex also invites children to use our swimming pool. If I find a traffic jam down our drive, I know it must be the cub's night or the brownies.

Alex helps parents as well as children. At times our telephone has become a helpline with Alex becoming the agony aunt on child care. Problems at school, difficult teenagers, "what do I do with my new baby" and, several times, "I don't think I can cope with our adopted child." When our telephone rings, I know it is for Alex. The clients of her helpline don't realise that there are times when Alex also has problems she needs to discuss – we too need time to talk.

We now have the answer to another dinner party question: "How do you find time for yourselves ?" The answer is simple. Regular holidays. Thanks for our star childminders, Janet and Eric Done, we are able to take two or even three holidays a year, without children. That is when we relax, get to know each other again and talk through the problems we left behind.

Whenever you think Alex has met every possible challenge, she finds another one.

In the early nineties, the news from Romania revealed the aftermath of the Ceaucescu regime and the number of helpless children in children's homes. Alex decided that two small Romanian children were just what we required to complete our family. We needed social services approval before we could talk to the Romania. We went through the vetting process again. Our friends were interviewed and this time we were asked searching questions about our attitude to cultural and ethnic links.We passed the test and set off to Romania on a fascinating four day trip. We visited four children's homes and stayed with a delightful family who had connections in Cheshire. We also met a Romanian lawyer who explained it was unlikely we could adopt due to difficulties in Romanian law. The lawyer was right, the rules did change, it was much more difficult to adopt from Romania. The children had to be offered to Romanians first, although Romanians were not interested in adoption. In addition, there was an age limit which disqualified both myself and Alex. For once Alex was unsuccessful. But we found Romania fascinating and went back to a wedding in the family where we had stayed. Our son Edward joined us on one of the most memorable trips of our lives. The Romanian wedding became the longest and most riotous party that we have attended and not one drop of alcohol was served.

As the dinner party draws to a close, there are still two more questions left to ask. "What are your most vivid memories?"

I remember the big groups for Sunday lunch – often a dozen or more sitting round the table.

I remember the particularly awkward 11 year old who ran away and hid in our large garden just as were about to drive to the airport to go on a skiing holiday. That child never ever did what he was told, so skiing lessons were impossible. He went up the tow bar and skied down on his own until he learned some skills. I took him up the mountain and he refused to take any advice as we tried to negotiate a very steep art of a red run. In despair, I shouted to the Almighty for help.

I remember the visit to Disney Paris with Alex leading a group of mother and children all on their first trip abroad – I was happy to go back to the office for a rest.

I remember the times I have driven through the night to collect Oliver after he has run away. But my most vivid and cherished memories are recent and they all relate to the three children born of Alex and myself.

The pleasure that Victoria now gets from teaching children. Equally, the boundless enthusiasm that Edward has for his career as a barrister and James' wedding to Roisin, undoubtedly the happiest day for our family since Alex and I were married 32 years ago.

Not long ago, three more short-term foster children came to stay. I took them one Sunday morning to the local garage to buy some newspapers and sweets before breakfast. The woman behind the counter gave me a sympathetic smile. She asked about the children and I explained that they were fostered. "I have always thought about doing that," she said. I have heard this remark many times. Lots of people think about fostering but few do anything about it.

I am lucky. Alex decided to do it and brought experiences into our lives that few people will have had the privilege to enjoy.

My final question from the dinner party: "How long are you going to continue fostering?" This is an impossible question. Alex is the only person who can answer it properly. Even Alex doesn't know what the future holds. There will be new challenges and they will almost certainly involve children.

I did think that perhaps things would change when grandchildren arrived. They have changed, of course. Alex has got a special excuse to welcome more children into our house. But why should I think that Alex would retire from her life as a foster carer? I have no plans to stop looking after the business, so I don't expect Alex will have any plans to stop looking after children!

Teenage parties

When my daughter was 15, I dramatically discovered that a teenage party with more than 20 guests produces a completely new set of management problems. Fortunately, my initiation to the teenage party scene only involved a day school. The problems increase considerably with a public school boy whose guests travel so far they have to stay the night.

Having survived several parties (but with the prospect of many more), I thought it prudent to put down on paper the lessons learned so far, as an aide-memoire and, perhaps as a guide to those who have not yet entered this world of the unknown.

Expect the worse and prepare for it. Don't worry about embarrassing your own children. Impose a strict set of rules before giving the party the go ahead. The objective is to allow the guests to enjoy themselves while avoiding serious disaster.

Don't think your child has "a particularly nice circle of friends." As the evening draws on even the mildest character is likely to enter into the party spirit. Certain monsters are renowned for causing a party to go off the rails. I found that some were friends of my teenage children and I suspect most teenagers will invite at least one tearaway. Your guests will find reasons to get into every accessible part of the house – anywhere not bolted and barred.

Different people measure success in different ways. For my part, teenage parties are successful if they result in little or no damage to my property.

Expectations

You can safely predict certain things will happen. A lot of children will drink and many will drink a lot. At least half of them smoke. The first two hours are concentrated on drinking and conversation. The conversation is almost entirely between members of the same sex. They will, at first, appear more sensible and mature than we were at their age. This impression will be proved largely false by the end of the night. When the food arrives at 10pm, it only gets a passing glance. It is seen as the interval between drinking and dancing. No one has taken any notice of the disco for two hours, then suddenly they jostle for position on the postage stamp sized dance floor. Half an hour after the dancing starts, people disappear and the trouble really begins. Everything happens very quickly. They have got the wanderlust. The hunt takes them all over your house. The girls look for lavatories (the boys just go in the garden), they all look for snogging spots, after 2am they search for food and even later somewhere to sleep. Don't expect the party to end at the time you put on the invitation. It is going to go on all night.

First steps

It is very important to send an invitation, not a cheap item from W H Smith but something formal or unique. A formal invitation discourages and almost excludes gate-crashers. No more than 65 per cent will reply to the invitation but don't assume the others have refused. Never allow your child to issue invitations by word of mouth because their message will be passed on to many more friends than you bargained for.

Before the invitation is printed, sit down with your son or daughter and list the ground rules. This will prepare them for the way you run the party and there is a chance they will encourage their guests to toe the line.

Planning

1. You need a disco. The guests will take very little notice of the music

but the disco man has an important role. He helps to provide the right atmosphere and is often cited in retrospect as the mark of a great party.. With the disco you acquire a man with considerable experience and a fund of advice. He knows how the party is going, where the problems are, and what to do next.

2. Provide an "outside" lavatory. You cannot insist that the girls go in the garden so make sure they can go to the loo without trudging through your house.

3. Decide which part of the house is to be used. If possible don't use any of it. Consider hiring a marquee (expensive but a good insurance policy), or even use the local hall. If you must use part of your house, take out anything that you don't want damaged.

4. Think through the sleeping arrangements. Guests travelling from far away will be staying the night and most locals will want to stay as well. The question is not whether they are going to stay but where you are going to put them.. If possible, find somewhere out of the house. Tents are a popular solution and a good reason for having the party in the summer. Do not be sensitive about mixed sleeping arrangements. The separate allocation of a room for the girls and a room for boys does not achieve its objective. Quite the reverse, it encourages couples to canoodle throughout your property. Communal sleeping is popular, works well, and when you think about it, is the most effective contraceptive you have at your disposal.

5. Have an adequate first aid kit – without being alarmist some minor accidents can be excepted.

6. Provide plenty of ashtrays. A large number of guests will smoke an awful lot during the course of the night. Use cheap bowls filled with sand, prominently displayed so their purpose is quite clear. .

7. Decorate the room with a party theme to create the right atmos-

phere. Show the guests that you have arranged a really good thrash otherwise they may take on the organisation themselves

8. If you are still nervous, employ two security guards – they will be seen as bouncers and will exert much more discipline than you will..

Before the party

Go through the guidelines again with your son or daughter and put up notices that clearly define the rules: "out of bounds, don't enter", "no glasses beyond this point,`` "please use the ashtrays" and "lavatories this way only."

Some guests arrive two days early. "You don't mind if Sue arrives on Thursday – there is nothing else she can do !". Don't get in any extra food. Sue will probably ring on Thursday to say she is coming on Friday. When she does arrive, she will visit friends in the area and use your house for bed and breakfast.

A fairly large gang will arrive far too early. Several guests will be coming from a long way, most by train. You will be expected to provide transport from the station for every one of them. Their instructions will be vague . Have a big pad by your telephone to list names, stations and train times. Despite doing your best, at least one will be missed. Expect a late arrival by taxi – asking for cash to pay the fare.Plan activities for the early arrivals. Fortunately, they are very simply entertained. It is better to encourage a game of football, tennis, darts or cards than to send them on a pub crawl. There will be enough drinking later in the evening. Don't start the party early. Keep them away from the bar until the time announced on your invitation.

Safety measures

Certain precautions can be taken well before you get involved with the early party arrivals. They are:
*   Lock up your house or those parts that are out of bounds (check all locks are working a week before the party).

- Lock up your car – it is amazing what can happen late at night !
- Lock any outbuildings that might store things of value or danger.
- Lock up your wine cellar and remove alcohol (especially spirits) from the house.
- Finally, be mentally prepared for the disco man arriving late. I have always had to call his home to see if he is coming. His wife always replies "he is on his way."

Drink

Alcohol is the root cause of most problems.

Supply enough drink (this will be more than you think you need). If you drastically under-cater, the boys will go off and hunt for more, especially if an off licence is within walking distance.

Draft beer is preferable to cans. Cider can be popular and you need to provide wine which will be drunk early by the girls and later on by the boys. White wine only – red is not as popular and probably not very good for them. Provide a large quantity of soft drinks.

Don't let them help themselves. (If you have beer in cans, break the packs up into singles. Otherwise guests will try to walk off with a six-pack.) You need a barman who must pour out every drink. Pick your barman carefully. Don't do it yourself. In doing so, you are excluded from some other vital activities; find someone, who you know and trust and who will work to your instructions. Don't choose another parent!

Don't allow drink or glasses outside the main party area. This rule will be broken and the following day you will find glasses and cans in the most extraordinary places. But the rule will limit this problem.

Arrange for extra supervision from 8.00 pm to 10.30 pm,when the bar will be busy, your wife will be worried about the catering and you may have to collect another guest marooned at the railway station.

Early on in the evening, watch out both for the inexperienced drinkers and the troublemakers. The troublemaker is easily identified. Quickly make sure that he (or she) knows you are keeping a careful watch.. The inexperienced drinker is often unfortunately the younger son or daughter from your own family !

As the evening develops, you will draw on the experience of your disco man who is in the best position to say when the music has to stop. For an extra £25 he will play for another hour.Hopefully when he stops, everyone will stop, and a large majority will go to sleep.

You cannot supervise the party by standing in one place. You have to circulate. Have a purpose in moving around the party – collect empty glasses, pick up litter, or generally patrol outside to see that all is well. Don't be embarrassed at stepping over courting couples – they will not even notice.

There is no definite time when danger has passed, it might 4, 5 or 6 in the morning. After 8 – 10 hours experience, you will be well placed to judge when it is safe to go to bed, locking the door behind you. However, it is sensible not to announce your departure by saying good-night.

Drugs

Drugs were not a problem when we started with teenage parties – but don't expect a drug free party today. I recommend zero tolerance – display a prominent notice: "If I find drugs I will call the police" and mean it.

The morning after

Some guests will plan to stay for an extra day ! This seldom happens, they thankfully disappear very quickly. A simple breakfast is appreciated and eaten very politely and quietly, coffee is particular welcome. Don't expect them to do any clearing up. Frankly you will prefer that they just cleared off ! Don't arrange to play golf on the day after the party – you are better employed driving the guests back to the station..

Finale

If all that puts you off and you have serious doubts, then don't have a party. We are still learning and are fortunate (or unfortunate) to have a number of children who give us the opportunity to gain from experience as each age group comes into the danger zone.

I am encouraged to do it again, not simply because we now think we are in control, but also because a majority of the partygoers take the trouble to write and say thank you. Their letters tell us what a lovely party it was even though I suspect they can remember very little about it.

Ending on a positive note

After one party, the disco man rang us up to say they were the best bunch he had met for a long while and, as a result, he was going to put his young son's name down for Uppingham, where most of the guests went to school.

Letter to our friends whose eldest child is 15

Dear George & Ann

Now that you feel experienced at dealing with the problems of puberty, it is time to give you some idea of what happens next.

Don't get too excited, this letter does not come with a guarantee that the spots and moods are coming to a speedy end. I am writing about another change you are about to see – the switch from schoolboy to student.

Having both graduated from Nottingham, you will know a lot about life at University. Let me warn you – much has changed in the last 25 years – financially, socially and academically. In your day, you could virtually decide whether you wished to go to University – frankly George, if you had worked hard you would have got that place at Oxford. Today, there is real competition for places – exam results are vital. Money, sporting ability and good looks do not impress most senior tutors.

Your son cannot afford to do as little work as you did – especially during the next 3 years. University offers are almost entirely based on the grade achieved at G.C.S.E. but are conditional on the A level results. A levels are ten times tougher than you remember.

You will have little influence on your son's choice of University. The nearest you will get is some carefully written detail from the school and, with luck, a meeting with the master responsible – neither the written nor the oral explanation will be of much help. The ways of University entry change completely as soon as parents start to understand how they work.

This is the first major decision your son is going to make for himself – you might as well get used to it because you are about to become a non-executive director of his life with purely financial responsibilities.

The best you can do is:

1. Forget secret aspirations of Oxford.
2. Make sure he has heard about UCCA forms.
3. Keep making subtle hints about Durham.

You may be asked about a "Gap Year." You will see this as a further year of financial dependency rather than a character building mix of world travel and work experience. My advice is to let him go – "Gap Years" are so successful most parents will retrospectively claim it was their idea.

If you drop the Durham hints with success, the next word to remember is Hatfield. Durham is a Collegiate University and the College to choose is Hatfield.

In three years time, don't go on holiday in August. Portugal is no place to be when the A level results appear. You will not be prepared for the "3B's" offer being matched by the "2B and a C" performance. It has happened to me twice ! Ringing up the school, university or college is impossible from abroad – you must immediately plead for your child, George, in every direction – it doesn't make any difference, but it will satisfy the desperate need for action from the head of the family.

With luck, patience and perhaps a retake, your 19 year old son, refreshed by the Gap Year, will be ready to take advantage of all that is on offer at Hatfield College.

The first day of the first term is your only opportunity to find out what goes on. There are no parents' evenings, no speech days – parents, frankly, are not required until graduation. I can only disclose a few snippets I have pieced together during four years listening to student conversation and visiting Durham more often that your child would wish.

Within a week the relationship between you and your son will have changed. Two reassuring telephone calls, which convince you he is homesick will be followed by silence. No news is good news – a sign of happiness and financial well-being.

Eventually he will ring to tell you he is coming home – an unscheduled visit not contained in the College calendar. You may be given very short notice and have to cancel a board meeting to meet the train. You may not recognise him – in a few weeks, young men can change their dress sense, have an ear pierced and grow a rather pathetic beard. The black bin bag contains the main reason for his visit – the dirty washing. He may not be travelling alone – perhaps you are about to meet his new girlfriend (don't worry, they all look the same !). You are probably providing free accommodation on route to a party.

You will be asked to pay for the return ticket. It's a hint that your talk of Mr Micawber has fallen on deaf ears.

This brings me to the thorny question of money. Most students are financial wizards. Whether funded by local authority loans, or by yourself, they have a modest amount to spend. Yet they manage to go to the Hatfield bar most nights, Rixy's once a week, curries, Chinese, pizzas (special deal before 6.30 pm), travel the country to parties and buy the special sweat shirt only worn by those who have devoured 12 pints in one session. Whatever you say he will run up a sizeable overdraft – let the bank manager sort it out – your son will learn a lot about budgeting at Barclays' expense.

I have mentioned Hatfield's main non-academic activities – eating and drinking.Music and drama also recruit the interest of a wide cross-section of students and there is a fanatical enthusiasm for sport. With such an active calendar it is amazing that undergraduates can still follow important world events, including *EastEnders*, *Neighbours*, *Coronation Street* and *Brookside*.

Don't worry about sex – this generation know a lot more about it than we do, you are better letting them make their own way down the sexual highway. Your advice is probably outdated, pretty useless and would be ignored.

Their independence is developed in the second year when they usually live out of college. They confidently arrange themselves into groups of three or four, looking forward to running a house together, sharing the cooking, washing up and cleaning while remaining the very best of friends. Domestic harmony rarely survives for more than six months. The mixed group is more likely to fail than single sex houses – an interesting lesson for the future!

Students have a lot of holidays. But your son won't be a permanent holiday resident – he will use your home as a hotel. Booking your own holidays can be tricky – he may come with you – especially skiing which he can't afford – but he may not – if he gets a better offer from his girlfriend. Students have reinvented the cheap package tour – a last minute booking to Greece sleeping on the beach can provide a week's holiday for less than you pay to park your car at the airport.

I have nearly reached the end without covering the academic side. At some point you will be asked to buy a powerful computer – an essential accessory for the modern student. This should not be viewed as the purchase of an expensive Game Boy. It shows real evidence that he is taking work seriously.

Don't ask me how they find the time, but quite a lot of work is done. They go to most lectures and give up a large chunk of their social life when completing a dissertation or revising for finals. In no time at all, the three years will have passed and you will attend the graduation ceremony with feelings of pride and envy at your son's achievements and experiences. Your fully educated child will from now on give you the benefit of his wise counsel and experience in return for your continued financial support.

In the meantime, I wish you the best of luck.

John Timpson